D0527951

Fragmented Faith?

Exposing the fault-lines in the Church of England

'Based on an extensive survey of readers of the *Church Times*, this book offers a fascinating insight into the current state of the Church of England. It highlights the growing importance of distinct theological and liturgical traditions, and assesses their influence and relevance in the context of a broad church. The authors not only describe the issues that distinguish different groups from one another, but also offer insights into those aspects of church life on which new alliances are emerging, as well as identifying some surprising divergences which might lead to potentially damaging disputes in the future. There will be many different assessments of the significance of this research, but no-one who wishes to understand the nature of Anglicanism today can afford to ignore it.'
John Drane, Author of *The McDonaldization of the Church*

'*Fragmented Faith* reveals a Church with fault lines so deep (views on homosexuality, for example) and so varied (age and gender polarisations as well as Catholic, Charismatic, and Evangelical divides) that we are faced with a Communion which is not merely fissiparous but one likely to explode.'
Andrew G. Walker, Canon Professor of Theology,
Culture and Education, King's College, London

'This well-informed, intelligent study offers a careful and empirically-based analysis of current fault-lines in the Church of England. It should be required reading for church leaders, bishops, clergy, laypeople alike.'
Robin Gill, Michael Ramsey Professor of Modern Theology,
University of Kent at Canterbury

Fragmented Faith?

Exposing the fault-lines in the Church of England

Leslie J. Francis
Mandy Robbins
Jeff Astley

Copyright © Leslie J. Francis, Mandy Robbins and Jeff Astley

First published 2005 by Paternoster Press

Paternoster Press is an imprint of Authentic Media
9 Holdom Avenue, Bletchley, Milton Keynes, Bucks., MK1 1QR, UK
and 129 Mobilization Drive, Waynesboro, GA 30830-4575, USA
www.authenticmedia.co.uk/paternoster

11 10 09 08 07 06 05   7 6 5 4 3 2 1

The right of Leslie J. Francis, Mandy Robbins and Jeff Astley to be identified as
the authors of this Work has been asserted by them in accordance with the
Copyright, Designs and Patents Act 1988.

*All rights reserved. No part of this publication may be reproduced, stored in a retrieval
system, or transmitted, in any form or by any means, electronic, mechanical, photocopying,
recording or otherwise, without the prior permission of the publisher or a license permitting
restricted copying. In the U.K. such licenses are issued by the Copyright Licensing Agency,
90 Tottenham Court Road, London WIP 9HE.*

British Library Cataloguing in Publication Data
A catalogue record for this book is available from the British Library

ISBN 1-84227-382-5

Typeset by Susan Thomas
Cover design by fourninezero design.
Printed and bound in Great Britain
for Paternoster Publishing
by Bell and Bain Ltd., Glasgow

Contents

FOREWORD

To be an Anglican Christian in 2005 is to live in an uncomfortable Church, as lay people and clergy struggle to deal with the fall-out from the ordination of Gene Robinson as Bishop of New Hampshire. The debate about that ordination was always about the 'h' word – not *homosexuality*, to quote Bishop Robinson himself, but *honesty*. This, however, is only the presenting symptom of our internal strife, which really revolves around the nature of Christianity itself, its mode of revelation, and the willingness of Christians to live together in the same Church with other Christians who – in good conscience – believe or do things which are in their view offensive to the Gospel.

I cannot be the only bishop to have been assailed from left and right. One layman – a graduate in theology, no less – writes to say that he regards himself as out of communion with Rowan Williams for 'kow-towing' to illiberal forces; an incumbent and his churchwardens write to insist on an assurance that the Church in Wales does not ordain those of a homosexual life-style. To the former, I replied that I hoped that he at least was still in communion with me, his diocesan bishop, given that I am still in communion with the Archbishop of Canterbury – and Bishop Robinson and Archbishop Akinola, for that matter. To the latter, I offered to conduct a teaching session in the parish on making moral judgements (against which the Lord Jesus has much to say) and reaching ethical decisions. I fear that neither side will be satisfied in the end.

One of the authors of *Fragmented Faith?*, in an earlier study of rural Anglicanism, proved to be the Cassandra of the Church of England, fated to prophesy the truth but never to be believed. It may be that the present work will incur similar disbelief and even animosity. I, however, take this piece of re-search to be a very useful snapshot of the way in which readers of the *Church Times* (and by extrapolation, Anglican Christians) feel and think about a variety of issues involved in our present predicament. It really does explore the fault-lines in our 'fragile consensus'. Although the readership of the *Church Times* may be a far cry from a truly representative sample of the Church of England, none of us who know the Anglican Church from within will fail to recognise ourselves in this study, and the way in which our Communion, our Churches and our churches are in danger of schism. This present volume is a useful guide to issues which face us all because of 'the licentiousness of the late times crept in among us' (Preface to BCP 1662 – *plus ça change, plus c'est la même chose*).

As a remarried divorcee, and therefore one whose episcopal ordination would appear to be disapproved of by 58% of the respondents in the *Church Times* survey, I live with the dis-ease of our Church, fragmented on this as on so many questions. (I have, however, to say that my personal history does not seem to be an obstacle to my ministry in the diocese of which I am bishop.) The issues dealt with in this book are, we know, ones which affect all Anglican churches, not just the Church of England. We should be grateful for the cool way in which the authors deal with the statistics. In the end, the great matter which will face synods and bishops will only be resolved by addressing not so much the 'is' question (as important as the data are), but the more difficult 'ought' question. In the resolution of our difficulties, 'the dialectic . . . between the teaching of the Church and the faith of its members' has an especially important role when informed by 'ecclesiastical and pastoral considerations' (Hans van der Ven, 1993), and in this, empirical theology comes into its own.

Fragmented Faith? uses the tools of empirical theology to lift the lid on a small section of the Anglican world, the Church of England, and to test both its diversity and fragility. The objective analysis in this book confirms one's subjective impressions. It provides a precision on the basis of which it is possible to predict developments and anticipate the consequences of action or inaction.

Many of us are convinced that the God in whom Anglicans believe is not a static God, nor a narrow God. The people of God, therefore, are not called to be static or narrow either. Movement and breadth, however, are often troublesome and problematic qualities with which to live. I should like to think that the enduring strength of the Anglican Church to date (of which this book is, in part, testimony) is not that of a stone edifice, but, rather, that of the tall eucalyptus tree in my garden which bends and turns in the breeze, but which continues to thrive. It is paradoxical that the flexibility and diversity which have been the mark of Anglicanism at its best, might also, in changed times, be its Achilles' heel. The analysis in this book points to tensions not only between evangelicals and catholics, but also between the old and not so old. Whether we can continue to live together will depend on whether we are prepared to exhibit forbearance, as has been the case in our Church from the days of Elizabeth I, rather than party spirit. The issue is whether we can allow each other to shelter under the same roof. Or is it the case that the battle is already set to destroy the Anglican consensus, that it is better to live together, acknowledging our differences, than to live apart by mutual consent or even recrimination?

We should be grateful to the authors of this fascinating work for the information and analysis which helps to set out the issues so clearly. It makes for disquieting reading, but only if we have lost sight of our belief in the God whose divine unity is stronger than the God-given diversity of Christian people in general, and Anglicans in particular.

The Venerable Anthony Crockett, Bishop of Bangor

PREFACE

The Practical Theology Unit within the University of Wales, Bangor has pioneered a distinctive tradition of empirical theology within the United Kingdom. Empirical theology has the capability of helping the Church to listen to God's people carefully and perceptively. This is no alien scientific enterprise peering at the Church from without. Empirical theology is able to hold up a mirror to the Church from within. Only a brave Church is willing and able to look into that mirror. Our conclusion, however, is that the alternative to such bravery is foolishness.

The present book grew out of a creative partnership between the Practical Theology Unit within the University of Wales, Bangor and the *Church Times*, which invited its readership to participate in a detailed survey. Within a matter of weeks, nearly 9,000 individuals had responded. The *Church Times* is of no insignificant influence in the life of the Church of England. It both reflects and shapes the continuing and developing response of the Church to secular and to ecclesiastical matters both at home and overseas. The *Church Times Survey* set out to listen to what Anglicans really think, believe and do. The findings from such a survey celebrate the fundamental points of consensus and strength in the Church of England, and reveal the fault-lines and points of fragility.

A project of this nature is both costly and time-consuming to undertake. Behind the three authors stands a dedicated team of colleagues without whose support, care, accuracy, and commitment research like this would never reach completion. We acknowledge with thanks the contributions made by: Paul Handley and Rachel Boulding at the *Church Times* for help in shaping the survey; colleagues, students and friends for critiquing draft editions of the questionnaire; over 9,000 readers for completing and returning the questionnaires to us; Calvin for carrying the sacks of post to our office; Carol Roberts and Heidi Broom for checking the returned questionnaires and preparing the data for analysis; Susan Thomas for skill in preparing the manuscript; Diane Drayson for copyediting; and Carol Roberts for compiling the indices.

Leslie J. Francis, Mandy Robbins, Jeff Astley
March 2005

CHAPTER 1

Testing the fault-lines

Introduction

In the summer of 2003 the Bishop of Oxford conducted a courageous experiment to test the strength of the bonds which maintain the *consensus Anglicanus* amid the creative diversities which comprise the Church of England. To fill the vacancy created by the translation of the Right Reverend Dominic Walker from being Bishop of Reading to becoming Bishop of Monmouth, he nominated the Reverend Canon Jeffrey John. Jeffrey John possessed, in the eyes of the Bishop of Oxford (and in the eyes of many other committed members of the Church of England), all the personal and professional qualities to qualify him for consecration to the episcopacy. The potentially controversial aspect of the nomination, however, was the fact that Canon John had publicly acknowledged his homosexual orientation and had publicly owned his long-term stable (and now celibate) same-sex relationship.

Those bonds which maintain the *consensus Anglicanus* quickly split under the experiment. The apparent split within the Church of England received detailed coverage from both the religious and the secular media, both at home and across the world. In the denouement, the Bishop of Oxford lost his candidate and the Archbishop of Canterbury lost some of the respect and admiration which so many from different sectors of the Anglican Church had invested in him. In all probability Jeffrey John did not survive unscathed either. The experiment clearly uncovered deep fault-lines in the Church of England.

There are, of course, other ways in which to test the fragility of the fault-lines within the Church of England, and the professional expertise is clearly available to the Church of England to try these other ways. The tools of empirical theology offer one such route.

Empirical theology

Empirical theology takes its name from the distinctive way in which practical theology has been shaped in the Catholic University of Nijmegen under the pioneering leadership of Professor Johannes van der Ven (see, for example, van der Ven, 1993, 1998). Since launching the journal *Empirical Theology* in 1987, van der Ven has been joined by an international team of theologians concerned with the application of empirical scientific methods in testing matters of crucial concern to the ministry and mission of the Church. In 2002 the International Society for Empirical Research in Theology was inaugurated.

Empirical theology also has well-established roots in England and Wales. The case was made persuasively in the 1970s by Robin Gill (1975) that theologians have a responsibility not only to take the evidence offered by the social sciences seriously, but also to apply the tools of the social sciences to examine theological claims made about the social world. Robin Gill's more recent books on *Churchgoing and Christian Ethics* and *The 'Empty' Church Revisited* provide good examples of how he continues to put that fundamental insight into practice (Gill, 1999, 2003).

A second foundation for empirical theology in England and Wales has been provided through the initiatives undertaken by Leslie Francis (see Cartledge, 1999). Over the past two decades Francis and his associates have employed the techniques of empirical theology to address a series of issues relevant to aspects of ministry and to aspects of mission, including areas like the distinctiveness and effectiveness of church schools (Francis, 1986, 1987) and the place of religion in shaping the lives of young people (Francis, 1984, 2001; Francis and Kay, 1995; Kay and Francis, 1996). Two of the more productive, and in some senses, the more controversial areas, have focused on the rural church and on the clergy.

LISTENING TO THE RURAL CHURCH

In *Rural Anglicanism: a future for young Christians?* Francis (1985) set out to examine in depth the strengths and weaknesses of one rural diocese. The project was initiated and facilitated by a rural diocese which wished to reflect creatively on the relationship between an empirically-grounded appraisal of recent trends, the current situation, and future educational strategy. It was also recognised that a detailed and professional case study of one diocese could illuminate the situation of rural Anglicanism more generally. By offering a clear and objective research programme based on one well-defined geographical location, other researchers could be placed in a strong position to replicate the study elsewhere and thereby to test the generalisability of the findings.

Rural Anglicanism employed three different empirical research methods to inform three distinct inter-related aspects of the book. The first section concentrated on what could be learnt from a careful reanalysis of historic statistics already in the public domain through diocesan and national church publications. Such reanalysis drew attention both to the weaknesses in such data and to the wealth of strategic information often left concealed within the data. An examination of trends from the early 1950s to the early 1980s began to explode the myth of the resilience of the rural church against the problems of modernisation and secularisation which were at that stage being taken somewhat more seriously in the study and critique of urban Anglicanism (see Archbishop of Canterbury's Commission on Urban Priority Areas, 1985).

The second section employed a detailed questionnaire which was sent to all clergy in the diocese who had responsibility for a church or for a congregation. The questionnaire clearly took time and commitment to complete and some considered advice warned against anticipating a good response rate. The fact that over 90% of the clergy completed and returned the questionnaire suggested that they were willing to see the potential in the exercise. The quality of the data began to illustrate for the first time with statistical objectivity issues like the way in which the creation of multi-parish benefices reduced the proportion of the local population participating actively in local church life.

The third section employed the method of participant observation. A team of ordinands who had been trained in observation techniques visited every church in one deanery during the Saturday, tried to discover the times of the Sunday services, and then set out to attend those services the following day. The exercise taught us just how unprepared the rural church had become to expect newcomers to its services.

The then Archbishop of Canterbury provided a foreword to *Rural Anglicanism* which recognised the overall usefulness of this kind of research to the Church, writing as follows.

> Dr Francis has written a timely, and devastating book. In it he documents not only the statistical demise of rural Anglicanism, but also the degree to which it no longer reflects its Barsetshire caricature. His research clearly demonstrates that the countryside is now as much a pastoral challenge to today's Church as the inner city. How, he asks, *does* rural Anglicanism successfully proclaim the Gospel of Christ, and what kind of spirituality *is* the Church able to offer those communities it was once designed to serve?
>
> Dr Francis' study is scrupulously researched and clearly presented, and buttressed by vivid case studies as well as statistics. It is a refreshing contrast to some of the blander and more theoretical writing currently available on pastoral issues. As such it deserves the widest possible readership and discussion.

Some bishops, however, were less convinced by the contribution of empirical theology. The *Church Times* for Friday, 19 July 1985 reported that:

> The Bishop of Taunton (the Right Reverend Peter Nott) had harsh words for the recent 'doom-laden document', *Rural Anglicanism*.
>
> 'It is partial, unbalanced, technically inaccurate and the title is misleading in that it is an examination of young membership in one diocese in East Anglia', said Bishop Nott.
>
> The book did 'a great deal of harm to the morale of the country Church', said Bishop Nott, and this he regretted. And he went on to commend a diocesan document, *Realism and Hope*, which was, he believed, 'equally honest and blunt but which offered a springboard for discovering the answers facing the rural Church'.

The Bishop of Reading (the Right Reverend Eric Wild) was also far from convinced about the value of the research, writing in the *Oxford Diocesan Magazine* for September 1985 as follows.

> We need not detain ourselves by paying too much attention to the details of his statistics; for those who know about the collection and collation of parochial statistics also have considerable reservations about their provenance and utility.

The book is a strange mixture of the pompous and the naive, but for all that it is useful to have it; it tells us to pay attention to what we know, and by implication raises questions of which Dr Francis seems to be only dimly aware . . . . And so one could go on - this is not only an irritating book, it is a bad and an ignorant book. But it ought to be read, and worried over by study groups; perhaps as a Lenten penance.

Rural Anglicanism was followed by three other initiatives. First, working in collaboration with David W Lankshear, the questionnaire completed by the clergy in the one anonymous rural diocese was developed for a national survey in which 24 dioceses and one additional archdeaconry participated. In addition to three statistical overviews of the Church of England as a whole (Francis and Lankshear, 1991, 1995a, 1995b), these data were employed to examine a series of focused questions on aspects of rural church life, including: the influence of church schools on local church life (Francis and Lankshear, 1990); the impact of children's work on church life in hamlets and small villages (Francis and Lankshear, 1992a); the implications of where the parsonage is located for growth and decline in rural congregations (Francis and Lankshear, 1992b); and the differential effectiveness of aging clergy on urban, suburban, and rural churches (Francis and Lankshear, 1993).

Second, in collaboration with a number of theological colleges and ministry courses, the participant observation protocol developed in *Rural Anglicanism* was extended to a number of different types of rural areas, employing both Russell's (1986) conceptualisation of four types of countryside (urban shadow, accessible, less accessible, and remote and marginal), and a distinction between seven types of rural communities (hamlets, small villages, medium villages, large villages, suburban villages, market towns, and resorts). The findings from the participant observation process were published by Francis (1996) in *Church Watch: Christianity in the countryside*.

Third, in collaboration with Jeremy Martineau, a series of focused studies have been undertaken on well-defined aspects of the rural church and published under the following titles: *Rural Praise* (Francis and Martineau, 1996), *Rural Ministry* (Francis, Littler and Martineau, 2000), *Rural Youth* (Francis and Martineau, 2001a), *Rural Visitors* (Francis and Martineau, 2001b), and *Rural Mission* (Francis and Martineau, 2002). Each volume in the series was based on a unique empirical study. For example, *Rural Youth* analysed the responses of nearly 10,000 young people growing up in rural England and rural Wales, while *Rural Visitors* analysed the responses of over 13,000 people who visited rural churches in England and Wales.

Perhaps studies like *Rural Anglicanism*, *Church Visitors*, *Rural Visitors*, and *Rural Mission* have begun to help the voices of the rural church to be heard.

LISTENING TO THE CLERGY

In *The Long Diaconate: 1987-1994,* Francis and Robbins (1999) set out to listen to the story of those women who had been ordained to the diaconate within an Anglican Church which had not yet come to a view of the acceptability of the ordination of women to the priesthood. A focus on England between the period 1987 and 1994 was complemented by the wider context of Britain and Ireland. Some months before the ordination of the first women to the priesthood in England, a very detailed questionnaire was mailed to all 1,698 deacons and deaconesses under the age of 71 identified by the Church Commissioners' database as living in England, Ireland, Scotland, and Wales. Three-quarters of them (73%) replied.

The Long Diaconate made good use both of statistical data generated by clearly focused questions and of qualitative data generated by open-ended questions. The analysis discussed the following themes: call to ministry, selection, first appointment, training incumbent, last appointment as deacon, last incumbent as deacon, clerical colleagues, parishioners, family, friends, collaborative ministry, stress in ministry, satisfaction in ministry, public role, pastoral role, social role, liturgical role, inclusive language, church's attitude to women, the ordination debate, legislation and ecumenism, and the future for women bishops.

Overall *The Long Diaconate* revealed a generation of women who served the Church of England with loyalty as deacons during a prolonged and painful period through which the vocation to priesthood experienced by the majority of them was being denied by their Church. On the positive side, the majority of the women deacons felt really supported by their local congregation and by the parishioners among whom they ministered. Thus, 84% said that their own congregation was always supportive of them. The proportion rose even higher to 93% who said that they felt accepted by most people in their ministry. Overall satisfaction in ministry was indicated in a number of ways. For example, 86% of the women deacons reported that they felt they were accomplishing things in their ministry. Over three-quarters (77%) felt that they were growing spiritually in their ministry.

There was, however, a darker and less positive side to the experiences of these women deacons. The negative side of the story revolved around the reactions of some of their male clerical colleagues. Thus, fewer than three-fifths (56%) of the women deacons had been made to feel part of the professional life of other clergy in their area. Over two-fifths (43%) of the women deacons reported that they had trouble with some clerical colleagues.

The survey also drew attention to some of the other pressures experienced by the women deacons. Over half (52%) found that as a consequence of the demands of ministry they often did not have enough time for their families. Nearly three-quarters (72%) found that they often did not have enough time for themselves and 75% said that they often did not have enough time for their hobbies and interests. One in three (32%) of the women deacons said that they often felt lonely and isolated in their ministry. It is, however, likely that similar pictures would emerge if the same questions were asked of clergymen. Such statistics raise real questions about the way in which the Church of England exercises pastoral care over the clergy.

In *The Naked Parish Priest: what priests really think they're doing*, Louden and Francis (2003) set out to listen to the story of the Roman Catholic clergy engaged in parochial ministry in England and Wales. This time a detailed questionnaire was sent to all Roman Catholic clergy identified as engaged in parochial ministry in the two nations. This time a less enthusiastic response was found than had been the case among the Anglican clergywomen. Fewer than half (42%) replied. At one stage it was even rumoured that one diocesan bishop had advised his clergy against participating.

Once again *The Naked Parish Priest* made good use both of the statistical data generated by clearly focused questions and of the qualitative data generated by open-ended questions. The analysis discussed the following themes: training for public ministry, training for pastoral ministry, training for work with people, training for the priestly life, theology and priesthood, experiencing priesthood, dress and deference, relating to the laity, celibacy and priesthood, fallen priests, Jesus and Mary, marriage, sex and death, church and sacrament, Rome and the Vatican, Catholic institutions, ecumenism and intercommunion, changes in the Catholic Church, ordination of women, emotional exhaustion, depersonalisation, personal accomplishment, and a future in priesthood.

Overall *The Naked Parish Priest* revealed a dedicated hardworking priesthood, committed to maintaining the integrity of the Catholic faith. There were, however, some key areas in which the priests wished to question the received wisdom of the Catholic Church, and inevitably it was to these areas that the press turned their attention. Of particular significance were the issues of artificial contraception and clerical celibacy. Overall, just two out of every five priests (39%) supported the Catholic Church's total ban on artificial contraception. Moreover, the evidence suggested that younger priests were growing more hesitant than their older colleagues about the official teaching of the Catholic Church on this issue. While 52% of the priests aged 60 or over supported the Catholic Church's total ban on artificial contraception, the proportion fell to 28% among the priests between the ages of 45 and 59 years.

The findings about clerical celibacy show that overall under half of the priests (46%) believed that celibacy should remain the norm for entry to the priesthood, and the proportion fell to 35% among the priests between the ages of 45 and 59 years. The vast majority of priests (91%) believed that a married man could validly be ordained priest and 45% argued that Catholic priests who left and married should be readmitted to ministry. Just 14% of the priests maintained that a priest who has sex with an unmarried woman should be barred from ministry. The proportion rose only slightly to 19% of the priests who maintained that a priest who has sex with a married woman should be barred from ministry. Such statistics raise real questions about the challenges which Catholic teaching on clerical celibacy may need to face.

The survey also drew attention to a darker side of the experience of Catholic priests engaged in parochial ministry by examining the levels of experienced professional burnout. One in every seven of the priests (14%) said that they felt burned out from their parish ministry. Similarly, 16% said that they felt fatigued when they got up in the morning and have to face another day in the parish. Over a third (36%) said that they felt used up at the end of the day in parish ministry. Such statistics raise real questions about the long-term physical, psychological, and spiritual health of the Catholic clergy working within the current pressures of parish ministry.

The Roman Catholic hierarchy responded quickly to news of the book's planned publication and issued a critical press release before the button had been pressed to print the copies. *The Tablet* for Saturday, 12 April 2003 reported as follows.

> Bishops in England and Wales have attacked a controversial survey that shows many parish priests disagree with Catholic teaching on contraception, clerical celibacy and homosexuality.
>
> In a prepared statement issued by the Catholic Communications Service on Monday, the bishops' conference complains that the survey is unofficial and was conducted by an Anglican clergyman and his doctoral student, a Catholic priest. They suggest only 26 per cent of priests responded, and that the questions posed in a multiple choice format were confused and confusing. Since the statistics were gathered in 1996 and 1997, the bishops believe the findings are out of date.

The discrepancy between the response rate of 42% reported in the book and 26% reported in the press release is consistent with the press release being published before copies of the book were available for reading.

Perhaps studies like *The Long Diaconate* and the *Naked Parish Priest* have begun to help the voices of the clergy to be heard.

Voices of Anglicanism

Against this background, the present study employed the tools of empirical theology to test the fault-lines in the Church of England by listening to the people, to the clergy and the laity who are the Church of England. In some ways listening to the clergy may be a relatively easy job to undertake. After all, the clergy constitute a well-defined group and are easily accessed through *Crockford's Clerical Directory*. Penetrating beyond the clergy, however, to try to listen to the wider voices of a denomination is much more problematic, and trying to capture the voice of lay Anglicans may be most problematic of all.

The first problem is that of recognising different categories of Anglicans within England. The spectrum runs from those who attend local churches Sunday by Sunday, through those who register their names on the electoral rolls of the parish church but attend only rarely, to those who see themselves as Anglicans but have absolutely no contact with any organised expression of religion. A Church which takes people seriously needs to listen to the different voices of this diverse constituency.

The second problem is that of developing appropriate research methods to sample these different groups of Anglicans. Previous studies have tried different techniques.

One well-established method focuses on churchgoers and does so through congregational surveys. The National Church Life Survey first pioneered in Australia by Peter Kaldor and his associates provides a good example of the fruitful data generated through congregational groups, as seen through books like: *First Look in the Mirror: initial findings of the 1991 National Church Life Survey* (Kaldor, Bellamy, Correy and Powell, 1992), *Views from the Pews: Australian church attenders speak out* (Kaldor, Powell, Bellamy, Castle, Correy and Moore, 1995), and *Taking Stock: a profile of Australian church attenders* (Kaldor, Dixon and Powell, 1999).

Congregational surveys have also played an important part in the tradition of empirical theology in England and Wales. For example, in a chapter entitled 'The pews talk back', Francis (2000) reports on a study conducted among four congregations in one town centre, worshipping in churches sponsored by the Church of England, Methodist Church, Roman Catholic Church, and United Reformed Church. The analysis discussed the following themes: motivation for churchgoing, a sense of belonging to the church, strengths and weaknesses of the local church, personal growth and learning in the faith, sources of spiritual help, religious experience, openness to change, religious beliefs, attitudes to the bible, understanding of the social gospel, and political and social concerns.

The study made explicit the beliefs and assumptions which these four congregations held in common, and the points (so often partly submerged) on which attempts at closer collaboration could founder. Some of the differences revealed by this survey may seem obvious. For example, while 71% of the Catholics said that they found ritual in services helpful, the proportion dropped slightly to 64% among the Anglicans and plummeted to 24% among the Methodists and 28% among those who attend the United Reformed Church. While 72% of the Methodists found reading the bible by themselves helpful, the proportions dropped by 62% among those who attend the United Reformed Church, to 49% among the Anglicans, and to 37% among the Catholics. Clearly the organisation of ecumenical worship in this context is quite difficult. Somewhat less obvious is the way in which the different denominations interpret scripture. The literalist view that God made the world in six days and rested on the seventh was taken by half of the Catholics (49%), compared with 32% of those who attend the United Reformed Church, 34% of the Anglicans, and 39% of the Methodists. What people look for in terms of fellowship within the local church also varies strongly from denomination to denomination.

While 69% of the Methodists said that they often turned to fellow members of their church when they needed help, the proportions fell to 55% among those who attend the United Reformed Church, 39% of the Anglicans, and 37% of the Catholics. Clearly there are quite different assumptions about the nature of the Church among these different groups. Such statistics demonstrate that a great deal can be gleaned from congregational surveys. The resources needed, however, to access a representative sample of congregations in this way could be quite extensive.

A very different approach was taken by Bibby (1986) in response to an invitation to listen to the voices of Anglicanism throughout the Anglican Diocese of Toronto, Canada. The findings from this study are published under the title *Anglitrends: a profile and prognosis*. In his preface to the book, Bibby (1986:ix) sets out his perception and commitment in the following way.

> I am very pleased to have had the opportunity to carry out this research for the Anglican Diocese of Toronto. An effective Church, like any other effective organisation, has to have a clear reading of the people with whom it is dealing. From the outset of my involvement in this project, I have been impressed by the commitment to such accurate perception on the part of the Diocese generally and Archbishop Garnsworthy specifically.

In order to reach a wider sample of Anglicans than those who sit in the pews on a given Sunday or even those who place their names on the local membership lists, Bibby drew his sample from the readership of the national Anglican newspaper, the *Canadian Churchman*. It was this study which provided both the precedent and the inspiration for the *Church Times Survey*.

Church Times Survey

IDENTIFYING THE ISSUES

The *Church Times Survey* was set up to provide a comprehensive picture of committed Anglicans in England today, in terms both of who they are and what they believe. The key problem concerned what to include in the questionnaire and what not to include, recognising the constraints on respondents' time. To begin with, a large map was compiled of questions included in previous surveys. This map then went out for consultation among a wide range of people who were invited to suggest revisions of questions and to propose new questions, but not to reject questions. The revised and larger map went out to a second stage of consultation to prioritise questions. The result was a questionnaire which included three main sections.

The first section of the questionnaire set out to discover the demographic characteristics of committed Anglicans in the broadest terms. These questions were generally asked in the pre-coded multiple-choice format. The respondents simply needed to tick the box which most accurately reflected their choice of answer. For example, the question about age was followed by nine categories beginning with 'under 10 years' and ending with '80 years or over'. Other questions in this section included a numerical rating scale in order to enable respondents to grade and nuance their replies. For example, the question designed to assess preferences for a liberal or for a conservative church tradition employed a seven-point semantic differential scale, following the model of Osgood, Suci and Tannenbaum (1957). The two poles of the scale were anchored by the terms 'conservative' and 'liberal'.

The second section of the questionnaire set out to discover the beliefs, attitudes, and values of committed Anglicans in the broadest terms. The main body of the present book builds on 15 of the key themes included. Each of these themes was explored by means of a set of up to ten short, precise, and well-framed statements. Within the questionnaire each statement was rated on a five-point scale, following the scaling principles first established by Likert (1932). The five points on the scale were defined as: agree strongly, agree, not certain, disagree, and disagree strongly.

Theme one on *patterns of belief* identified three doctrinal areas against which to assess the orthodoxy of committed Anglicans: beliefs about God, beliefs about Jesus, and beliefs about life after death.

Theme two on *paths of truth* identified three ways in which truth claims are asserted and tested: beliefs about the bible, beliefs about the exclusivity of Christianity, and beliefs about evolution versus creationism.

Theme three on *paths of spirituality* distinguished between three kinds of issues: personal and private sources of spiritual sustenance, group-based and shared sources of spiritual sustenance within the local area, and wider resources like religious retreats and secular means of spiritual sustenance.

Theme four on *public worship* included three sets of questions to assess responses to different aspects of public worship: the first set focused on the debate between traditional and modern forms of public worship, the second set focused on different aspects of the service, and the third set focused on the initiation of children into the worshipping community.

Theme five on *local church life* included three groups of questions to assess different aspects of commitment to the local church: questions concerning stages in the cycle of increasing and reducing commitment, questions concerning the nature of commitment, and questions concerning the relationship between commitment and power.

Theme six on *ordained ministry* identified four issues of contention within Anglicanism: the ordination of women, the ordination of divorced people, the ordination of divorced and remarried people, and the ordination of practising homosexuals. Each issue distinguished between ordination as priests and ordination as bishops.

Theme seven on *church leadership* focused on two sets of issues: strategic issues concerned with the development and future of ordained ministry, including stipends, freehold and parsonages, and issues concerned with the development and future of lay ministry, including lay presidency at the eucharist.

Theme eight on' *churches and cathedrals* included two types of questions: the first focused on attitude toward the individual respondent's local church, while the second focused on wider issues of policy, including closing rural churches, charging entry fees to cathedrals, and having church buildings taken over by the state.

Theme nine on *money and policy* posed a series of questions to gauge the priorities of committed Anglicans for their local church funds. The four specific areas identified as having potential calls on funds were: central church structures, the clergy, development and mission, and community regeneration.

Theme ten on *Anglican identity* examined the way in which committed Anglicans viewed the Church of England by examining two specific issues: the first issue concentrated on willingness to merge Anglican identity with other denominations, and the second issue concentrated on the future of establishment.

Theme eleven on *confidence and the future* recognised the importance of confidence for future development and growth. In order to gauge the level of confidence which committed Anglicans hold in the future, the survey examined two main issues: the first issue concerned confidence in the Church of England's leadership, including bishops, General Synod and the Archbishops' Council, while the second issue concerned confidence in the future of their own local church to survive or to grow.

Theme twelve on *sex and family life* identified four specific areas in which to test the orthodoxy of Anglican views today: views on sex and cohabitation before marriage, views on divorce, views on same sex relationships, and views on caring for children and teenagers.

Theme thirteen on *social concerns* included a set of items on global concerns and a set of items on community concerns. The global concerns included environmental and development issues, AIDS, and genetic research. The community concerns included violence on television, paedophiles in the community, and the effects of the National Lottery.

Theme fourteen on *social conscience* followed a style of question generally used in the British Social Attitudes Survey (see, for example, Park, Curtice, Thomson, Jarvis and Bromley, 2001). The aim was to gauge commitment to and priorities concerning expenditure from the public purse by asking people to assess their willingness to pay more tax to fund specific areas. The three broad areas identified were: health and education, social security and prisons, and defence and development aid.

Theme fifteen on *education* recognised the Church of England's long involvement in education and set out to gauge current Anglican opinion on three key issues. The first issue concerned the debate between state provision and the independent sector of schools. The second issue concerned the nature of religious education and school worship in a multi-faith environment. The third issue concerned the case for expanding the number of Church of England primary schools and secondary schools, and the case for other faith communities benefiting from public funding for faith-based schools.

The third section of the questionnaire included a standard personality test, namely the abbreviated form of the Eysenck Personality Questionnaire, as developed by Francis, Brown and Philipchalk (1992) and modified by Francis, Robbins, Louden and Haley (2001). The personality test was included because a great deal of the recent research conducted within the Wales school of empirical theology has identified the key importance of personality theory in understanding differences in church life and in theological orientation. The findings from this part of the survey are not included in the present book, but need to be dealt with in a separate volume.

CONDUCTING THE SURVEY

The questionnaire was designed and typeset to occupy a full four-page inset to the *Church Times* and was included in two editions published at the end of March and the beginning of April 2001. The questionnaire was introduced to the readership with the following letter signed by the editor, Paul Handley.

> The *Church Times* is compiling one of the widest-ranging surveys of church people ever undertaken in the United Kingdom. Our aim is to collect both facts and opinions in order to give the Anglican Church a chance to reflect on how it wishes to proceed in the twenty-first century. The survey will identify strengths and weaknesses in the Church's present practice, and will encourage its members to debate these, and suggest improvements. The survey is independent, and there will be no doctoring of results . . . .
>
> All responses will be confidential. They will be used only by the *Church Times*, its sister companies and Professor Francis and his team. They will not be passed on or sold to any outside organisation or individual. The questionnaire can be completed anonymously.

The questionnaires were returned by freepost to the University of Wales, Bangor. The response outstripped our expectation. Within a matter of weeks over 9,000 envelopes passed through our letter box. Given the *Church Times* circulation of around 33,000 copies, this represents an impressive response rate of around 27%. Some envelopes carried detailed letters explaining why the project was misconceived, some contained long letters explaining why some people did not have the time to complete the questionnaire, and a few contained blank questionnaires sent purely to incur the freepost charge. The overwhelming majority, however, contained carefully completed questionnaires, and some even included complimentary letters commending the project and wishing the researchers well with the enormous task of analysis.

The incoming post kept us busy checking each questionnaire for completeness. If large sections had been ignored these copies were either rejected or, if name and address had been supplied, sent back for further attention. Overall, 8,577 thoroughly completed questionnaires were keyed into the computer for data analysis.

Since the purpose of the present book is to profile committed members of the Church of England, three key questions on the survey were examined with care. The first of these three questions asked, 'Where do you live?' All told, 8,004 (93%) of the respondents lived in England. Of the remaining 5%, 250 lived in Wales, 95 in Scotland, 35 in Ireland, and 13 on the Channel Islands. Others lived in Austria, Australia, Belgium, Canada, Denmark, France, Germany, Gibraltar, Italy, Luxemburg, Netherlands, New Zealand, Norway, Russia, South Africa, Spain, Sri Lanka, Switzerland, and the United States of America. Only those who lived in England are included in the following analyses.

The second of these three questions asked, 'What type of church do you normally attend?' All told, 8,349 (97%) of the respondents attended Anglican churches. Of the remaining 3%, 48 attended Methodist churches, 32 Roman Catholic churches, 29 ecumenical churches or Local Ecumenical Projects, 17 United Reformed Churches, 16 Baptist churches, and 16 attended Quaker meetings. Others attended Brethren, Congregational, Episcopal, Evangelical House Church, Lutheran, Moravian, Orthodox, Pentecostal, Reformed and Salvation Army places of worship. Only those who attended Anglican churches are included in the following analyses.

The third of these three questions asked, 'How often do you attend church (apart from weddings, baptisms and funerals)?' All told, 8,055 (94%) attended church at least once a week and a further 296 (4%) attended at least twice a month. Of the remaining 2%, 73 attended at least once a month, 61 at least six times a year, 36 at least once a year, and 37 attended church less often than once a year. Only those who attended church at least twice a month are included in the following analyses. Attendance at an Anglican church at least twice a month serves in this study as the operational definition of a committed Anglican. Twice a month rather than weekly was selected as the cutting off point on the grounds that in some rural parishes it may now be very difficult for elderly non-car driving Anglicans to maintain a pattern of weekly attendance.

PLANNING THE ANALYSIS

Having excluded those respondents who lived outside England, who did not normally attend an Anglican church, and who attended church less frequently than twice a month, the data set was reduced by 11% to 7,611 individuals. The rest of this book examines these 7,611 individuals.

Chapter two on *profiling laity and clergy* begins the tale by offering careful profiles of the committed Anglicans who participated in the survey. Separate profiles are provided for the 5,762 laity and for the 1,849 clergy included in the survey. Laity and clergy are treated separately because, as the data demonstrate, the two groups have somewhat different demographic characteristics and such differences may be important for understanding and interpreting the differences which later emerge in terms of beliefs, attitudes, and values.

Chapter three on *fragile consensus* takes a broad overview of the responses of the whole sample of committed Anglicans who responded to the *Church Times Survey*, in order to assess just how much the Church of England is today a broad church. Here laity and clergy are put together into the same melting pot of Anglican opinion. Here men and women, young and old, Catholic and Evangelical, charismatic and non-charismatic are viewed together through a single lens. There will be some issues on which there may be close consensus, perhaps almost unanimity. There will be other issues on which opinion may be sharply divided, perhaps almost equally divided down the middle.

The argument of the following chapters is that the divisions in Anglican opinions are not random and haphazard, but that they reflect clearly identifiable fault-lines in the very structure and composition of the Church of England. Grasping and understanding these fault-lines should enable the Church of England to be more aware of the major points of fragility and danger, and at the same time to be more certain of the major points of strength and unity.

For many people the most obvious fault-line in the Church of England may be thought to be the uneasy tension of church orientation between the Evangelical wing and the Catholic wing (see, for example, Saward, 1987, Penhale, 1986). If that were the Church of England's only fault-line, life for the Church of England could still be relatively straightforward, since that fault-line has been well mapped and chronicled over the years. A second fault-line has been detected between those influenced by the charismatic movement and those left uninfluenced by the charismatic movement. This fault-line has appeared more recently in the Church of England, the map has not yet been fully drawn, and the implications have been less well chronicled (see, for example, Bax, 1986).

What the *Church Times Survey* has done, however, is to draw attention to three other major fault-lines in the Church of England which have been there for all to see but which, for some reason, have attracted less attention. It is these fault-lines which may still catch us unawares and unprepared. It is these fault-lines which need to be more fully explored and understood if that fragile consensus which defines the very essence of the Church of England is to remain intact. It is these fault-lines which may have taken the Bishop of Oxford so much by surprise when he conducted his courageous experiment in the summer of 2003. These are the fault-lines which stand between lay and ordained Anglicans, between male and female Anglicans, and between Anglicans of different generations.

The examination of all these fault-lines in the depth which they deserve stretches beyond the scope of a single volume. Chapters four through eight have selected five of the fault-lines to explore in depth. This is sufficient to illustrate the basic thesis that fault-lines matter and to put down some serious guidelines about the significance of key fault-lines.

Chapter four begins the argument by examining the *fault-line between clergy and laity*. In this chapter age, sex and church orientation are not taken into account. All the 5,762 laity included in the analysis are compared with all the 1,849 clergy included in the analysis. In many ways ordained Anglicans look out onto a somewhat different world from the world viewed by lay Anglicans.

Chapter five turns attention to the *fault-line between men and women in the pews*. In this chapter age and church orientation are not taken into account. All the 3,318 lay women included in the analysis are compared with all the 2,428 lay men included in the analysis. In many ways the men and the women sitting in the pews have a distinctive perspective on issues which are important to the Anglican Church. Recognising the differences between clergymen and clergywomen is also important, but space precludes this additional analysis. The chapter has decided to focus on sex differences among laity rather than among clergy because this fault-line has been less anticipated and has remained less visible among the laity.

Chapter six turns attention to the *fault-line between young and old in the pews*. In this chapter sex and church orientation are not taken into account. The comparison is made between three age groups. Anglicans in their fifties or sixties are regarded as the largest, most active and most influential group in many congregations. There were 3,006 lay people in this age group included in the analysis. Anglicans under the age of fifty are generally in a minority in church congregations. There were 1,093 lay people in this age group included in the analysis. Anglicans aged seventy and over, who have often been the backbone of their church for many years, are now beginning to experience the in-roads made into their territory by those in their fifties and sixties. There were 1,659 lay people in this age group included in the analysis. The three age groups will be referred to as young Anglicans (under fifty), middle-aged Anglicans (in their fifties and sixties) and senior Anglicans (aged seventy and over). This odd use of language makes sense within the peculiar age profile of Anglican congregations. Recognising age differences among the clergy is also important, but space precludes this additional analysis. This chapter has decided to focus on age differences among laity rather than among clergy because this fault-line has been less anticipated and has remained less visible among the laity.

Chapter seven focuses on the *fault-line between Catholics and Evangelicals in the pulpit*. In this chapter sex and age are not taken into account. The division between Catholics and Evangelicals has been made on the basis of responses to the seven-point semantic differential scale included in the survey. Clergy who checked the two values closest to the Catholic end of the continuum have been regarded as Catholics. A total of 846 clergy came into this category. Clergy who checked the two values closest to the Evangelical end of the continuum have been regarded as Evangelicals. A total of 366 clergy came into this category. The remaining clergy who either checked the three middle values on the scale or omitted the question have been excluded from the analysis. Recognising differences between commitment to the Catholic and Evangelical wings of the Anglican Church among the laity is also important, but space precludes this additional analysis. This chapter has decided to focus on church orientation differences among clergy rather than among laity because it is here that the fault-line is most pronounced.

Chapter eight focuses on the *fault-line between charismatics and non-charismatics in the pulpit.* In this chapter sex and age are not taken into account. The division between charismatics and non-charismatics has been made on the basis of responses to the seven-point semantic differential scale included in the survey. Clergy who checked the two values closest to the charismatic end of the continuum have been regarded as charismatics. A total of 193 clergy came into this category. Clergy who checked the two values closest to the non-charismatic end of the continuum have been regarded as non-charismatics. A total of 818 clergy came into this category. The remaining clergy who either checked the three middle categories on the scale or omitted the question have been excluded from the analysis. Recognising the differences between charismatic lay-people and non-charismatic lay-people is also important, but space precludes this additional analysis. This chapter has decided to focus on the clergy rather than on the laity because it is here that the fault-line is most pronounced.

Finally chapter nine draws the threads together and takes stock of that fragile consensus which holds the Church of England together. In the light of this kind of empirical evidence, perhaps it is not all that surprising that the Bishop of Oxford's courageous experiment to test the bonds which maintain the *consensus Anglicanus* found how quickly those bonds tend to snap under pressure.

STATISTICAL NOTE

The figures on which the narrative of the main chapters has been based are provided in the statistical appendix. Two features of these statistics require commentary. In chapter three the percentages have been rounded to whole numbers without decimal places. As a consequence the rows may sum to 99%, 100% or 101%. This is common practice. In the following chapters the statistical significance of differences in the responses of different groups has been calculated by the chi square test in respect of dichotomized data. The division has been made between those who agree or agree strongly with the question on the one hand, and those who check the disagree, disagree strongly, or uncertain categories on the other hand. Differences which do not reach the five percent probability threshold will be regarded as non-significant.

CHAPTER 2

Meeting the people

Introduction

Before subsequent chapters examine the pattern of beliefs and values held by the committed Anglicans identified through the *Church Times Survey*, the present chapter sets out to profile the identity of those who were included in the analysis. The laity and the clergy are treated separately because the distinctive profiles of these two groups may help to explain some of the characteristics of the fragility of the *consensus Anglicanus*. The method adopted by the chapter is not to compare and to contrast the laity and the clergy, but to treat the two groups separately in two clear sections of the chapter. The profile of the laity will be discussed first, followed by the profile of the clergy.

The three key issues addressed in both sections relate to personal characteristics, Anglican formation, and participation in services. As far as it is sensible to do so, the same sequence of issues will be addressed in respect of both the clergy and the laity. Not all issues are of equal relevance, however, to both groups, and for this reason the two sections do not follow identical paths. Broadly, however, the same kinds of issues are discussed.

The section on personal characteristics explores five areas. First, we need to begin by understanding who committed Anglicans are in terms of basic demographic information concerned with sex, age, and marital status. Second, we need to know something about their educational background. The two issues here concern the type of school they attended and the level of education attained. To what extent have committed Anglicans been shaped by the independent sector of schools? To what extent do committed Anglicans constitute a community of graduates? Third, we need to know about the employment status of committed Anglicans. To what extent do committed Anglicans constitute a community of the retired? Among those who are engaged in full-time employment, how wide is the range of work-experience represented among committed Anglicans? Related to both of these issues is the question regarding overall household income. How well placed are committed Anglicans to support the financial costs of their church? Fourth, we need to know something about the geographical location of committed Anglicans. How well-rooted is Anglicanism in rural, urban, and suburban environments? Fifth, we need to know how strongly committed Anglicans are connected with their local community and with the wider society of which they are part. How much do

committed Anglicans contribute to voluntary work within their local communities? How much do committed Anglicans give active support to matters of
local, national, and international concern?

The section on Anglican formation explores five areas. First, we need to
begin by understanding the path which led participants in the study to become
committed Anglicans. Were they born into an Anglican family and baptised at
an Anglican font as infants? Have they remained as committed Anglicans all
their lives, or have they experienced periods of absence from the church? Have
they experienced a religious turning point or conversion at some stage in their
lives? How much has their faith been based on intellectual decisions or on
religious experience? How important has been the influence of friends, of
family, and of other people on the formation of their identity as Anglicans?
Second, we need to know something about the church traditions represented by
the sample. What proportions of the participants in the survey identify with the
Catholic or with the Evangelical wings of the Church of England? What proportions of the participants in the survey identify themselves as liberals or as
conservatives? What proportion of the participants in the survey identify
themselves with the charismatic movement? Third, we need to know about the
way in which committed Anglicans contribute financially to their church. What
proportion of them make good use of gift aid, and how much do they actually
give? Fourth, we need to examine what commitment to Anglicanism means in
terms of personal religious practice. What commitment is shown to personal
bible reading, and to personal prayer? How much commitment is shown to
reading books on theology and faith? Fifth, we need to know about the ways in
which the faith of committed Anglicans continues to be nurtured. To what
extent do committed Anglicans draw on resources like Alpha courses, Emmaus
programmes, parish-based courses, diocesan-based courses, or courses rooted
in the further education and higher education sectors?

The section on participation in services explores five areas. First, we need to
begin by understanding how committed Anglicans relate to the parish structure.
To what extent do committed Anglicans worship in their own parish church?
How far do they travel to the church in which they worship? Are they members
of the electoral roll? Second, we need to know about the types of services
committed Anglicans generally attend. To what extent is committed
Anglicanism currently seen as a eucharistically-based faith? What part do
morning prayer and evening prayer play in the life of committed Anglicans?
What place is given to family services? Third, we need to know about the
preferred times for Sunday church attendance. To what extent is committed
Anglicanism currently seen as a mid-morning faith? What part do early
morning services, afternoon services, and evening services currently play in the
life of committed Anglicans? Fourth, we need to know more about the
experience of Sunday worship. With how many other people do committed
Anglicans tend to worship on a Sunday? Is the general experience of committed
Anglicans that of worshipping in large congregations or in small groups? How

are these services generally led? How general for committed Anglicans is the experience of services led by clergywomen or by lay people? Fifth, we need to know something about the experience of weekday services. What proportions of committed Anglicans generally attend communion services, morning prayer, or evening prayer on a weekday?

Profiling laity

PERSONAL CHARACTERISTICS

Anglican congregations are clearly weighted toward women rather than toward men. Often the estimates suggest that there are two women in the Anglican congregation for every one man (see Francis, 1996). In the present survey, the gender bias is not quite so pronounced: 42% of the lay participants were male and 58% were female.

The general impression of Anglican congregations is that they constitute a community of the retired (see Francis, 1996). In the present survey the best represented age group comprises men and women in their sixties. Of the total sample of lay participants, 7% were under the age of forty, 12% were in their forties, 24% were in their fifties, 28% were in their sixties, 21% were in their seventies, and 7% were aged eighty or over.

A lot of church activity seems to be shaped toward people who are living as part of a family. The present data demonstrate that this assumption does not hold true for one out of every three committed Anglicans. Of the total sample of lay participants, 18% were single, 12% were widowed and 4% were either separated or divorced. Of the remaining lay participants, 2% described themselves as divorced and remarried, 1% as living with a partner, and 62% as married.

The relationship between Anglicanism and the independent educational sector remains strong, with one in every three of the lay participants in the survey having been educated in an independent school. Of the total sample of lay participants, 29% received all their education in the independent sector, with a further 7% receiving part of their education in the independent sector. The remaining 64% received all their education within the state-maintained sector of schools.

Committed lay Anglicans are heavily weighted toward graduates. Nearly two out of every three (63%) of the lay participants in the survey had gained a degree. This high level of graduates is not typical of the population as a whole within the age group of the participants in the survey.

Committed lay Anglicans tend not to be people who are engaged in the full-time labour market. Fewer than one in four (24%) of the lay participants in the survey reported that they were engaged in full-time employment, with a further 14% engaged in part-time employment. By far the largest group among the lay participants in the survey was the retired (52%). Among the remaining lay participants in the survey, 8% described themselves as housewives, 2% as students and 1% as unemployed. The high proportion of committed lay Anglicans not engaged in full-time employment may carry two implications for the Church of England. On the one hand, the Church of England may be hard pressed to raise more and more money from its core constituency. On the other hand, the Church of England may find it much easier to release the potential of commitment in terms of time from the very same core constituency. The Anglican Church may be very rich in terms of human capital, if not so rich in terms of financial resources.

The majority of committed lay Anglicans had been employed at some stage of their lives. Only 4% did not identify experience in the work place. Two out of every three (69%) of the lay participants in the survey regarded themselves as having experience in professional spheres of work and a further 19% in semi-professional spheres of work. This left 8% who identified non-manual work, 2% skilled manual work, 1% semi-skilled manual work, and 1% unskilled manual work.

The fact that such a large proportion of committed lay Anglicans are currently unwaged is reflected in the level of household income, but the level of household income also reflects the status of those who have retired from professional positions. Just 2% of the lay participants in the survey reported an annual household income of less than £5,000, while a further 8% had an income of between £5,000 and £9,999; 17% had an income of between £10,000 and £14,999 and 15% between £15,000 and £19,999; 24% had an income of between £20,000 and £29,999 and 14% between £30,000 and £39,000. In the higher income brackets, 7% checked between £40,000 and £49,999, 8% between £50,000 and £69,999, 3% between £70,000 and £99,999, and 2% over £100,000. Clearly there remain significant pockets of affluence among committed lay Anglicans.

Higher numbers of committed lay Anglicans live in rural and in suburban areas than in urban areas. Thus 38% of the lay participants in the survey reported that they were currently living in rural areas and 36% reported that they were currently living in suburban areas, compared with 26% who reported that they were currently living in urban areas. As a consequence lay opinion in Anglicanism may be less well attuned to priorities in urban areas than to priorities in rural areas and to priorities in suburban areas.

Overall committed lay Anglicans are highly involved in a wide range of voluntary work, both within their local communities and on a wider stage. Given a check list of 11 different spheres of voluntary work, 15% of the lay participants in the survey reported that they undertook voluntary work related to education, 14% to cultural activities, 14% to community activities, 11% to social welfare activities, 8% to health-related groups, 7% to activities among children, 6% to environmental groups, 6% to political groups, 5% to world development activities, 5% to youth work, and 4% to human rights groups. At the same time, 16% reported that they were engaged in voluntary work in spheres not listed in the survey. These figures illustrate the large contribution being made by committed lay Anglicans to the social capital of their community through their voluntary work.

The majority, but by no means all, of the committed lay Anglicans in the survey were cradle Anglicans. While 84% had been originally baptised at Anglican fonts, the remaining 16% had transferred from other denominational backgrounds. Only 9% of the 5,762 committed lay Anglicans in the survey had come to Anglicanism from a totally unchurched background. The most significant sources of transfer were from the Methodist Church (3%), the Baptist Church (2%), the Roman Catholic Church (2%), the Congregational Church (2%), and the Presbyterian Church (1%). Other transfers had taken place from the Assemblies of God, the Brethren, the Catholic Apostolic Church, the Christadelphians, the Church of Christ, the Church of the Nazarene, Elim, the Free Evangelical Independent Church, the Lutheran Church, the Moravian Church, the New Covenant Church, the Salvation Army, the Seventh-day Adventist Church, and the Unitarian Church. Clearly there is a wide range of experience of other denominations among committed lay Anglicans.

In their book, *Gone but not Forgotten*, Richter and Francis (1998) defined church leavers as people who had been regular churchgoers, but who then at some stage in their lives had reduced their church attendance to less than six times a year. In this study Richter and Francis (1998) recognised that some church leavers became church returners, while others continued to keep away from church. In the present sample one in every four committed lay Anglicans (27%) had themselves experienced being church leavers and church returners. Such a body of experience within Anglicanism should help local congregations to understand better the processes of enabling other church leavers to become church returners.

Participants in the survey were invited to assess the part played by five different factors in their journey to faith, namely conversion experience, intellectual decision, Christian upbringing, influence of friends and family, and influence by someone outside the circle of friends and family. These were not presented as mutually exclusive categories, so that individuals could draw attention to more than one factor. By far the largest vote went to the influence of a Christian upbringing, which was identified by three-quarters of the lay participants (76%) in the survey. The influence of friends and family was identified by 28% and the influence of someone outside the circle of friends and family was identified by 25%. A quarter of the committed lay Anglicans felt that they had come to faith by making an intellectual decision (26%), compared with a fifth who felt that they had come to faith through a religious conversion experience (20%).

While committed lay Anglicans were generally reluctant to attribute their path to faith to a conversion experience, there was room among many of them to talk about religious experience more generally. When asked whether or not they have had a religious experience, the lay participants responded as follows: 41% said yes definitely, 13% said probably but not certain, and 19% said perhaps but not sure, leaving only 27% who said no.

Church tradition was assessed in the survey by three seven-point semantic scales, anchored by Catholic and Evangelical, by conservative and liberal, and by charismatic and non-charismatic. In the analysis the scale was collapsed into three categories. In respect of the continuum between Catholic and Evangelical, 44% of the lay participants in the survey checked the two categories at the Catholic end, and 16% checked the two categories at the Evangelical end, leaving 40% in the middle three categories. In respect of the continuum between conservative and liberal, 27% of the lay participants in the survey checked the two categories at the conservative end, and 31% checked the two categories at the liberal end, leaving 42% in the middle three categories. In respect of the continuum between charismatic and non-charismatic, 8% of the lay participants in the survey checked the two categories at the charismatic end, and 55% checked the two categories at the non-charismatic end, leaving 37% in the middle three categories. The profile of committed Anglicans in the present survey veers toward non-charismatic liberal Catholics.

The majority of committed lay Anglicans contribute to their church through gift aid (85%), leaving one in every seven (15%) who do not do so. The amount given each week varies considerably. One in ten (10%) contribute less than £3 per week; one in five (22%) contribute between £3 and £5 per week; 28% contribute between £6 and £10 per week; 16% contribute between £11 and £15 per week; 9% contribute between £16 and £20 per week; 13% contribute between £21 and £50 per week; and 3% contribute more than £50 per week.

Committed lay Anglicans take the discipline of personal prayer seriously: 84% say that they pray nearly every day, while a further 10% pray at least once a week. This leaves 6% who are not committed to the practice of regular personal prayer.

Committed lay Anglicans take the discipline of bible reading less seriously than they take the discipline of personal prayer. Nonetheless, over half (53%) of the lay participants in the survey say that they read the bible nearly every day, while a further 23% read the bible at least once a week. This leaves 5% who read the bible at least once a month, 18% who read the bible less often than once a month, and 1% who say that they never read the bible.

The majority of committed lay Anglicans are used to reading books on theology and faith. Only 12% had read no books of this nature during the past year, while 57% had read between one and five such books and 31% had read more than six.

The majority of committed lay Anglicans are also keen to participate in various kinds of educational programmes. More than one in three (36%) had taken part in a parish-based programme during the past five years, while one in four (25%) had taken part in a diocesan-based programme. Committed lay Anglicans also give due attention to nationally-based programmes. During the past year, one in five (19%) had taken part in an Alpha course and one in eight (13%) had taken part in an Emmaus programme.

In order to develop an understanding of faith further, a number of committed lay Anglicans had also participated in theology or religious studies programmes operated through colleges of further education or institutions of higher education. During the past year one in ten (9%) had taken part in a further education programme and one in fourteen (7%) had taken part in a higher education programme. There is clearly good scope for Anglican churches to collaborate with providers of further and higher education in order to build on this interest in learning among committed lay Anglicans.

PARTICIPATION IN SERVICES

The operational definition of a committed lay Anglican employed by the present study included attendance at church at least once a fortnight. Closer inspection of the data revealed that 32% of the lay participants in the survey attended several times each week, with a further 64% attending weekly. This leaves just 4% who attended once a fortnight.

The idea that committed lay Anglicans are also highly committed to the parochial structure of the Church of England is not well supported by the data. Two out of every five committed lay Anglicans (39%) travel outside the parish in which they reside in order to attend an Anglican church. For nearly one in five committed lay Anglicans (18%) this means travelling more than a couple of miles. For 10% the distance travelled is up to four miles, while for 6% it means travelling between five and nine miles, and for 2% it means travelling ten miles or more.

Whether or not they live in the parish in which they choose to worship, the majority of committed lay Anglicans are registered on the electoral roll (96%) of the church they attend, with only 4% not being so registered.

The types of services attended confirm that, while Anglicanism promotes a eucharistically-based form of worship, the emphasis is far from exclusively on eucharistic services. Over the past four Sundays, 56% of committed lay Anglicans attended a eucharist each week, with a further 20% attending a eucharist on three of the four weeks. This left 15% who attended a eucharist on two Sundays and 6% who attended a eucharist on one Sunday. The remaining 3% did not attend a eucharist at all during the previous four Sundays.

By way of comparison, morning prayer is no longer part of the general experience of committed lay Anglicans worshipping on a Sunday. Three out of every four committed lay Anglicans (73%) did not attend morning prayer on a Sunday at all during the previous four weeks. Of the remaining lay participants in the survey, 14% attended morning prayer on one Sunday, 7% on two Sundays, 2% on three Sundays, and 4% on all four Sundays.

Evening prayer remains better established than morning prayer in the experience of committed lay Anglicans. Nevertheless, well over half (56%) of the lay participants in the survey did not attend a service of evening prayer during the previous four Sundays. Looked at from the opposite perspective, 11% attended evening prayer on all of the previous four Sundays, 7% on three of the previous four Sundays, 10% on two of the previous four Sundays, and 17% on one of the previous four Sundays.

Alongside the services of communion, morning prayer and evening prayer, a number of Anglican churches promote a pattern of family services, a term which can cover a wide variety of different experiences. Two out of every five committed lay Anglicans (40%) attended at least one family service during the previous four Sundays. Within this number, 31% attended a family service on just one of the four previous Sundays, 5% on two of the previous four Sundays, 1% on three of the four previous Sundays, and 3% on all of the previous four Sundays.

The preferred time for committed lay Anglicans to come out to worship on a Sunday is mid-morning before 11.00am. Early morning Sunday services before 9.00am are largely unattractive: only 22% of committed lay Anglicans attended a service beginning that early during the previous four Sundays. Sunday services beginning at 11.00am or later are equally unpopular: only 24% of committed lay Anglicans attended a service beginning that late during the previous four Sundays. By way of comparison, 85% of committed lay Anglicans attended a service beginning between 9.00am and 10.45am during the previous four Sundays. Sunday afternoon is the least popular time of day: only 10% of committed lay Anglicans attended a service beginning between 1.00pm and 5.45pm during the previous four Sundays. Anglicanism comes partly back into life on Sunday evening at 6.00pm or 6.30pm: 45% of committed lay Anglicans attended a service beginning at that time in the evening during the previous four Sundays. The concentration of services within such a narrow time band on Sunday mornings has clear implications for the ways in which services need to be led in an age when the number of stipendiary clergy is declining. Requiring fewer clergy to take more services more widely spread throughout the day may just fail to coincide with the expectations of committed Anglicans regarding the time when they expect services to take place in their local community.

Although the majority of committed lay Anglicans (62%) now have the experience of clergywomen leading services in their church, two out of every five (38%) reported that this never happens in the churches they attend. Looked at from a different perspective, 7% of committed lay Anglicans attend churches where the services are generally led by a female priest and a further 55% of committed lay Anglicans attend churches where the services are sometimes led by a female priest.

Although the majority of committed lay Anglicans (76%) now have the experience of lay people leading services in their church, one out of every four

(24%) reported that this never happens in the churches they attend. Looked at from a different perspective, 40% of committed lay Anglicans attend churches where the services are sometimes led by lay people in the absence of clergy and a further 36% of committed lay Anglicans attend churches when the services are sometimes led by lay people working alongside clergy.

Clearly Anglican congregations vary greatly in size. A small number (2%) of committed lay Anglicans find themselves generally worshipping in congregations of fewer than ten people and a further 12% in congregations of between 10 and 24 people. One in five committed lay Anglicans (21%) worship in congregations of between 25 and 49 people, and a further one in five (20%) in congregations of between 50 and 74 people. One in six committed lay Anglicans (16%) worship in congregations of between 75 and 99 people, and a further one in six (17%) in congregations of between 100 and 149 people. This leaves 12% of committed lay Anglicans who worship in congregations of at least 150 people.

A number of committed lay Anglicans are also likely to attend some services on a weekday as well as on a Sunday. During the past week, 46% of committed lay Anglicans attended at least one weekday communion service, 14% attended at least one weekday service of evening prayer, and 11% attended at least one weekday service of morning prayer. A high level of devotional commitment is indicated by the fact that, during the past week, 8% of committed lay Anglicans attended at least three weekday communion services, 3% attended at least three weekday services of evening prayer, and 3% attended at least three weekday services of morning prayer.

Profiling the clergy

PERSONAL CHARACTERISTICS

The Anglican clergy who participated in the survey include a range of different forms of ministry. Two out of every five (41%) of them were engaged in stipendiary parochial ministry, and a further 8% were engaged in stipendiary extra-parochial ministry. One in every seven (14%) described themselves as engaged in non-stipendiary ministry, and a further 3% as engaged in ordained local ministry. The remaining 35% were retired.

About one in five (19%) of the Anglican clergy who participated in the survey were female and 81% were male. This imbalance between the sexes fairly reflects the much longer period of time over which the Church of England has ordained men into priesthood.

The age profile of the Anglican clergy who participated in the survey reflects the important contribution of retired clergy to the total body of Anglican clergy in England. Overall, 10% of the clergy were under the age of forty, 17% were in their forties, 24% in their fifties, 25% in their sixties, 18% in their seventies, and 6% were aged eighty or over.

The majority of Anglican clergy are married. Overall, 72% of the clergy said that they were married. A further 3% described themselves as divorced and remarried, and 1% described themselves as living with a partner. Of those living alone, 4% were widowed, 4% were separated or divorced, and the remaining 16% were single.

Quite a high proportion of Anglican clergy had been educated in the independent sector. One in every three (33%) had received all of their schooling in independent schools and a further 7% had received at least part of their schooling in independent schools. This leaves three out of every five (60%) of the Anglican clergy who had received all of their schooling within the state-maintained sector.

Although ministry in the Church of England is not an all-graduate profession, a high proportion of Anglican clergy are themselves graduates: 88% are graduates, compared with 12% who are not graduates. By no means all of the graduates, however, hold degrees in theology.

The overall household income of the Anglican clergy varies considerably, depending on whether they are retired or in active ministry, on whether they are engaged in secular employment, whether their spouse is in paid employment, and whether they have other independent means. Thus, 3% of the clergy have an annual household income of less than £10,000 per year and 15% have between £10,000 and £14,999 per year. One in three (33%) of the clergy come into the category between £15,000 and £19,999 per year, and a further one in four (26%) come into the category between £20,000 and £29,999 per year. Just 11% of the clergy come into the category between £30,000 and £39,999, 6% into the category between £40,000 and £49,999, and 6% into the category of £50,000 and above per year.

The geographical distribution of the clergy indicates that higher proportions of Anglican clergy live in rural and suburban areas than in urban areas. Thus 37% described their environment as rural, and 34% described their environment as suburban, compared with 28% who described their environment as urban.

Like the committed lay Anglicans, the clergy invest a lot of energy and time in spheres of voluntary work, relevant both to the local community and to wider national and international issues. Thus, one in three (31%) of the Anglican clergy reported that they undertook voluntary work in the sphere of education; 16% did so in the sphere of community activities, and 11% in the sphere of cultural activities. Similarly, 9% reported engagement with social welfare activities, 8% with work among children, 7% with work among youth, and 7% with work among health-related groups. Anglican clergy were also involved with work concerned with world development (7%), environmental issues (4%), and human rights issues (4%). Like the committed lay Anglicans, the Anglican clergy appear to be making a significant contribution to the infrastructure of social capital within their communities.

ANGLICAN FORMATION

The majority (84%) of men and women currently ordained in the Church of England had themselves been originally baptised into the Anglican Church. The remaining 16% had transferred from other Christian denominations. The largest areas of transfer had been from the Methodist Church (3%), the Baptist Church (2%), the Congregational Church (2%), the Roman Catholic Church (2%), the Presbyterian Church (1%), and the Lutheran Church (1%). Other transfers had taken place from the Assemblies of God, the Brethren, the Church of Christ, the Free Independent Evangelical Church, the Society of Friends, and the Unitarian Church.

The path which led to faith for Anglican clergy followed a somewhat different route from that followed by the committed lay Anglicans. The clergy were almost twice as likely to have come to faith by means of a religious conversion (35%, compared with 20% of the laity). The clergy were more likely than the laity to have come to faith by means of an intellectual decision (33%, compared with 26% of the laity). The clergy were also more likely than the laity to trace their path of faith as influenced by someone outside the immediate sphere of family and friends (38%, compared with 25%). At the same time, 28% of the laity and 32% of the clergy traced their path to faith as influenced by family and friends. The clergy were less likely than the laity to attribute their path to faith to a Christian upbringing (69%, compared with 76%).

Religious experience has played a much more central part in the lives of Anglican clergy than in the lives of the committed lay Anglicans. When asked whether or not they have had a religious experience, 41% of the lay participants in the survey said yes definitely. Among the clergy the proportion rose to 71%. Among the remaining clergy, 10% said probably but not certain, and 10% said perhaps but not sure, leaving only 10% who said no.

Church tradition was assessed in the survey by three seven-point semantic scales, anchored by Catholic and Evangelical, by conservative and liberal, and by charismatic and non-charismatic. In the analysis the scale was collapsed into three categories. In respect of the continuum between Catholic and Evangelical, 47% of the clergy checked the two categories at the Catholic end, and 21% checked the two categories at the Evangelical end, leaving 32% in the middle three categories. In respect of the continuum between conservative and liberal, 21% of the clergy checked the two categories at the conservative end, and 44% checked the two categories at the liberal end, leaving 35% in the middle three categories. In respect of the continuum between charismatic and non-charismatic, 12% of the clergy checked the two categories at the charismatic end, and 50% checked the two categories at the non-charismatic end, leaving 38% in the middle three categories. The profile of Anglican clergy in the present survey veers toward non-charismatic liberal Catholics.

The majority of clergy contribute to their church through gift aid (83%), leaving one in every six (17%) who do not do so. The amount given each week varies considerably. A small number (6%) contribute less than £3 per week; one in six (17%) contribute between £3 and £5 per week; 28% contribute between £6 and £10 per week; 20% contribute between £11 and £15 per week; 11% contribute between £16 and £20 per week; 16% contribute between £21 and £50 per week; and 2% contribute more than £50 per week.

The clergy who participated in the survey clearly regard themselves as people who take the religious life of personal devotions very seriously. Thus, 98% say that they pray nearly every day, and 89% say that they read the bible nearly every day. Very few say that they engage in personal prayer less than once a week (1%), or that they read the bible less than once a week (3%).

The majority of Anglican clergy, both active and retired, maintain an interest in reading books about theology and about the faith. Just 1% claim to have read no books of this nature during the past year. One in three (35%) have read between one and five books in the past year, and nearly half (46%) have read between six and twenty books in the past year. The remaining 17% have read more than twenty books on theology and faith in the past year.

The Anglican clergy who participated in the survey are quite heavily involved in a range of educational and outreach programmes. During the past five years, one in four of the clergy (24%) were involved in an Alpha course, and one in five (19%) were involved in an Emmaus programme. One in three (33%) were involved in a parish-based programme during the past year, while one in four (27%) were involved in a diocesan-based programme.

A number of the Anglican clergy are also looking to programmes operated through colleges of further education and institutions of higher education. During the past year, one in ten (9%) had taken part in a further education programme and one in five (22%) had taken part in a higher education programme. There may be a particular role for institutions of higher education to support the continuing professional development of the clergy.

PARTICIPATION IN SERVICES

The operational definition of a committed Anglican employed by the present study included attendance at church at least once a fortnight. The retired clergy included in the present analysis are restricted, therefore, to those active retired who are able to participate in regular attendance at services. Closer inspection of the data revealed that 56% of the clergy in the sample are attending services several times a week and a further 43% are attending weekly. This leaves just 1% who attend once a fortnight.

The majority of Anglican clergy, active and retired, are highly focused on eucharistic worship. Four out of every five (82%) attended at least one communion service on all four of the previous four Sundays, while a further 11% attended communion services on three of the previous four Sundays. This left just 7% who attended communion services on less than three of the previous four Sundays.

By way of comparison, morning prayer is no longer part of the general experience of Anglican clergy on a Sunday morning. During the previous four Sundays two-thirds (64%) of the Anglican clergy did not participate in morning prayer at all. Looked at from the opposite perspective, 12% participated in morning prayer on one Sunday during the previous four weeks, 8% on two Sundays, 3% on three Sundays, and 13% on all four Sundays.

Evening prayer remains better established than morning prayer in the pattern of services conducted or attended by Anglican clergy on a Sunday. Nevertheless, between two-fifths and half of the Anglican clergy (45%) had not participated in evening prayer on any of the previous four Sundays. Looked at from the opposite perspective, 14% participated in evening prayer on one Sunday during the previous four weeks, 12% on two Sundays, 8% on three Sundays, and 22% on all four Sundays.

Slightly more than two out of every five (44%) of the Anglican clergy attended at least one family service during the previous four Sundays. Within this number 33% attended a family service on one of the four previous Sundays, 8% on two of the four previous Sundays, 1% on three of the four previous Sundays, and 2% on all four Sundays.

The majority of Anglican clergy, both active and retired, participate in worship during the week as well as on Sundays. Just over one-third (35%) of the clergy attended a communion service on at least two weekdays during the previous week and just over another third (35%) attended one mid-week communion service during the previous week, leaving 30% who attended no weekday communion services during the previous week.

Anglican clergy are much less likely to attend public services of morning prayer and evening prayer on a weekday than they are to attend mid-week communion services. While 70% attended at least one weekday communion service during the previous week, the proportions fell to 39% who had attended at least one service of morning prayer and to 27% who had attended at least one service of evening prayer. Looked at in greater detail, 26% had attended morning prayer on four days, 3% on three days, 4% on two days, and 6% on one day during the previous week. Similarly, 16% had attended evening prayer on four days, 2% on three days, 2% on two days, and 7% on one day during the previous week.

CHAPTER 3

Fragile consensus

Introduction

The Church of England is a broad church. The aim of the present chapter is to assess just how broad by providing an overview of the responses of the whole sample of committed Anglicans who responded to the *Church Times Survey*. Here clergy and laity are put together into the same melting pot of Anglican opinion. Here men and women, young and old, Catholic and Evangelical, charismatic and non-charismatic are viewed together through a single lens. There will be some issues on which there may be close consensus, perhaps almost unanimity. There will be other issues on which opinion may be sharply divided, perhaps almost equally divided down the middle.

Each of the fifteen themes highlighted in the *Church Times Survey* will be examined in turn. The analysis will be straightforward and direct. Each theme will be introduced briefly and analysed into its constituent sub-components. Then an overview of the responses will be discussed by distinguishing three categories of response to each individual question included in the survey. The 'agree strongly' and 'agree' responses have been collapsed into the single category of 'agree' or 'yes'. The 'disagree strongly' and 'disagree' responses have been collapsed into the single category of 'disagree' or 'no'. The 'not certain' response has been treated as an unwillingness or inability to take a decisive stance on one side of the issue or the other. In this chapter the responses are presented and discussed in narrative form. The tables on which the narrative is based are presented in full at the end of the book.

What is crucial about this chapter is the clear presentation of the way in which our sample of committed Anglicans responded to the precise questions in the survey. The authors' commentary and interpretation are but secondary. Individual readers are not only welcomed but positively urged to formulate their own interpretation of these multi-faceted data, and their own assessment of just how strong or how fragile the Anglican consensus may prove to be in the coming decade.

Patterns of belief

The *Church Times Survey* identified three doctrinal areas against which to assess the orthodoxy of Anglican belief: beliefs about God, beliefs about Jesus, and beliefs about life after death.

If committed Anglicans are clear about one thing, it is about the existence of God: 97% of committed Anglicans have no hesitation in affirming belief in the existence of God. It is nonetheless important to recognise that three in every hundred committed Anglicans have moved from the theistic position into the agnostic position. When invited to stand to recite the creed in liturgy such Anglicans may experience some difficulty.

While the majority of Anglicans have little difficulty in affirming belief in the existence of God, the God in whom they all believe may not necessarily reflect the historic vision of the creeds. Eight out of ten (82%) Anglicans believe that God is a personal being, but the remaining 18% either disagree (5%) or are unsure (15%). Indeed one in every eight Anglicans (13%) has moved to the position of seeing God as an impersonal power. Belief that God is an impersonal power is far removed from belief that God is the loving Father of Our Lord Jesus Christ.

The historic creeds base much of their understanding of the person of Jesus on the birth narratives and on the resurrection narratives. The Jesus of the creeds was born of a virgin and rose physically from the dead. Contemporary Anglican belief clings more strongly to the physical resurrection than to the virgin birth. Nearly four out of every five Anglicans (78%) affirm faith in the physical resurrection of Jesus, compared with three out of every five who affirm faith in the virgin birth (62%). The proportion of Anglicans who actually deny such beliefs, rather than adopting a position of agnosticism about them, remains quite low: 12% deny belief in the virgin birth and 6% deny belief in the physical resurrection.

Two out of every three committed Anglicans believe in the literal nature of the miracles attributed to Jesus by the gospel writers: 64% believe that Jesus really turned water into wine.

Belief in life after death is also a core component of faith in the historic creeds. Nine out of every ten committed Anglicans (88%) find belief in life after death remains core to their faith. One in ten (10%) are agnostic about life after death and just 2% reject such belief.

While the majority of committed Anglicans have little difficulty in affirming belief in life after death, the image which they carry of life after death may be at some variance with the historic creeds. Of this traditional imagery, belief in heaven has survived much more strongly than belief in hell. More than three-quarters (79%) of committed Anglicans believe that heaven really exists, compared with less than one half (46%) who believe that hell really exists. Once again most of those who are now reluctant to affirm these components of the ancient creeds (regarding heaven and hell) lean more toward agnosticism than toward clear disbelief. Thus, 17% of committed Anglicans remain agnostic about the existence of heaven, compared with 4% who reject such belief outright. Similarly, 34% of committed Anglicans remain agnostic about the existence of hell, compared with 20% who reject such belief outright.

Paths of truth

The *Church Times Survey* identified three means of examining the ways in which truth claims are asserted: beliefs about the bible, beliefs about the exclusivity of Christianity, and beliefs about evolution versus creationism.

The distinctive emphasis of Anglicanism is commitment to revelation and to reason. Committed Anglicans remain clear that the bible is not the *only* source for their faith. While one in eight Anglicans (12%) take the view that the bible is without any errors, six times that number (70%) are firm in their rejection of that position. The remaining 18% feel confident neither to affirm nor to deny this position.

Overall Anglicanism promotes a critical approach to the study of scripture. Three out of every five committed Anglicans (62%) argue that biblical truths are culturally conditioned, compared with only 15% who reject this position. The remaining 23% feel confident neither to affirm nor to deny this position.

Historically the Christian faith has made strong exclusivity claims about the nature of salvation. Today fewer than half (46%) of committed Anglicans believe that Christianity is the only true religion and a third (32%) flatly reject the idea. This leaves one in five (22%) who have no formal view on the matter.

Although many committed Anglicans (54%) are disinclined to support the view that Christianity is the only true religion, only a small number (11%) would go as far as claiming that all religions are of equal value. Two-thirds (67%) of committed Anglicans flatly deny that all religions are of equal value and the remaining 22% keep an open mind on the matter.

Creationism comprises one of those areas which clearly divide one group of Christians from another and which separate out some Christian groups very strongly from the society in which they live. The data demonstrate that among committed Anglicans there are creationists who take the view that God made the world in six days and rested on the seventh, but that those who take that view are in a minority. While one in every six Anglicans (16%) signs up to a creationist position, four times that number (62%) reject the creationist position and the remaining 23% keep an open mind on the matter.

The basic notion of evolution is, however, well integrated within the Anglican worldview. Seven out of every ten committed Anglicans (69%) believe that all living things evolved, compared with just a sixth of that number (11%) who firmly reject the evolutionary account of life. Once again, one in five committed Anglicans (21%) remain unclear about where precisely they stand on this issue.

Paths of spirituality

In order to gauge different pathways of spirituality, the *Church Times Survey* distinguished between three kinds of issues: personal and private sources of spiritual sustenance, group-based and shared sources of spiritual sustenance, and drawing on wider resources for spiritual sustenance.

Committed Anglicans claim to be well grounded in the traditional practices of personal prayer and bible reading. Just 3% say that they are not helped in their faith by praying by themselves. Just 5% say that they are not helped in their faith by reading the bible. Additionally, a further one in every ten are not really sure that they are helped in their faith by praying by themselves (11%) or by reading the bible (10%). So, if Anglican spirituality is really grounded in personal prayer and bible reading (as evidenced by the daily offices), it may be a matter of some significance that a sizeable minority (one in every seven) no longer feels profitably part of that tradition.

Committed Anglicans resource their faith by reading Christian books. Four out of every five Anglicans (82%) say that they are helped in their faith by reading Christian books, compared with only 5% who are not helped in this way and a further 14% who are not so sure.

Committed Anglicans are much less likely to resource their faith by reading non-religious books. While 82% of Anglicans say that they are helped in their faith by reading Christian books, the proportion more than halves to 36% who say that they are helped in their faith by reading non-religious books. As many as 28% are clear that they are not helped in their faith by reading non-religious books and another 36% are not really sure one way or the other.

Committed Anglicans generally recognise the value of discussing matters of faith with others. Four out of every five Anglicans (82%) say that they are helped in their faith by discussing their faith with others, compared with just 6% who deny that this is the case and 12% who are not really sure about it.

Although the majority of committed Anglicans generally recognise the benefits of discussing matters of faith with other people, there is overall less enthusiasm for bible study groups and for prayer groups. Just over half (55%) say that they are helped in their faith by bible study groups, and slightly fewer (50%) say that they are helped in their faith by prayer groups. Looked at from the opposite perspective, one in five committed Anglicans are clear that they are not helped in their faith by bible study groups (19%) or by prayer groups (20%). Quite large proportions are uncertain regarding whether or not they are helped by bible study groups (26%) or by prayer groups (30%). This may reflect the lack of opportunity in some Anglican churches to experience such groups in the first place.

Seven out of every ten committed Anglicans (69%) are helped in their faith by considering the natural world, compared with just 10% who are clear that this has not been the case for them and a further 22% who are unclear about the matter. These data are consistent with the view that Anglicanism continues to place reason alongside scripture as a primary source of revelation.

Nearly three out of every five committed Anglicans (56%) affirm that they are helped in their faith by going on retreat, compared with just 15% who are clear that this has not been the case for them and a further 29% who are unclear about the matter. The high proportion who are unclear about the matter may reflect the fact that significant sectors of committed Anglicans have not experienced the practice of retreats.

For the majority of committed Anglicans their spiritual path is well defined within the church itself. Nonetheless, as many as one in seven (15%) feel that they often get more spiritual help outside the church than within it. This compares with 66% who are clear that they get more spiritual help from inside the church than from outside, and 19% who just wonder if they might be getting more help outside the church than from within it.

Public worship

The definition of committed Anglicans in the present analysis involves attendance at Sunday church services at least twice a month. The *Church Times Survey* included three sets of questions to assess responses to public worship: the first set focused on the debate between traditional and modern forms of public worship, the second set focused on different aspects of the service, and the third set focused on the initiation of children into the worshipping community.

Overall among committed Anglicans there is more support for the traditional forms of worship than for the modern forms of worship. Thus, 68% of Anglicans feel that they are helped in their faith by traditional forms of service, compared with 51% who feel that they are helped in their faith by new forms of service. Similarly, 76% of Anglicans feel that they are helped in their faith by traditional hymns in services, compared with 60% who feel that they are helped in their faith by new hymns in services.

As well as indicating that there is greater support for the traditional than for the modern, these statistics also reveal three other important features regarding the approach of committed Anglicans to public worship. The first important feature is that there is comparatively little hostility among committed Anglicans against their non preferred forms of public worship. Only 14% say that they are not helped by traditional forms of service and 19% say that they are not helped by new forms of service. Similarly, only 8% say that they are not helped by traditional hymns in services and 15% say that they are not helped by new hymns in services.

The second important feature is that there is considerable overlap between those who are helped by traditional and by modern features in public worship. In other words, many committed Anglicans appear to be supported in their faith by a mixture of the traditional and the new.

The third important feature is that more Anglicans are uncertain about the contribution of modern aspects of public worship to their faith than are uncertain about the contribution of traditional aspects of public worship to their faith. Thus, 30% of Anglicans are unclear about the extent to which new forms of service help them in their faith, compared with 18% who are unclear about the extent to which traditional forms of service help them in their faith.

Similarly, 25% of Anglicans are unclear about the extent to which new hymns in services help them in their faith, compared with 16% who are unclear about the extent to which traditional hymns in services help them in their faith.

The diversity in forms of worship from one church to another is often considered one of the strengths of Anglicanism. The survey examined the extent to which three specific aspects of public worship are now generally found helpful by committed Anglicans, namely periods of silence, sermons, and ritual.

The data demonstrate considerable support for periods of silence in service. Four out of every five committed Anglicans (78%) say that they are helped in their faith by periods of silence in services, with only 7% saying that they find silence to be unhelpful. A further 16% are not really sure.

The idea that preaching has lost its power in the twenty-first century is clearly contradicted by the data. Three out of every four committed Anglicans (76%) say that they are helped in their faith by listening to sermons, with only 6% saying that they find sermons to be unhelpful. A further 18% are not really sure.

Ritual continues to play an important part in the spiritual lives of committed Anglicans. More than two out of every three committed Anglicans (70%) say that they are helped in their faith by ritual in services, with only 13% saying that they find ritual unhelpful. A further 17% are not really sure.

Considerable variation is thought to exist in contemporary baptism policy in Anglican parishes. The charge given to the clergy in the *Book of Common Prayer* to ensure that all infants born in their parish should be baptised has been eroded by a growing awareness of secularisation. The majority of committed Anglicans, however, resist the idea that baptism should be restricted to church-going families. Thus almost three-quarters of committed Anglicans (72%) are against churches baptising only babies of regular churchgoers, compared with only 13% who are in favour of such restrictions. A further 15% are not clear how they feel about this issue.

The *Book of Common Prayer* restricted communion to those who had been confirmed by the bishop or who were >desirous= of so being confirmed. As a radical departure from this Anglican practice, contemporary thinking, both on baptism as a total rite of Christian initiation and on the place of children within the church, has promoted the practice of the admission of children to communion prior to confirmation. Slightly over a half of committed Anglicans (53%) are in favour of this new practice, compared with slightly over a quarter (27%) who are against it. A further 21% are not clear how they feel about this issue.

Local church life

The kind of committed Anglicans on whom the present study is based are those who signal their commitment through association with a local church. In order to assess the nature of this commitment to a local church, the *Church Times Survey* included three groups of questions: questions concerning stages in the cycle of commitment, questions concerning the nature of commitment, and questions concerning the relationship between commitment and power.

Local church membership is far from static. Figuratively speaking, the entrance to each church is guarded by a revolving door. From time to time new members come in and old members drift away. Those who were very committed to being in the pews week-by-week gradually begin to attend less frequently. Those who were on the fringes take their place at the centre and start to attend every Sunday. The present snapshot of committed Anglicans focuses on those who are there in church most Sundays. The data show that as many as 41% of these committed Anglicans are people who say that they are coming to their church more regularly nowadays. In other words, these are the people who are on the way in through the revolving door.

The fact that such a high proportion of committed Anglicans are people whose commitment is on the increase demonstrates the ability of Anglicanism to continue to renew itself. It also raises questions about the stability of local Anglican churches and about what is happening on the other side of the revolving door. Since Anglicanism is not noticeably growing in England, those who are increasing their level of commitment seem to be doing no more than filling the places of whose who are decreasing their commitment.

The data also show that 6% of the current sample describe themselves as coming to their church less regularly nowadays. To have been included in the present definition of committed Anglicans these individuals who are already conscious of beginning the process of disengagement are nonetheless still attending at least twice a month. These figures suggest that, at any given time, among every seventeen apparently committed members one may be on the way out through the revolving doors.

Clearly one of the strong dynamics which keep committed Anglicans bonded to their local church is a sense of belonging. Nine out of every ten committed Anglicans (90%) say that they feel a strong sense of belonging to their church, compared with just 4% who deny that this is the case and a further 6% who are not so sure about their sense of belonging.

For seven out of every ten committed Anglicans (70%) their church is important for their social life, with just 18% denying that this is the case and 12% being uncertain about it. Not only is the church central to social life, but it is also central to personal support systems. Three out of every five committed Anglicans (60%) turn to fellow members of their church when they need help, with just 22% denying that this is the case and 18% being uncertain about it.

Being committed to a local church also often means exercising some control or power over the management and life of that church. Almost two-thirds of committed Anglicans (63%) say that they can influence their church=s decisions, compared with just 17% who feel powerless over their church=s decisions and a further 21% who are unsure if they have influence or not.

Looking at the same issue from the negative perspective, one in every seven committed Anglicans (15%) feel that they have too little control over the running of their church, with a further 20% unwilling to deny that this is the case.

The committed Anglicans at the centre of the local church are those on whom the church relies for financial resources and for human resources. The majority of these key people never complain that the church is asking too much of them. The figures show that 69% feel that the church does not make too many demands on their time, and 79% feel that the church does not make too many demands on their money. Nevertheless, the proportions who feel that the demands are too great may send significant warnings about the future direction of Anglicanism. One in every six committed Anglicans (16%) say that the church makes too many demands on their time, and one in every twelve (8%) say that the church makes too many demands on their money. These are the individuals who are likely to withdraw, either through burnout or through exasperation.

Ordained ministry

The Anglican Church has remained committed to the three-fold ordained ministry of deacon, priest, and bishop. The question of the moment is not whether the three-fold ministry itself should be reviewed, but who can properly be called to fulfil such sacred ministry. The debates in Anglicanism have focused on the ordination of women, the ordination of individuals who are divorced, the ordination of individuals who are divorced and remarried, and the ordination of practising homosexuals. The *Church Times Survey* included all four issues and distinguished between ordination as priest and ordination as bishop.

The debate about the ordination of women as priests has been largely won among committed Anglicans following the first ordinations of women in 1994. More than three-quarters of committed Anglicans (77%) say that they are in favour of the ordination of women as priests. For every ten committed Anglicans in favour of women priests there are now two firmly against (15%), and one who is undecided (8%).

Although women are not yet ordained as bishops in the Church of England (as they are elsewhere in the Anglican communion), almost two-thirds of committed Anglicans in England (64%) are of the view that women should be ordained as bishops. One in five committed Anglicans (21%) are against the ordination of women as bishops, and a further 15% are undecided.

The ordination of divorced people is as yet less clearly decided in the minds of committed Anglicans. Just over half (55%) are in favour of divorced people as priests, with 18% against and 27% undecided. Just under half (47%) are in favour of divorced people as bishops, with 27% against, and 27% undecided.

The ordination of those who are divorced and remarried is a little less acceptable to committed Anglicans than the ordination of those who are divorced and not remarried. While 55% are in favour of divorced people as priests, the proportion falls to 50% who are in favour of divorced and remarried priests. While 47% are in favour of divorced people as bishops, the proportion falls to 42% who are in favour of divorced and remarried bishops.

It is the ordination of practising homosexuals which attracts least support from committed Anglicans. More than half of committed Anglicans (53%) are clear that they are against the ordination of practising homosexuals as priests. The proportion increases further to 58% of committed Anglicans who are clear that they are against the ordination of practising homosexuals as bishops. Looked at from the opposite perspective, just one in every four committed Anglicans (25%) is in favour of the ordination of practising homosexuals as priests. Just one in every five committed Anglicans (21%) is in favour of the ordination of practising homosexuals as bishops.

One other feature of these data is worth comment and that concerns the proportions of committed Anglicans who register uncertainty on these issues. While just 8% of committed Anglicans are now uncertain about the ordination of women as priests, the proportion rises to 22% who are uncertain about the ordination of practising homosexuals as priests, and then the proportion rises further to 28% who are uncertain about the ordination of divorced and re-married people as priests. These issues may now need to be debated in a properly informed way in the Church of England in order to reduce such a pool of uncertainty.

Church leadership

Practical pressures from three different directions (in addition to profound theological reflection) have encouraged the Church of England in recent years to give serious reconsideration to issues of church leadership and ministry. The practical pressures have come from declining membership, erosion of historic financial resources, and falling vocations. As a consequence attention has been focused on practical aspects of the deployment and remuneration of the clergy and on practical aspects of lay ministry. The *Church Times Survey* gave proper attention to both issues.

Among committed Anglicans, there is clearly significant support for increasing clergy stipends, at least in principle. Three out of every five committed Anglicans (62%) believe that clergy should be paid a better wage, compared with 12% who disagree with that view. A further 26% are unsure about the matter.

Among committed Anglicans there is much less support, however, for changing other aspects of the current employment practices affecting the clergy. While two in every five committed Anglicans (39%) take the view that clergy freehold should be abolished, this still means that three in every five are not ready to support such a change, with 29% being firmly against the proposal and a further 32% being undecided.

The notion of employing clergy on short-term contracts would, in theory, enable greater and more responsive mobility among the clergy. Just 29% of committed Anglicans are in favour of this idea, with nearly half (48%) being decided against it. The remaining 23% have not made up their minds on this issue.

One of the very distinctive features of current employment practices among the clergy concerns the provision of a tied house. For one in four committed Anglicans (25%) the idea of the parsonage going with the job should now be a thing of the past with clergy living in their own houses. A considerably larger vote (43%), however, goes against this proposal. The remaining 32% have not made up their minds.

Overall there is considerable support among committed Anglicans for the involvement of lay people in the leadership of worship. At the same time, the level of support clearly varies from one liturgical function to another. At the top end of the scale, nearly nine out of every ten committed Anglicans (88%) are in favour of lay people leading morning and evening prayer and eight out of every ten (82%) are in favour of lay people preaching at morning and evening prayer. Looked at from the opposite perspective, just 6% are not in favour of lay people leading morning and evening prayer and only 9% are against lay people preaching at morning and evening prayer. It is clear, therefore, that for the majority of committed Anglicans it would be quite acceptable to leave the offices in the hands of the laity.

Lay leadership at communion services is somewhat less acceptable to committed Anglicans. While 88% of committed Anglicans are in favour of lay people leading morning and evening prayer, the proportion falls to 69% who are in favour of lay people leading the first part of the communion service (the ministry of the word). While 82% of committed Anglicans are in favour of lay people preaching at morning and evening prayer, the proportion falls to 74% who are in favour of lay people preaching at communion services. Looked at from the opposite perspective, 15% of committed Anglicans are against lay people preaching at communion services and 19% are against lay people leading the first part of the communion service. With as many as one in five committed Anglicans against this form of lay leadership, it could be pastorally disruptive to promote too quickly patterns of shared ministry which devolve more liturgical leadership onto laity and which allow priests to service more worship centres on a Sunday.

Lay presidency at the eucharist has never been part of Anglican theology or practice. The facts that one in every five committed Anglicans (18%) are now in favour of lay people taking the whole communion service and that a further 15% are not closed to the possibility signals a radical departure from tradition. Nevertheless, the majority (67%) remain committed to the traditional view. Change on this issue of practice and principle is unlikely to be welcomed in the near future.

Churches and cathedrals

The Church of England possesses a wonderful heritage of churches and cathedrals, medieval, Victorian, and twentieth-century buildings, in city centres, in remote and inaccessible rural areas and in suburbia. These buildings may be seen either as blessing or as liability, or perhaps a mixture of both. In order to assess divergent Anglican opinion on this issue, the *Church Times Survey* included two types of questions: the first focused on attitude toward the individual respondent=s local church, while the second focused on wider issues of policy.

The fact that one in every five committed Anglicans (20%) has come to the view that their congregation can no longer afford to pay for their church building may be a significant warning regarding the future capability of the Church of England for maintaining its architectural heritage. The additional fact that a further 18% are uncertain about the ability of their congregation to continue to pay for their church building may accentuate the sense of crisis. The good news, however, is that the maintenance of buildings has not yet reached crisis point in the eyes of 61% of committed Anglicans.

A significant minority of committed Anglicans are now clearly looking beyond the church community itself for ways of maintaining the church buildings. One in three committed Anglicans (32%) argue that, in order to survive, their church building needs more money from the state. One in four committed Anglicans (24%) argue that, in order to survive, their church building needs more money from tourists and visitors. Here are further indicators that the upkeep of church buildings may be becoming too burdensome for some parishes. The good news, however, is that in the eyes of many Anglicans the local church congregation is still in a strong enough position to take responsibility for the building. Thus, 47% of committed Anglicans reject the view that more grants are needed from the state, and 56% reject the view that more money is needed from tourists and visitors.

On the wider front, Anglican opinion is split over whether or not too much money is being spent on keeping old churches. A third of committed Anglicans (35%) believe that this is the case. Two-fifths of committed Anglicans (42%) believe that this is not the case. A quarter of committed Anglicans (23%) remain undecided one way or the other.

Opinion is divided, too, on the best strategy for dealing with the opportunities and challenges presented by the heritage of church buildings. A third of committed Anglicans (34%) believe that more church buildings should be taken over by the state, but two-fifths (42%) reject this solution and a further quarter (24%) are unsure about it. One in every seven committed Anglicans (15%) see part of the solution to be in closing more rural churches (where often the maintenance costs are high and the membership small), but 65% reject this solution and a further 21% are unsure about it.

The idea of charging visitors to enter cathedrals has sparked considerable controversy in recent years. Once again Anglican opinion is divided on this issue, but the weight of opinion is against entry charges. Thus more than half of committed Anglicans (55%) are against charging entry fees to cathedrals, compared with 24% who support the principle and 21% who have not yet made up their minds.

Money and policy

As the purchasing power of the historic resources of the Church of England available to meet recurrent running costs declines, so more and more of the annual budget devolves to the parishes themselves. As other denominations have been quick to learn, those who pay the piper also have some power over determining the tune. Increasingly, when local churches disagree fundamentally with diocesan or provincial policy they can threaten the sanction of withholding payment to the central purse. Through such mechanisms church policy can be impacted significantly. In order to gauge the priorities of committed Anglicans, the *Church Times Survey* posed a series of questions about how they envisaged the use of their church funds. Four specific areas were identified: central church structures, the clergy, development and mission, and community regeneration.

The current willingness and ability of parishes to meet their parish share (or quota) must remain a matter of concern to church authorities and to those responsible for setting diocesan and national budgets. The data demonstrate that only two out of every five committed Anglicans (40%) agree that the parish share has not been over-assessed. Of the remaining 60%, half (29%) are quite clear that their parish pays too much for its parish share and the other half (32%) appear at least to be feeling uneasy abut the level of assessment. The crisis comes when local churches are no longer able to increase their giving.

Overall, the majority of committed Anglicans feel quite positively about the financial needs of the diocesan structure. Seven out of every ten committed Anglicans (71%) are happy for some money given to their church to go to diocesan funds, compared with 12% who are unhappy about this. Another 18% are undecided. Committed Anglicans feel less positively, however, about the financial needs of the central church structures. While 71% of committed Anglicans are happy to contribute toward diocesan funds, the proportion falls to 55% who are happy for some money given to their church to go to church central funds. While 12% of committed Anglicans are unhappy to contribute toward diocesan funds, the proportion rises to 19% who are unhappy for some money given to their church to go to church central funds.

The majority of committed Anglicans remain content to want to support a professional clergy. Thus, 89% are happy for money given to their church to go to training new priests, and 82% are happy for money given to their church to go to clergy pensions. The proportions of committed Anglicans who are unhappy supporting a professional clergy are by comparison very small. Just 2% are unhappy for money given to their church to go to training new priests.

Just 5% are unhappy for their money to go to clergy pensions.

The majority of committed Anglicans also remain committed to funding aspects of development and mission, both at home and overseas. Thus, 86% of committed Anglicans are happy for money given to their church to go to struggling parishes. There is here a sense of richer and more affluent parishes helping the mission and pastoral work in poorer areas. Similarly, 83% of committed Anglicans are happy for money given to their churches to go to churches in developing countries. There is here a sense of being part of and supporting the world-wide presence of the church. Only a small minority of committed Anglicans are unhappy to use their money to support struggling parishes at home (4%) or to help churches in developing countries (4%).

Overall committed Anglicans are less sure about the use of their resources for community regeneration, and, where support is given to community development, there is more support for urban issues than for rural issues. Thus, 61% of committed Anglicans are happy for money given to their church to go to urban regeneration, and a slightly smaller proportion (55%) are happy for money given to their church to go to the farming community. Among those who are not positively supporting such use of church funds, there are twice as many who are uncertain about the issue as who are positively opposed to such use of church funds. Only 13% are against supporting urban regeneration, compared with 26% who are undecided. Only 16% are against supporting the farming community, compared with 29% who are undecided. Despite the educational programme initiated by the reports *Faith in the City* in 1985 and *Faith in the Countryside* in 1990, a number of committed Anglicans appear to be either uninformed or undecided about the issues involved.

Anglican identity

The Church of England occupies a unique position within the denominational landscape of England. As the established church of the land, the monarch remains the Supreme Governor of the Church of England, diocesan bishops are appointed by the state, and Parliament retains control of Church of England legislation. Implicitly and explicitly establishment is part of the identity of Anglicanism in England. The *Church Times Survey* focused two kinds of questions on Anglican identity: the first concentrated on willingness to merge Anglican identity with other denominations, and the second concentrated on the future of establishment.

The days appear to be over when committed Anglicans see their denominational loyalty in such strict terms that they would feel unhappy contemplating switching their allegiance. Today committed Anglicans seem to fall into three equally-sized groups. Just over a third (36%) remain convinced that they would never become a member of another denomination. Just over a third (35%) are clear that they would contemplate becoming a member of another denomination. Just under a third (30%) are not sure about their willingness to switch denominations, but neither are they sure that they would never do so.

In an age of ecumenical cooperation and denominational realignment, just 20% of committed Anglicans feel that they would not want the Church of England to join with another denomination, compared with 53% who would not resist such a development and 27% who are uncertain about their views on the matter.

Just over half of the committed Anglicans (53%) would be happy to be a member of an ecumenical church or a local ecumenical project, compared with 23% who say that they would not be happy to be a member of an ecumenical church or a local ecumenical project. The remaining 24% are undecided.

Church unity under papal supremacy remains unacceptable to a large number of committed Anglicans. While 29% would be prepared to accept the Pope as their church leader, 48% are clear that this would not be acceptable to them and the remaining 22% have sufficient reservations not to vote in favour of the suggestion.

Committed Anglicans are very ambivalent over the question of establishment. On the one hand, only between a quarter and a third of committed Anglicans (28%) sign up to the view that the Church of England should be disestablished. Four out of every five committed Anglicans (81%) believe that senior bishops should continue to sit in the reformed House of Lords. Twice as many committed Anglicans believe that the monarch should continue to be the Supreme Governor of the Church of England as believe that this should no longer be the case (49% compared with 26%); nonetheless, these figures show that less than half positively desire the monarch to remain as head of their Church.

On the other hand, the vast majority of committed Anglicans have clearly grown impatient with state control over key aspects of church life. Only 14% of committed Anglicans believe that Parliament should retain control of Church of England legislation. An even smaller proportion of committed Anglicans (5%) believe that diocesan bishops should be appointed by the state.

Confidence and the future

Psychologically speaking, confidence is crucial for the Church=s future. People who are confident in themselves and in the organisations which they support invest energy in making the future work. People who have lost confidence in themselves and in the organisations which they support also lose energy and lose commitment for the future. In order to gauge the level of confidence which committed Anglicans hold in the future, the *Church Times Survey* asked questions about two main issues: the first issue concerned confidence in the church=s leadership, and the second issue concerned confidence in the future of their own local church.

These data indicate that, overall, the majority of committed Anglicans display a reasonable level of confidence in the local and in the diocesan leadership, but a much lower level of confidence in the national leadership. The local parish clergy emerge from the survey as enjoying a high level of confidence among committed Anglicans. Three-quarters of committed Anglicans (75%) say that they have confidence in the leadership given by their local clergy, compared with just 7% who have no confidence in the leadership given by their local clergy and with 18% who are uncertain about the confidence they can place in the leadership given by their local clergy.

Diocesan bishops also emerge from the survey as enjoying a high level of confidence among committed Anglicans. Between three-quarters and two-thirds of committed Anglicans (71%) say that they have confidence in the leadership given by their diocesan bishop, compared with just 9% who have no confidence in the leadership given by their diocesan bishop and with 20% who are uncertain about the confidence they can place in the leadership given by their diocesan bishop.

By way of comparison, the General Synod and the Archbishops= Council emerge from the survey as not inspiring a high level of confidence among committed Anglicans. Just two out of every five committed Anglicans (41%) say that they have confidence in the leadership given by the General Synod, compared with 59% who cannot own that level of confidence. Just two out of every five committed Anglicans (38%) say that they have confidence in the leadership given by the Archbishops= Council, compared with 62% who cannot own that level of confidence. At the same time, it is important to note that the majority of those who are unwilling to express confidence in the leadership given by the General Synod or by the Archbishops= Council prefer to reserve their judgement on the matter rather than to signal complete lack of confidence. In other words, for many Anglicans the jury is still out and they are waiting to see if the General Synod and the Archbishops= Council are able to earn their confidence.

Nearer to home, there is cautious optimism about the future of the local church. Two out of every five committed Anglicans (40%) believe that the membership of their church will grow in the next 12 months, compared with just a third of that number (13%) who are convinced that their church is not going to grow in the next 12 months. The largest group (47%), however, has no firm grounds for anticipating growth, but nonetheless just wonders if it might be a possibility.

Churches grow by new people beginning to attend. These people are either invited by existing members or just turn up. It is not always easy, however, for newcomers to feel at home. It is a salutary reflection on the health of local Anglican churches that more committed Anglicans feel unable to invite other people to come to their church than actually feel able to invite others to come (44% compared with 37%). A further 19% of committed Anglicans are uncertain about inviting other people to their church.

One in every four committed Anglicans (23%) acknowledge that it is not easy for newcomers in their church and a further one in every four (23%) are not convinced that it is easy for newcomers in their church. Such a process of self-evaluation may help to explain why so many Anglican churches may find growth difficult to stimulate. Looked at from the opposite perspective, 54% of committed Anglicans reject the suggestion that it is difficult for newcomers to join their church.

Sex and family life

Traditionally, sexual relationships and family life are areas which have been closely policed by religious organisations and by religious teaching. The *Church Times Survey* identified four specific areas in which to test the orthodoxy of Anglican views today: views on sex and cohabitation before marriage, views on divorce, views on same sex relationships, and views on caring for children and teenagers.

Committed Anglicans today have tended to adopt a relatively liberal attitude concerning sex before marriage. Just over two out of every five committed Anglicans (43%) hold to the traditional view that it is wrong for men and women to have sex before marriage. One in three committed Anglicans (34%) are confident that they now reject this traditional view on sex before marriage and the remaining 23% feel that they want neither to accept the traditional view nor to affirm positively the alternative.

While 34% of committed Anglicans agree that sex before marriage is acceptable, the proportion falls slightly to 26% who agree that it is all right for a couple to live together without intending to get married. Twice that number of committed Anglicans (50%) take the view that it is not right for a couple to live together without intending to get married, and the remaining 24% feel that they want neither to accept the traditional view nor to affirm positively the alternative.

One in every five committed Anglicans (18%) are happy to recommend couples who intend to get married to live together first, but nearly three times that number (50%) maintain the more traditional view that this is not appropriate behaviour. At the same time, as many as one in three committed Anglicans (32%) find that they want neither to accept the traditional view nor to affirm positively the alternative.

Committed Anglicans today have tended to accept the inevitability of marriage breakdown. Three out of every four committed Anglicans (75%) agree that some marriages can come to a natural end in divorce or separation. By way of comparison, only one in every ten committed Anglicans (10%) would take the more traditional view that divorce or separation is not a natural end to marriage, and a further 16% have not formed a clear view on the issue.

Anglican opinion appears fairly evenly divided on whether or not couples should stay together for the sake of the children. Just over a third (38%) believe that they should do so. Just under a third (31%) believe that they should not do so. The remaining third (32%) have not formed a clear view on the issue.

Anglicans remain less liberal in their views on homosexual relations than in their views on heterosexual relations. Just over half of committed Anglicans (54%) take the view that it is wrong for people of the same gender to have sex together, compared with half that number (27%) who support same gender sexual activity. One in five committed Anglicans (18%) remain unsure about where they stand on this issue.

Looked at from another perspective, however, support for same sex marriage is not insignificant among committed Anglicans. One in every seven committed Anglicans (14%) take the view that homosexual couples should have the right to marry one another. For every one Anglican who takes this liberal view, five others (69%) are clearly opposed to the idea and one (17%) has not formed a firm opinion.

Committed Anglicans tend to remain committed to traditional gender roles in the upbringing of children. Just three out of every ten Anglicans (30%) take the view that children thrive equally whether cared for primarily by their father or mother, while four out of every ten (38%) are clear that this is not the case and the remaining 33% are unwilling to vote either way.

Not all committed Anglicans are averse to making contraception available to teenagers under 16 who want it. While 42% are firmly against the availability of contraception under the legal age, 35% support such availability and a further 23% appear open to persuasion.

Social concerns

In order to assess the levels of social concern expressed by committed Anglicans, the *Church Times Survey* included a set of items on global concerns and a set of items on community concerns. The global concerns included environmental and development issues, AIDS and genetic research. The community concerns included violence on television, paedophiles in the community, and the effects of the National Lottery.

Committed Anglicans record a very high level of concern regarding those global issues which affect the future lives of men and women across the world. The vast majority are concerned about environmental pollution (94%), about the poverty of the developing world (95%), and about the spread of AIDS (95%). Only 1% or 2% say that these matters are of no concern to them and a further 4% remain uncertain about their personal level of concern. If concern really leads to action, committed Anglicans are likely to be involved in environmentally-friendly behaviour, are likely to support development education initiatives, and are likely to be involved in initiatives concerned with responding to the AIDS crisis across the globe.

Research into human genes has raised a number of weighty ethical issues and the churches have been properly involved in that debate. Currently two-thirds of committed Anglicans (68%) express concern about research into human genes, compared with a quarter of that number (17%) who say that they are not concerned about this issue. At the same time, one out of every seven committed Anglicans (15%) has not formed an opinion on this issue.

Turning to issues that are closer to home, committed Anglicans register quite a high level of concern about the potentially detrimental influence of television on social values. Four out of every five Anglicans (81%) express concern about violence on television. For every twelve Anglicans who express concern about violence on television only one (7%) reports no concern about this issue and only two (13%) are unsure as to whether this should be a matter of concern or not. If concern leads to action, Anglicans might be well involved in protesting to the Broadcast Standards Authority at times when programmes portray excessive violence.

The safety of children and the proper care of convicted paedophiles is a matter of both theological and pastoral concern. Just over half of committed Anglicans (52%) express concern about paedophiles living in the community, compared with 16% who express no concern about the issue. One in three (32%), however, have not made up their minds on this issue.

The National Lottery has divided the opinion of Christians in England and Wales. There are those who see the National Lottery as propagating the evils of gambling and enticing those in society who can least afford it to waste their scarce resources on lottery tickets. There are those who have welcomed the support of lottery funds for the upkeep of ancient churches and cathedrals. This ambivalence is reflected among committed Anglicans. While just under half of committed Anglicans (47%) register concern about the National Lottery, just over half (54%) do not, with 27% saying definitely that they have no concern about the National Lottery and another 27% saying that it is an issue regarding which they have no clear opinion.

Social conscience

One of the standard devices used by the well-established British Social Attitudes Survey to gauge commitment to and priorities concerning expenditure from the public purse is through asking people to assess their willingness to pay more tax to fund specific areas. The *Church Times Survey* identified three such broad areas: health and education, social security and prisons, and defence and development aid.

The National Health Service and the state-maintained sector of education clearly remain close to the heart of many Anglicans, whether or not they are fully aware of the historic role of the churches in the establishment of hospitals and in the building of schools long before the 1870 Education Act. Four out of every five Anglicans (82%) say that they would pay more tax to fund spending on health. Three out of every four Anglicans (75%) say that they would pay more tax to fund spending on schools. Only a small minority clearly say that they would not pay more tax for better funding for health (7%) and for schools

(9%). What is also clear is that there are more Anglicans who have not made up their minds about their commitment to schools (16%) than is the case regarding commitment to health (12%).

The priority of the university sector is much lower in the minds of Anglicans than the priority of the school sector. While 75% of committed Anglicans would pay more tax to fund spending on schools, the proportion drops to 44% who would pay more tax to fund spending on universities. While just 9% of committed Anglicans are clear that they would not pay more tax to fund spending on schools, the proportion more than doubles to 21% who would not pay more tax to fund spending on universities. This leaves one in every three of committed Anglicans (36%) who appear uncertain about the value of providing more funding for universities from the public purse.

Two out of every five committed Anglicans would pay more tax to fund spending on prisons (43%) or to fund spending on social security benefits (42%). Almost as many committed Anglicans are uncertain about their willingness to contribute more to prisons (36%) or to social security benefits (35%). One out of every five committed Anglicans are clear that they would not pay more tax to fund better provision for prisons (21%) or for social security benefits (23%).

Two out of every three committed Anglicans (66%) say that they would pay more tax to fund spending on overseas aid. Of the remaining 34%, 12% are clear that they would not pay more tax to improve spending on overseas aid, and 22% have not really made up their minds on the issue.

Of all the seven specific issues identified in the *Church Times Survey*, it is the issue of increased spending on security forces which attracts least support from committed Anglicans. While 35% of committed Anglicans are clear that they would not pay more tax to fund spending on security forces, the proportion falls to 29% who are clear that they would pay more tax for this purpose. One in every three committed Anglicans (36%) has not formed a clear opinion on the issue.

The comparatively high proportion of committed Anglicans who have not formed a clear opinion on their willingness to fund universities, prisons, social security benefits and security forces from the public purse may reflect the lack of willingness or opportunity to debate these issues in church circles.

Education

The Church of England has had a long history of involvement in schools, both in the state-funded sector and in the independent or private sector. The statutory provisions of religious education and the daily act of worship throughout the whole of the state-maintained sector reflect the Church of England's astute negotiations over the future of church schools at the time of the 1944 Education Act. Again at the beginning of the twenty-first century, in the Dearing Report (2001), *The Way Ahead,* the Church of England renewed its commitment to the expansion of the church school system. In response to these issues, the *Church Times Survey* framed questions on three key topics: the debate between the state-funded and the independent sector, the place of religious education and worship in schools, and the future for faith-based schools.

The majority of committed Anglicans clearly continue to support the place of the independent sector of schools alongside the state-maintained sector. Thus, three-quarters of committed Anglicans (74%) speak clearly against the proposal that private schools should be abolished, compared with just 12% who vote in favour of the abolition of independent schools. A further 14% remain uncertain on the issue.

One in every five committed Anglicans (20%) have no confidence in the state-funded education system, and a further 28% are doubtful about their confidence in the system. This leaves 53% of committed Anglicans who have confidence in the state-funded education system.

The vast majority of committed Anglicans (93%) remain convinced that religious education should be taught in schools, with only 3% arguing against the provision and 5% adopting an uncommitted stance. The religious education envisaged by these committed Anglicans is, however, a far cry from the Christian education envisaged by the architects of the 1944 Education Act. Today four-fifths of committed Anglicans (81%) sign up to the view that religious education in schools should teach about world religions. Only 6% argue against teaching about world religions and 13% adopt an uncommitted stance.

Arguing for school worship and religious assemblies is generally regarded as more problematic than arguing for the place of religious education. To teach pupils about religion is one thing, but to expect them to engage in religious practices (like singing hymns) is something rather different. This distinction seems to be reflected in the responses to the survey. While 93% of committed Anglicans agree that religious education should be taught in schools, the proportion falls to 66% who agree that schools should hold a religious assembly every day. This leaves 12% of committed Anglicans who are against the provision of a daily religious assembly in schools and 22% who seem to be uncertain about it.

The majority of committed Anglicans clearly remain supportive of the church school system. Thus, 85% say that they are in favour of state-funded church schools, compared with only 4% who are against state-funded church schools and a further 11% who are undecided. The majority of committed Anglicans are also behind the recommendation of *The Way Ahead* to expand the Church of England's stake in the state-maintained sector of schools. Thus, 73% of committed Anglicans argue that the Church of England should fund more new church primary schools and 77% argue that the Church of England should fund more new church secondary schools. By way of comparison, only 6% of committed Anglicans are against the expansion of the number of church primary schools or the expansion of the number of church secondary schools.

Many might argue that a sense of fairness and justice should extend the facility of state funding for schools to other faith communities as well as to the Christian churches. The Jewish community has long enjoyed that provision in England, and more recently Islamic and Sikh schools have been added to the state-maintained sector. Committed Anglicans, however, are much more reticent in their support for Jewish and Islamic schools than in their support for Christian schools. While 85% of committed Anglicans are in favour of state-funded church schools, the proportions drop to 42% who are in favour of state-funded Jewish schools and to 38% who are in favour of state-funded Islamic schools. Looked at from the opposite perspective, while only 4% of committed Anglicans are against state-funded church schools, the proportions rise to 26% who are against state-funded Jewish schools and 30% who are against state-funded Islamic schools.

CHAPTER 4

Clergy and laity

Introduction

The first of the potential fault-lines within the Church of England to be examined by the present study concerns the relationship between the views of the committed laity and the views of the ordained clergy. Each of the fifteen themes highlighted in the *Church Times Survey* will be examined in turn.

The statistical tables on which this chapter is based are presented in the appendix at the end of the book. These tables have been designed to display the percentages of clergy and the percentages of the laity who have said 'yes' to the statements. As in the previous chapter the two responses of 'agree strongly' and 'agree' have been collapsed into the single category 'yes'. The statistical significance of the difference between the responses of the clergy and of the laity have been calculated by the chi square test, for which the responses have been dichotomised. The dichotomy is between those who say 'yes' and those who do not say yes, which is the product of the 'disagree strongly', 'disagree', and 'not certain' responses. Differences which do not reach the five percent probability threshold will be regarded as non-significant.

Patterns of belief

The *Church Times Survey* identified three doctrinal areas against which to assess the orthodoxy of Anglican belief: beliefs about God, beliefs about Jesus, and beliefs about life after death.

Very high proportions of committed lay Anglicans (97%) and clergy (97%) are firm in their belief in the existence of God. Nonetheless, it may just be worth noting that one in every thirty-three Anglican clergy doubt the existence of God. The God in whom the committed laity believe and the God in whom the clergy believe, however, are not necessarily identical. The laity are less likely than the clergy to believe that God is a personal being (79% compared with 90%). The laity are significantly more likely than the clergy to think of God in terms of an impersonal power (14% compared with 9%). In other words, the personal God of the historic creeds is likely to make less sense to the committed laity than to the clergy.

The clergy and the committed laity hold very similar views on the person of Jesus. Nearly four out of every five of the clergy (78%) and nearly four out of every five of the laity (78%) are firm in the belief that Jesus rose physically from the dead. Both clergy and laity are less inclined to believe in the virgin birth than in the physical resurrection. Thus, 62% of the laity and 60% of the clergy believe that Jesus' birth was a virgin birth. On the other hand, the clergy are significantly less inclined than the laity to believe that Jesus really turned water into wine, with 61% of the clergy believing this really happened, compared with 65% of the laity.

There is a significant, but not large, difference in the beliefs held by the clergy and by the committed laity regarding life after death. The clergy are slightly more orthodox than the laity. Thus, 91% of the clergy are firm in their belief that there is life after death, compared with 87% of the laity. A higher proportion of the clergy believe that heaven really exists (84%, compared with 78% of the laity). A higher proportion of the clergy believe that hell really exists (48%, compared with 46% of the laity).

Overall, Anglican clergy and committed lay Anglicans hold similar patterns of core beliefs. The fault-line is there, but not pronounced.

Paths of truth

The *Church Times Survey* identified three means of examining the ways in which truth claims are asserted: beliefs about the bible, beliefs about the exclusivity of Christianity, and beliefs about evolution versus creation.

As clergy receive a structured theological education, a situation which obtains with only some lay people, on the whole the clergy are likely to be more competent than the committed laity in handling the complexity of truth claims based on the bible. On the one hand, similarly low proportions of clergy (13%) and laity (11%) alike see the bible as an absolute authority without any errors. On the other hand, the clergy are much more at home with the idea that biblical truths are culturally conditioned. Three-quarters (74%) of the clergy agree that biblical truths are culturally conditioned, compared with 58% of the laity.

The clergy are more convinced than the committed laity about the strong exclusivity claims made by the Christian faith. While only 7% of the clergy take the view that all religions are of equal value, the proportion rises significantly to 12% among the committed laity. At the same time, 46% of the committed laity and 48% of the clergy believe that Christianity is the only true religion.

The gap between the beliefs of the clergy and the committed laity begins to widen a little further in the debate about creation versus evolution. While just 10% of the clergy take the creationist view that God made the world in six days and rested on the seventh, the proportion rises to 17% among the laity. While 74% of the clergy take the evolutionist view that all things living evolved, the proportion drops to 67% among the laity. Overall, there are many ways in which Anglican clergy and committed lay Anglicans hold similar views on the paths to religious truth. Now, however, a more serious fault-line begins to emerge as the committed laity show signs of being significantly less comfortable with the nuances of professional theological debate.

Paths of spirituality

In order to gauge different pathways of spirituality the *Church Times Survey* distinguished between three kinds of issues: personal and private sources of spiritual sustenance, group-based and shared sources of spiritual sustenance, and drawing on wider resources for spiritual sustenance.

The clergy have clearly developed greater reliance than the committed laity on the personal practices of spirituality. The clergy are more likely than the laity to feel that they are helped in their faith by praying by themselves (92% compared with 85%). The clergy are more likely than the laity to feel that they are helped in their faith by reading the bible (94% compared with 82%). The clergy are more likely than the laity to feel that they are helped in their faith by reading Christian books (90% compared with 79%). Most pronounced of all, the clergy are more likely than the laity to feel that they are helped in their faith by reading non-religious books (55% compared with 30%).

The committed laity are also somewhat less convinced than the clergy about group-based and shared sources of spiritual sustenance. While 90% of the clergy feel that they are helped in their faith by discussing their faith with others, the proportion falls to 79% among the laity. While 58% of the clergy feel that they are helped in their faith by bible study groups, the proportion falls to 54% among the laity. While 54% of the clergy feel that they are helped in their faith by prayer groups, the proportion falls to 49% among the laity.

While the spiritual benefits of retreats are well recognised by the committed laity, retreats remain significantly better grounded in the spirituality of the clergy. Thus, 51% of the committed laity say that they are helped in their faith by going on retreat, but the proportion rises to 74% among the clergy.

Clergy and committed laity are equally helped in their faith by considering the natural world (69% and 68%). The clergy are slightly more likely than the committed laity to feel that they often get more spiritual help outside the church than within it (18% compared with 15%).

Overall, the main fault-line between the spirituality of the clergy and the spirituality of the committed laity concerns the ways in which the clergy=s spirituality is more likely to be resourced by retreats and by reading non-religious books. Experience gained from both resources may, as a consequence, be less communicable, say through preaching, then some clergy may imagine.

Public worship

The *Church Times Survey* included three sets of questions to assess responses to public worship: the first set focused on the debate between traditional and modern forms of public worship, the second set focused on different aspects of the service, and the third set focused on the initiation of children into the worshipping community.

The clergy are clearly more likely than the committed laity to want to support modern forms of public worship. Thus, 65% of the clergy feel that they are helped in their faith by new forms of services, compared with 47% of the laity. Similarly, 67% of the clergy feel that they are helped in their faith by new hymns in services, compared with 58% of the laity.

As well as giving more support to new forms of public worship, the clergy are likely to give less support than the committed laity to traditional forms of public worship. The difference this time, however, is not so pronounced. While 71% of the laity feel that they are helped in their faith by traditional forms of services, the proportion falls to 59% among the clergy. While 77% of the laity feel that they are helped in their faith by traditional hymns in services, the proportion falls to 72% among the clergy.

There are much less pronounced differences between clergy and committed laity in terms of their preferences for different styles of worship. Three-quarters (76%) of the laity feel that they are helped in their faith by listening to sermons, and so do 75% of the clergy. Just over three-quarters (77%) of the laity feel that they are helped in their faith by periods of silence in services, and the proportion rises slightly to 81% among the clergy. Similarly, 69% of the laity feel that they are helped in their faith by rituals in services, and the proportion rises slightly to 73% among the clergy.

Both clergy and committed laity are clearly in favour of an open baptismal policy. Just 13% of the clergy and 13% of the laity take the view that churches should baptise only babies of regular churchgoers. The clergy and laity are quite clearly divided, however, on the issue of the admission of baptised children to communion prior to confirmation. While two-thirds (68%) of the clergy are in favour of this change in Anglican practice, the proportion falls to 48% among the committed laity.

Overall, the fault-line between the clergy and the committed laity begins to widen when tradition in public worship is at stake. Clergy who are keen on changing the Sunday service by introducing new forms of services or by introducing new practices, like the admission of children to communion prior to confirmation, may well need to expect some resistance and incomprehension from their key and committed lay people.

Local church life

In order to assess commitment to local church life, the *Church Times Survey* included two groups of questions useful for comparing the perspectives of the clergy and of the committed laity: questions concerning the sense of belonging, and questions concerning the relationship between commitment and power.

In several ways the clergy and the committed laity display a very similar sense of belonging to the local church. Thus, 91% of the laity say that they feel a strong sense of belonging to their church, and so do 90% of the clergy. Similarly, 60% of the committed laity say that they turn to fellow members of their church when they need help, and so do 60% of the clergy. There is a significant difference, however, regarding the way in which clergy and laity see the local church as key for their social life. While 71% of the committed laity see the local church as important for their social life, the proportion falls to 65% among the clergy.

The clergy feel significantly more in control of the local church than is the case among the committed laity. While 60% of the laity feel that they can influence their church=s decisions, the proportion rises to 72% among the clergy. While 16% of the laity feel that they have too little control over the running of their church, the proportion falls further among the clergy to 11%.

The clergy and the committed laity feel equally comfortable about the demands made by the church on their money. Just 8% of the laity and 7% of the clergy feel that their church makes too many demands on their money. The clergy are, however, twice as likely as the laity to feel that their church makes too many demands on their time (24% compared with 13%).

Overall, there are three aspects to the fault-line which runs between clergy and committed laity concerning the local church. The clergy may feel resentment that the local church is making too many demands on their time. The laity may feel resentment that they have too little control over running their local church.

Ordained ministry

The *Church Times Survey* included questions about four issues which divide opinion in the Church of England on the question of ordained ministry: the ordination of women, the ordination of individuals who are divorced and remarried, and the ordination of practising homosexuals. In respect of each of these issues the survey distinguished between ordination as priest and ordination as bishop.

On the issue of the ordination of women, the clergy and the committed laity hold quite similar views, with marginally more support coming from the clergy. Thus, 77% of the laity and 80% of the clergy are in favour of the ordination of women as priests; 63% of the laity and 66% of the clergy are in favour of the ordination of women as bishops.

The committed laity are, however, significantly more conservative than the clergy in their views regarding the ordination of individuals who have experienced divorce. While two-thirds (66%) of the clergy are in favour of divorced people as priests, the proportion falls to half (51%) among the laity. While 58% of the clergy are in favour of divorced people as bishops, the proportion falls to 43% among the laity. The same pattern is reproduced in respect of individuals who are divorced and remarried. While three-fifths (60%)

of the clergy are in favour of divorced and remarried priests, the proportion falls to 46% among the laity. While half (51%) of the clergy are in favour of divorced and remarried bishops, the proportion falls to 39% among the laity.

Neither clergy nor committed laity are strongly in favour of the ordination of practising homosexuals, but once again it is the clergy who are more likely to adopt an inclusive view. While one-third (33%) of the clergy are in favour of the ordination of practising homosexuals as priests, the proportion falls to 23% among the laity. While 29% of the clergy are in favour of the ordination of practising homosexuals as bishops, the proportion falls to 19% among the laity.

Overall, the fault-line between the clergy and the committed laity is quite significant when it comes to judging who should and who should not be ordained. In some senses the committed laity may be looking for more conservative standards of sexual behaviour among the clergy than the clergy are looking for among themselves. Here is an area in which it may be all too easy for clergy to misjudge the attitudes of the committed laity.

Church leadership

In order to assess attitudes toward two major areas of change in church leadership, the *Church Times Survey* included a section on the development of ordained ministry and a section on the development of lay ministry.

The clergy and the committed laity hold very similar views on the future of clergy freehold and on the future of the parsonage. Two-fifths (40%) of the laity argue that clergy freehold should be abolished, and so do 38% of the clergy. A quarter (26%) of the laity argue that clergy should live in their own houses, and so do 25% of the clergy.

In a couple of other ways, however, the committed laity are keener than the clergy to modernise the clerical profession. Thus, 30% of the laity consider that clergy should be employed on short-term renewable contracts, compared with 26% of the clergy themselves. Similarly, 64% of the laity consider that clergy should be paid a better wage, compared with 56% of the clergy themselves.

The gap between the views of the clergy and of the committed laity widens a little further on the subject of lay ministry. The clergy are keener than the laity themselves on developing many aspects of lay ministry. Thus, while 94% of the clergy are in favour of lay people leading morning and evening prayer, the proportion falls to 85% among the laity. While 85% of the clergy are in favour of lay people preaching at morning and evening prayer, the proportion falls to 81% among the laity. While 79% of the clergy are in favour of lay people preaching at communion services, the proportion falls to 72% among the laity. While 72% of the clergy are in favour of lay people leading the first part of the communion service, the proportion falls to 68% among the laity.

The one exception to these consistent differences between the attitudes of the clergy and of the committed laity toward lay ministry concerns lay presidency at the eucharist. While just 12% of the clergy are in favour of lay people taking the whole communion service, the proportion rises to 20% among the laity.

Overall, the fault-line between the clergy and the committed laity regarding the future of lay ministry may signal a significant problem for the Church of England if clergy are being encouraged or forced to develop systems of lay leadership before the laity are ready to welcome such changes.

Churches and cathedrals

The *Church Times Survey* included two sets of questions to assess attitudes toward churches and cathedrals, the buildings used for worship. The first set of questions focused on attitude toward the individual respondent=s local church, while the second set of questions focused on wider issues of policy.

The clergy and the committed laity hold very similar views on the costs incurred by their own churches. One in five (20%) of the laity and one in five (21%) of the clergy agree that their local congregation can no longer afford to pay for its church building. One in four (25%) of the laity and one in four (23%) of the clergy agree that their church building needs more money from tourists and visitors in order to survive. The clergy are, however, slightly more likely than the laity to argue that their church building needs more grants from the state in order to survive (35% compared with 31%).

The gap between the clergy and the committed laity widens considerably when the question changes to the future of church buildings. The clergy are much more radical than the laity regarding the future of church buildings. To begin with, a much higher proportion of the clergy say that too much money is spent on keeping old churches (47% compared with 30% of the laity). The clergy are much more likely than the laity to argue that more church buildings should be taken over by the state (48% compared with 29%). The clergy are also more likely than the laity to argue that many rural churches should be closed (22% compared with 12%).

On the other hand, the clergy and the committed laity hold similar views on levying entrance charges at cathedrals: 22% of the clergy and 25% of the laity argue that cathedrals should charge visitors for entry.

Overall, the fault-line between the clergy and the committed laity regarding the future of church buildings may signal a further problem for the Church of England. Clergy may run into significant opposition over the threatened closure of churches if they do not properly anticipate the higher levels of attachment toward the building displayed by the laity.

Money and policy

In order to gauge the priorities of committed Anglicans, the *Church Times Survey* posed a series of questions about how they envisaged the use of their church funds. Four specific areas were identified: central church structures, the clergy, development and mission, and community regeneration.

The committed laity hold a significantly less positive attitude than the clergy toward bearing the costs of the central church structures. While one in five (20%) of the clergy feel that their parish pays too much for its parish share, the proportion rises to one in three (32%) among the laity. While 75% of the clergy are happy for some money given to their church to go to diocesan funds, the proportion falls to 69% among the laity. While 64% of the clergy are happy for some money given to their church to go to church central funds, the proportion falls to 52% among the laity.

The committed laity also hold a significantly less positive attitude than the clergy toward bearing the costs of the clergy themselves. While 92% of the clergy are happy for some of the money given to their church to go to training new priests, the proportion falls to 88% among the laity. While 89% of the clergy are happy for some money given to their church to go to clergy pensions, the proportion falls to 81% among the laity.

The committed laity are less likely than the clergy to endorse the outflow of parish funds to support development and mission. While 90% of the clergy are happy for some money given to their church to go to struggling parishes, the proportion falls to 85% among the laity. While 88% of the clergy are happy for some money given to their church to go to churches in developing countries, the proportion falls to 81% among the laity.

The committed laity are also less likely than the clergy to endorse the outflow of parish funds to support community regeneration. While 67% of the clergy are happy for some money given to their church to go to urban regeneration, the proportion falls to 59% among the laity. While 58% of the clergy are happy for some money given to their church to go to the farming community, the proportion falls to 54% among the laity.

Overall, the fault-line between the clergy and the committed laity over money and policy suggests that there may be a fundamental tension between committed laity thinking more in terms of the congregational church which needs to secure its own internal finances first and the clergy thinking more in terms of the wider church needing to resource ministry and mission further afield.

Anglican identity

The *Church Times Survey* focused two kinds of questions on Anglican identity: the first concentrated on willingness to merge Anglican identity with other denominations, and the second concentrated on the future of establishment for the Church of England.

The committed laity are significantly more reluctant than the clergy to risk their Anglican identity through too much ecumenical involvement. While 17% of the clergy would not want to be a member of an ecumenical church or local ecumenical project, the proportion rises to 25% among the laity. While 15% of the clergy would not want their denomination to merge with another, the proportion rises to 21% among the laity. While 38% of the clergy would be prepared to accept the Pope as their church leader in some situations, the proportion falls to 26% among the laity.

Similar proportions of the clergy and of the committed laity are, however, clear that they would never become a member of another denomination (37% and 35% respectively).

The committed laity are also significantly more reluctant than the clergy to lose the status of being the established Church of England. While 32% of the clergy believe that the Church of England should be disestablished, the proportion falls to 27% among the laity. Looked at from the opposite perspective, 51% of the laity believe that the monarch should continue to be the Supreme Governor of the Church of England, compared with 43% of the clergy. Similarly, 82% of the laity believe that senior bishops should continue to sit in the reformed House of Lords, compared with 76% of the clergy.

On the other hand, there are aspects of establishment concerning which the clergy and the committed laity are in close agreement. Only 5% of the laity and 6% of the clergy believe that diocesan bishops should be appointed by the state. Only 13% of the laity and 14% of the clergy believe that Parliament should retain control of Church of England legislation.

Overall, the fault-line between the clergy and the committed laity over Anglican identity may lead to tensions in the local church in respect both of ecumenical cooperation and in terms of attitude toward establishment.

Confidence and the future

In order to gauge the level of confidence which committed Anglicans hold in the future of their Church, the *Church Times Survey* asked questions about two main issues: the first issue concerned confidence in the Church's leadership, and the second issue concerned confidence in the future of their own local church.

There are some interesting differences in the ways in which the clergy and the committed laity view the leadership of the Church of England. On the one hand, the clergy are more optimistic than the laity regarding their diocesan bishop. While 70% of the laity have confidence in the leadership given by their diocesan bishops, the proportion rises to 74% among the clergy. On the other hand, the clergy are less optimistic than the laity regarding the local clergy and regarding the Archbishops' Council. While 77% of the laity have confidence in the leadership given by their local clergy, the proportion falls to 68% among the clergy themselves. While 39% of the laity have confidence in the leadership given by the Archbishops= Council, the proportion falls to 35% among the clergy.

At the same time, the clergy and the committed laity have formed very similar evaluations of the General Synod. Thus, 42% of the laity and 40% of the clergy have confidence in the leadership given by the General Synod.

The clergy are significantly more optimistic than the committed laity regarding the future of their own congregation. Nearly half (47%) of the clergy believe that the membership of their church will grow in the next twelve months, compared with 38% of the laity. Moreover, twice as many of the clergy, as compared with the laity, feel that they can invite other people to come to their church (57% compared with 30%).

At the same time, the clergy and the committed laity have formed very similar evaluations of the difficulties faced by newcomers to their church. Thus, 25% of the clergy and 23% of the laity feel that it is not easy for newcomers in their church.

Overall, the fault-line between the clergy and the committed laity over the future potential of their local church may lead to considerable misunderstanding between the two groups. Clergy may well run the risk of feeling resentful that their committed laity neither share their own optimism for the growth of the local church, nor show the same level of enthusiasm for inviting other people to come to their church.

Sex and family life

The *Church Times Survey* identified four specific areas in which to test the orthodoxy of Anglican views on sex and family life: views on sex and cohabitation before marriage, views on divorce, views on same sex relationships, and views on caring for children and teenagers.

The clergy and the committed laity share some very similar views on the question of sex before marriage. Thus, 43% of the laity consider that it is wrong for men and women to have sex before marriage, and so do 45% of the clergy. A quarter (25%) of the laity consider that it is all right for a couple to live together without intending to get married, and so do 27% of the clergy. The laity are slightly more liberal than the clergy, however, in other respects. One in five (19%) of the laity consider that it is a good idea for couples who intend to get married to live together first, compared with 15% of the clergy.

The clergy are significantly more accepting of divorce than the committed laity. Four-fifths (80%) of the clergy accept that some marriages can come to a natural end in divorce or separation, compared with 74% of the laity. On the other hand, similar proportions of the clergy (39%) and of the laity (37%) maintain that couples should stay together for the sake of the children.

The clergy are also significantly more accepting of homosexuality than the committed laity. While 56% of the laity believe that it is wrong for people of the same gender to have sex together, the proportion falls to 48% among the clergy. Similarly, 18% of the clergy believe that homosexual couples should have the right to marry one another, compared with 13% of the laity.

The clergy are slightly more likely than the committed laity to argue that contraception should be available to teenagers under 16 who want it (37%

compared with 34%). Equal proportions of the clergy (30%) and of the laity (30%) believe that children thrive equally whether cared for primarily by their father or mother.

Overall, it is the fault-line between the clergy and the committed laity on the issue of homosexuality which may take the Church of England most by surprise. Clergy who wish to liberalise the Church=s attitude toward homosexuality may not be fully prepared for the more conservative approach advocated by the committed laity.

Social concerns

In order to assess the levels of social concern expressed by committed Anglicans, the *Church Times Survey* included a set of items on global issues and a set of items on community issues. The global issues included the environment, world development, AIDS and genetic research. The community issues included violence on television, paedophiles living in the community, and the effects of the National Lottery.

The clergy and the committed laity share very similar levels of concern regarding global issues. Thus, 94% of the laity are concerned about environmental pollution, and so are 95% of the clergy; 95% of the laity are concerned about the spread of AIDS, and so are 96% of the clergy. The clergy are slightly, but significantly, more concerned than the laity about the poverty of the developing world (97% and 95%). The clergy are also slightly, but significantly, more concerned than the laity about research into human genes (70% and 67%).

It is in respect of community concerns that the gap widens somewhat between the views of the clergy and the views of the committed laity. On the one hand, the laity are more concerned than the clergy about violence on television (82% compared with 76%) and about paedophiles living in the community (55% compared with 43%). On the other hand, the clergy are more concerned than the laity about the National Lottery (51% compared with 45%).

Overall, the fault-line between the clergy and the committed laity on community concerns is not huge, but nonetheless may be indicative of ways in which the two groups view the local community through somewhat different lenses. In other words, the clergy cannot always expect the committed laity to share their own enthusiasms for specific issues.

Social conscience

The *Church Times Survey* assessed social conscience by means of a series of questions exploring the willingness of committed Anglicans to pay more tax in order to fund specific areas of social life. The three broad areas included in the survey concerned health and education, social security and prisons, and defence and development aid.

Across six of the seven specific areas listed in the survey the clergy are consistently more willing than the committed laity to pay more tax in order to fund aspects of social life. To begin with, the clergy show more concern regarding the health service. Thus, 85% of the clergy would pay more tax to fund spending on health, compared with 80% of the laity.

In the area of education the clergy are more supportive than the committed laity in respect of both the school system and higher education. While three-quarters (74%) of the laity would pay more tax to fund spending on schools, the proportion rises to 81% among the clergy. While 42% of the laity would pay more tax to fund spending on universities, the proportion rises to 47% among the clergy.

The clergy are also more supportive than the committed laity in respect of the social security system and the prison service. Thus, 49% of the clergy would pay more tax to fund spending on social security benefits, compared with 39% of the laity. Similarly, 48% of the clergy would pay more tax to fund spending on prisons, compared with 42% of the laity.

The biggest difference of all between the priorities of the clergy and the priorities of the committed laity concerns development aid. While 62% of the laity would pay more tax to fund spending on overseas aid, the proportion rises to 77% among the clergy.

The one area for which the laity show more concern than the clergy is in respect of defence. Thus, 30% of the laity would pay more tax to fund spending on security forces, compared with 24% of the clergy.

Overall, the fault-line between the clergy and the committed laity in respect of social conscience reveals some quite fundamental differences of perspective. Once again the clergy cannot take for granted that the committed laity share their own priorities when they are offering leadership and teaching on matters of social concern.

Education

The *Church Times Survey* framed questions on three key topics of relevance to the Church of England=s concerns with education. These topics related to the debate between the state-funded and the independent sector of schools, the place of religious education and worship in schools, and the future for faith-based schools.

The clergy are significantly more in favour of the state-funded system of education than is the case among the committed laity. Thus, 62% of the clergy express confidence in the state-funded education system, compared with 50% of the laity. Taking a more aggressive stance, 16% of the clergy argue that private schools should be abolished, compared with 10% of the laity.

The clergy and the committed laity hold somewhat different views on the place of religion in schools. High proportions of both the clergy (91%) and the laity (93%) believe that religious education should be taught in schools, but their views differ on the nature of that religious education. The clergy are significantly more supportive than the laity of a multi-faith approach to religious education. While 79% of the laity believe that religious education in schools should teach about world religions, the proportion rises further among the clergy to 85%. In a similar vein the clergy are less convinced than the laity about the place of worship within schools. While 69% of the laity believe that schools should hold a religious assembly every day, the proportion drops to 59% among the clergy.

The clergy and the committed laity hold similar views on some of the issues raised in the survey about church schools. Thus, 85% of the laity and 86% of the clergy are in favour of state-funded church schools. Similarly, 77% of the laity and 75% of the clergy maintain that the Church of England should fund more new church secondary schools. On the other hand, the clergy are significantly less likely than the laity to support the expansion of church schools in the primary sector. While 75% of the laity maintain that the Church of England should fund more new primary schools, the proportion falls to 68% of the clergy.

The gap between the clergy and the committed laity widens further, however, over the issue of extending public funding to schools operated by other faith communities. While 51% of the clergy are in favour of state-funded Jewish schools, the proportion falls to 39% among the laity. While 47% of the clergy are in favour of state-funded Islamic schools, the proportion falls to 35% among the laity.

Overall, the fault-line between the clergy and the committed laity on the subject of education reveals some quite fundamental differences of perspective. Some of the committed laity may be disappointed by clerical lack of support for the independent sector of schools and for Christian education and worship within the state-maintained sector. They may be equally disappointed by clerical sympathy for state funding of schools supported by other faith groups.

Conclusion

There is sufficient evidence in the present analysis to alert the Church of England to the wisdom of taking seriously the fault-line between clergy and committed laity. Decisions made on the basis of well-informed clerical opinion may not in fact be all that representative of what the key lay people believe and of how the key lay people feel.

CHAPTER 5

Men and women in the pews

Introduction

The second of the potential fault-lines within the Church of England to be examined by the present study concerns the ways in which beliefs, attitudes, and values may vary between the men and women in the pews. The present sample of committed lay Anglicans included 2,428 men and 3,318 women.

In calculating the statistical significance between the responses of men and women, the chi square test has been employed in respect of dichotomised data within each of the two sexes. The division has been made between those who agree or agree strongly with the question on the one hand, and those who check the disagree, disagree strongly, or uncertain categories on the other hand. Differences which do not reach the five percent probability threshold will be regarded as non-significant.

Patterns of belief

The *Church Times Survey* identified three doctrinal areas against which to assess the orthodoxy of Anglican belief: beliefs about God, beliefs about Jesus, and beliefs about life after death.

The men and women in the pews are united rather than divided by their religious beliefs. Committed lay Anglicans of both sexes share a high level of belief in the existence of God. This is the case for 97% of the men and for 97% of the women. Moreover, the vast majority of men and women in the pews conceptualise the God in whom they believe in personal terms. Thus, 78% of the men believe that God is a personal being, and so do 80% of the women. At the same time, the small proportion of committed lay Anglicans who conceptualise God in impersonal terms contains three men for every two women. While 17% of the men believe that God is an impersonal power, the proportion falls to 12% among the women.

The two sexes also hold highly similar views on the person of Jesus. Around two-thirds of the men (66%) believe that Jesus really turned water into wine, and so do 65% of the women. Just under two-thirds of the men (63%) believe that Jesus' birth was a virgin birth, and so do 61% of the women. Although the men adopt a slightly more conservative position on the physical resurrection, the difference between men and women on this aspect of doctrine is far from large. Four-fifths of the men (80%) believe that Jesus rose physically from the dead, and the proportion falls marginally to 76% among the women.

The two sexes also hold highly similar views on life after death. Almost nine out of every ten men (87%) believe in life after death, and so do 88% of the women. Almost eight out of every ten men (78%) believe that heaven really exists, and so do 77% of the women. Although the men adopt a slightly more conservative position on the existence of hell, the difference between men and women on this aspect of doctrine is far from large. Almost half of the men (48%) believe that hell really exists, and the proportion falls marginally to 43% among the women.

Overall, the fault-line between men and women in the pews is hardly noticeable in respect of orthodoxy of belief. Nonetheless, there is just a hint that on some issues the men may be significantly more conservative than the women. This finding suggests that men may be somewhat more anxious than women to defend what they understand to be orthodox beliefs. Consequently men may tend to be more critical than women of preaching and teaching which calls into question the credibility of traditionally expressed doctrines.

Paths of truth

The *Church Times Survey* identified three means of examining the ways in which truth claims are asserted: beliefs about the bible, beliefs about the exclusivity of Christianity, and beliefs about evolution versus creation.

The men and women in the pews are also united rather than divided by their understanding of the nature of religious truth. Committed lay Anglicans of both sexes tend to espouse a liberal understanding of scripture. Three-fifths of the men (60%) agree that biblical truths are culturally conditioned, and so do 57% of the women. Just one in ten of the women (10%) take the fundamentalist line that the bible is without any errors. Although the men are significantly more likely to agree with this view of scripture, the percentage only rises to 13% of the men who believe that the bible is without any error.

Similar proportions of the men and women in the pews agree with the exclusivity claims of Christianity. Just under half of the men (47%) believe that Christianity is the only true religion. The proportion falls only slightly among the women to 44%. Looking at the same issue from the opposite perspective, around one in every eight of the men (12%) and one in every eight of the women (12%) believe that all religions are of equal value.

Finally, there is no disagreement between the men and women in the pews on the debate between creationism and evolutionary theory. The creationist view that God made the world in six days and rested on the seventh is supported by fewer than one in five of the men (17%) and by fewer than one in five of the women (18%). The creationist view that all living things evolved is supported by two-thirds of the men (68%) and by two-thirds of the women (67%).

Overall, there is no significant fault-line between men and women in the pews in respect of their understanding of the nature of religious truth.

Paths of spirituality

In order to gauge different pathways of spirituality the *Church Times Survey* distinguished between three kinds of issues: personal and private sources of spiritual sustenance, group-based and shared sources of spiritual sustenance, and drawing on wider resources for spiritual sustenance.

An analysis of the paths of spirituality preferred by the men and by the women in the pews begins to open up some interesting ways in which the two sexes differ. Men and women show significantly different levels of interest in some of the forms of spirituality often promoted or assumed in Anglican churches. Three main trends emerge from the data presented in this section.

First, the women show a slightly higher commitment than the men to a range of personal and private spiritual practices. While 83% of the men say that they are helped in their faith by praying by themselves, the proportion rises slightly among the women to 86%. While 81% of the men say that they are helped in their faith by reading the bible, the proportion rises slightly among the women to 84%. While 76% of the men say that they are helped in their faith by reading Christian books, the proportion rises slightly among the women to 81%. On the other hand, there is no significant difference in the proportions of men and women in the pews who identify non-religious books as core to their spirituality. Thus, 29% of the men say that they are helped in their faith by reading non-religious books, and so do 31% of the women.

Second, the women show a much higher commitment than the men to a range of group-based and shared spiritual practices. While 75% of the men say that they are helped in their faith by discussing their faith with others, the proportion rises to 82% among the women. While 46% of the men say that they are helped in their faith by bible study groups, the proportion rises to 60% among the women. While 39% of the men say that they are helped in their faith by prayer groups, the proportion rises to 56% among the women.

Third, the women show a much higher commitment than the men to a range of wider resources available to promote spiritual growth. While three-fifths of the men (60%) say that they are helped in their faith by considering the natural world, the proportion rises to three-quarters among the women (74%). While 43% of the men say that they are helped in their faith by going on retreat, the proportion rises to 57% among the women. On the other hand, there is no significant difference in the proportions of men and women in the pews who feel that their main source of spiritual sustenance is found outside the churches rather than within them. Thus, 15% of the men say that they often get more spiritual help outside the church than within the church, and so do 15% of the women.

Overall, the fault-line between men and women in the pews begins to become quite noticeable in respect of different preferences for developing and expressing spirituality. The women are inclined to take such matters more seriously than the men and, as a consequence, may be prepared to devote more time to such activities. Parishes which arrange prayer groups, bible study groups, and discussion groups will find that such activities appeal more strongly to the women in the pews than to the men in the pews. Given the fact that women generally outnumber men in Anglican congregations at a ratio of two women to every one man, the gender imbalance in prayer groups, bible study groups, and discussion groups is likely to be even more pronounced.

Public worship

The *Church Times Survey* included three sets of questions to assess responses to public worship: the first set focused on the debate between traditional and modern forms of public worship, the second set focused on different aspects of the service, and the third set focused on the initiation of children into the worshipping community.

The men and women in the pews hold some significantly different views on the nature of the services they like to attend. While both sexes hold a similar level of appreciation for the traditional forms of worship, the women are much more open than the men to benefiting from new forms of worship. The point is illustrated by the following statistics.

On the one hand, there is agreement between the sexes on traditional forms of worship. Thus, 73% of the men say that they are helped in their faith by traditional forms of service, and so are 70% of the women. Similarly, 78% of the men say that they are helped in their faith by traditional hymns in services, and so are 76% of the women.

On the other hand, there is disagreement between the sexes on new forms of worship. Thus, half of the women (51%) say that they are helped in their faith by new forms of service, but the proportion falls to 42% among the men. Nearly, nearly two-thirds of the women (63%) say that they are helped in their faith by new hymns in services, but the proportion falls to 50% among the men.

There are some aspects of church services which are more highly rated by women than by men. The particular issue highlighted by the survey concerns the use of silence in services. Four out of every five women in the pews (80%) say that they are helped in their faith by periods of silence in services, compared with 72% of the men.

There are other aspects of church services, however, which are rated equally by both sexes. The particular issues highlighted in the survey concern listening to sermons and appreciating ritual in services. Three-quarters of the men in the pews (76%) say that they are helped in their faith by listening to sermons, and so do three-quarters of the women (76%). Two-thirds of the men in the pews (68%) say that they are helped in their faith by ritual in services, and so do 70% of the women.

There is a slight but statistically significant difference in the attitudes of men and women in the pews to baptismal policy. Men are significantly more likely to be in favour of a restrictive baptism policy. While only one in ten of the women (11%) are in favour of churches baptising only babies of regular churchgoers, the proportion rises to 15% among the men.

There is also a slight but statistically significant difference in the attitudes of men and women in the pews to the admission of children to communion prior to confirmation. Women are significantly more likely to break with tradition. While 46% of the men are in favour of baptised children being admitted to communion before confirmation, the proportion rises to 49% among the women.

Overall, the fault-line between men and women in the pews may begin to impact the local congregation quite powerfully when there is disagreement over forms of worship. Not only are the women more likely than the men to support new forms of services and new hymns, but women also outnumber men in most Anglican congregations. Different worship preferences between men and women may help to marginalise men ever further from the heart of Anglican church life, if women support moves for modernisation which men are likely to resent.

Local church life

In order to assess commitment to the local church, the *Church Times Survey* included three groups of questions: questions concerning the cycle of commitment, questions concerning the sense of belonging, and questions concerning the relationship between commitment and power.

The men and women in the pews show similar profiles in respect of the cycle of commitment to the Anglican Church. These men and women are the committed lay people who are currently much more likely to be in the process of increasing their commitment to local church life than in the process of reducing their commitment to local church life. Just 6% of the men and 6% of the women say that they are coming to their church less regularly nowadays. Examining this issue from the opposite perspective, more than two in every five of the men in the pews (42%) say that they are coming to their church more regularly nowadays. Among the women in the pews the proportion is even slightly higher with 45% saying that they are coming to their church more regularly nowadays.

Both the men and the women in the pews show a strong sense of belonging to their church. Nine out of every ten of the men (90%) feel a strong sense of belonging to their church, and so do 91% of the women. For 69% of the men, their church is important for their social life. The proportion increases slightly but significantly to 72% among the women.

The first major difference between the sexes in terms of their attitude toward local church life concerns the ways in which they draw on fellow church members for support. The women are much more likely than the men to establish personal ties with fellow members of the congregation. Thus, although as many as half of the men (49%) turn to fellow members of their church when they need help, the proportion rises to two-thirds among the women (68%).

The second significant difference between the sexes in terms of their attitude toward local church life concerns the perceptions of power and powerlessness. The women are much more likely than the men to feel excluded from the power structures of the local church. While nearly two-thirds of the men (64%) feel that they can influence their church's decisions, the proportion falls significantly among the women to 56%.

In spite of this significant difference between the sexes in terms of perceptions of power and powerlessness, the women are no more likely than the men to complain about their position in local church life. Just 17% of the men complain that they have too little control over the running of their church, and so do 16% of the women. Just 14% of the men complain that their churches make too many demands on their time, and so do 13% of the women. Just 9% of the men complain that their church makes too many demands on their money, and so do 8% of the women.

Overall, the fault-line between men and women in the pews reveals some fundamental differences concerning the kind of church community with which men and women may wish to engage. The men in the pews are more likely than the women to want to be part of a local organisation which they can influence and help to shape. The women in the pews are more likely than the men to want to be part of a local network on which they can draw for personal support and friendship. These two very different expectations on local church life may be indicative of more fundamental differences in the model of church life espoused by the men and by the women in the pews.

Ordained ministry

The *Church Times Survey* included questions about four issues which divide opinion in the Church of England on the question of ordained ministry: the ordination of women, the ordination of individuals who are divorced, the ordination of individuals who are divorced and remarried, and the ordination of practising homosexuals. In respect of each of these issues the survey distinguished between ordination as priest and ordination as bishop.

There are significant differences between the men and women in the pews on the question of the ordination of women. The women hold a more positive attitude than the men on this issue. Four-fifths of the women (80%) are in favour of the ordination of women as priests, but the proportion falls significantly to 73% among the men. Two-thirds of the women (67%) are in favour of the ordination of women as bishops, but the proportion falls significantly to 59% among the men.

There is much greater unanimity between the men and the women in the pews on the question of the ordination of individuals who have experienced divorce. Half of the men (49%) are in favour of divorced people as priests. The proportion rises significantly, but only slightly, to 52% among the women. Just under half of the men (47%) are in favour of divorced and remarried people as priests. The proportion remains at a similar level among the women (46%).

Both the men and the women in the pews are less sympathetic toward divorced bishops than toward divorced priests. While 49% of the men are in favour of divorced people as priests, the proportion drops to 43% of the men who are in favour of divorced people as bishops. While 47% of the men are in favour of divorced and remarried people as priests, the proportion drops to 40% of the men who are in favour of divorced and remarried people as bishops. While 52% of the women are in favour of divorced people as priests, the proportion drops to 43% of the women who are in favour of divorced people as bishops. While 46% of the women are in favour of divorced and remarried people as priests, the proportion falls to 38% of the women who are in favour of divorced and remarried people as bishops.

There is also unanimity between the men and the women in the pews on the question of the ordination of practising homosexuals. Less than a quarter of the men (22%) and less than a quarter of the women (23%) are in favour of the ordination of practising homosexuals as priests. The proportion declines further to 19% of the men and 20% of the women who are in favour of the ordination of practising homosexuals as bishops.

Overall, the fault-line between the men and the women in the pews will not impact the Anglican Church's debate on the ordination of divorced people or the ordination of practising homosexuals. The fault-line between men and women in the pews is highly relevant, however, to debates about the acceptability of women priests and the future possibility of women bishops. Divisions in local congregations over these issues may well continue to emerge along gender lines.

Church leadership

In order to assess attitudes toward two major areas of change in church leadership, the *Church Times Survey* included a section on the development of ordained ministry and a section on the development of lay ministry.

The men and the women in the pews are much more united than divided in respect of their attitudes toward changes and developments in church leadership, both in terms of ordained leadership and in terms of lay leadership.

First, there is agreement on the need to enhance the remuneration of clergy. Nearly two-thirds of both sexes believe that clergy should be paid a better wage. The case is supported by 63% of the men and by 64% of the women.

Second, there is no serious disagreement between the sexes on the relative priority that should be given to various reforms affecting the ways in which clergy work. Two out of every five men (42%) maintain that clergy freehold should be abolished. Although the women are significantly less in favour of this reform, the proportion drops only slightly to 38%. Over a quarter of the men (28%) maintain that clergy should be paid on short-term renewable contracts, and so do 31% of the women. A quarter of the men sitting in the pews (26%) maintain that clergy should live in their own houses rather than in provided housing, and so do 26% of the women.

Third, there is close agreement between both sexes in terms of the future potential for lay liturgical ministry in the context of morning and evening prayer. A clear majority among both the men and the women in the pews are in favour of lay leadership of the offices. Thus, 85% of the men and 86% of the women are in favour of lay people leading morning and evening prayer. Moreover, the proportions only drop slightly when the question changes from one concerned with leadership to one concerned with preaching. Thus, 81% of the men and 81% of the women are in favour of lay people preaching at morning and evening prayer.

Fourth, there is close agreement between both sexes in terms of the future potential for lay liturgical ministry in the context of the first part of the communion service. Between two-thirds and three-quarters of the men and women in the pews are in favour of lay leadership of aspects of the ministry of the word at communion services. Thus, 73% of the men and 72% of the women are in favour of lay people preaching at communion services. Similarly, 69% of the men and 68% of the women are in favour of lay people leading the first part of the communion service.

Fifth, a small but significant gap opens up between the men and the women in the pews on the controversial issue of lay presidency of the eucharist. In this case the women are even more reluctant than the men to depart from the traditional insistence of Anglicanism on priestly presidency. While 22% of the men are in favour of lay people taking the whole communion service, the proportion drops significantly to 18% among the women.

Overall, the fault-line between men and women in the pews is unlikely to cause great problems for the Church of England in respect of developments in the structure of the ordained ministry or in respect of developments in the expectations placed on lay liturgical ministry. Moreover, the most radical change envisaged by the survey, namely lay eucharistic presidency, remains without significant support from either the men or the women in the pews.

Churches and cathedrals

The *Church Times Survey* included two sets of questions to assess attitudes toward churches and cathedrals, the buildings used for worship. The first set of questions focused on attitudes toward the individual respondent's local church, while the second set of questions focused on wider issues of policy.

The two sexes are in basic agreement about the future viability of their own church building. One in five of the men in the pews (20%) feel that their congregation can no longer afford to pay for its church building. Exactly the same proportion of the women (20%) have formed the same view. One in four of the men in the pews (25%) argue that, in order to survive, their church building needs more money from tourists and visitors. Exactly the same proportion of the women (25%) have formed the same view. Nearly one in three of the men in the pews (31%) argue that, in order to survive, their church building needs more grants from the state. Nearly the same proportion of the women (30%) have formed the same view.

There is less agreement among the two sexes, however, on the wider issues of church policy regarding the future of church buildings. On these issues the women are less likely than the men to support the more radical solutions. While one in three of the men in the pews (32%) argue that too much money is spent on keeping old churches, the proportion drops significantly to 29% among the women. While one in three of the men in the pews (33%) argue that more church buildings should be taken over by the state, the proportion drops even more significantly among the women to 26%. While 15% of the men in the pews take the tough line that many rural churches should be closed, the proportion drops significantly among the women to 10%.

There is also a small but statistically significant difference between the sexes in their attitude toward the funding of cathedrals. Once again the women are less likely than the men to back an unpopular solution to a tough problem. While more than a quarter of the men in the pews (26%) back the idea that cathedrals should charge visitors for entry, the proportion drops to less than a quarter among the women (23%).

The fault-line between the men and the women in the pews over the future of church buildings is neither wide nor greatly damaging. Nonetheless, this fault-line is sufficient to alert the Church of England to ways in which radical solutions to the problems posed by the current stock of aging buildings are likely to be even less acceptable to the women than to the men.

Money and policy

In order to gauge the priorities of committed Anglicans, the *Church Times Survey* posed a series of questions about how they envisaged the use of their church funds. Four specific areas were identified: central church structures, the clergy, development and mission, and community regeneration.

The priorities chosen by committed lay Anglicans for the use of their church funds reveal some significant differences between the sexes, alongside a number of areas in which there is basic agreement between the men and the women sitting in the pews.

On the issues concerned with church structures, there is much more agreement than disagreement between the sexes. Just under a third of the men (31%) and of the women (32%) in the pews argue that their parish pays too much for its parish share (quota). Looked at from the opposite perspective, just over two-thirds of the men (69%) and of the women (69%) in the pews are happy for some of the money given to their church to go to diocesan funds. On the other hand, women are slightly less supportive than men of the needs of central church structures, as distinct from diocesan structures. While more then half of the men in the pews (54%) are happy for money given to their church to go to church central funds, the proportion drops significantly among the women to 50%.

On the issues concerned with clergy support, the views of the men and the women in the pews remain very close. Nine out of every ten men (90%) are happy for money given to their church to go to training new priests. Although the women are significantly less supportive of this objective, the level still remains at 87%. At the same time, almost exactly the same proportions of men (80%) and of women (81%) are happy for money given to their church to go to clergy pensions.

The gap between the two sexes begins to open up more noticeably on issues concerned with development and mission. The men are more attracted than the women to supporting struggling parishes. The women are more attracted than the men to supporting developing countries. Thus, while 87% of the men in the pews are happy for money given to their church to go to struggling parishes, the proportion falls significantly to 83% among the women. While 82% of the women in the pews are happy for money given to their church to go to churches in developing countries, the proportion falls significantly to 79% among the men.

The gap between the two sexes opens up even more noticeably on issues concerned with community regeneration. The women have much larger hearts than the men both for supporting urban projects and for supporting rural projects. While 62% of the women in the pews are happy for money given to their churches to go to urban regeneration, the proportion falls to 56% among the men. While 60% of the women in the pews are happy for money given to their church to go to the farming community, the proportion falls to 45% among the men.

Overall, the fault-line between men and women in the pews on policy-related issues linked to spending church money is most visible in the areas of community regeneration. The women may judge the men in the pews alongside them as ungenerous, even as un-Christian, in their greater reluctance to deploy church funding on community regeneration projects. The men may judge the women in the pews alongside them as naively generous in dedicating such hard-earned church funding to support essentially secular enterprises.

Anglican identity

The *Church Times Survey* focused two kinds of questions on Anglican identity: the first concentrated on willingness to merge Anglican identity with other denominations, and the second concentrated on the future of establishment for the Church of England.

There are both similarities and dissimilarities regarding the ways in which the men and the women in the pews feel about ecumenism. On the one hand, the two sexes hold highly similar views on losing their identity as Anglicans. Over a third of the men (36%) would never become a member of another denomination. A similar proportion of the women (34%) also adopt this position. A fifth of the men (21%) would not want their denomination to merge with another. The same proportion of women (21%) also adopt this position.

On the other hand, the two sexes adopt significantly different profiles on other aspects of the ecumenical future. The women are more supportive of shared churches. While 28% of the men in the pews would not want to be a member of an ecumenical church or local ecumenical project, the proportion falls to 22% among the women. The men are more sympathetic to an ecumenical future incorporating the papacy. While 21% of the women in the pews would be prepared to accept the Pope as their church leader in some situations, the proportion rises to 34% among the men.

There are also both similarities and dissimilarities regarding the ways in which the men and the women in the pews feel about the established status of the Church of England. On the one hand, the two sexes hold highly similar views on the role of bishops in the House of Lords and on the role of the monarch as head of the Church. Over four-fifths of the men in the pews (82%) maintain that senior bishops should continue to sit in the reformed House of Lords. A similar proportion of the women (83%) also adopt this position. Half of the men in the pews (52%) maintain that the monarch should continue to be the Supreme Governor of the Church of England. A similar proportion of the women (50%) also adopt this position.

On the other hand, the two sexes adopt significantly different profiles on other aspects of the future of establishment. The women are even less supportive than the men of the part played by the secular authorities in the internal life of the church. While only 7% of the men in the pews believe that diocesan bishops should be appointed by the state, the proportion drops even further to 4% among the women. While only 17% of the men in the pews believe that Parliament should retain control of Church of England legislation, the proportion drops to 10% among the women.

The most significant difference between the two sexes in this section concerns response to the direct question on disestablishment. A significantly higher proportion of the men are convinced by the case for disestablishment. While a fifth of the women in the pews (23%) argue that the Church of England should be disestablished, as many as a third of the men (33%) support disestablishment.

Overall, the fault-line between the men and the women in the pews over the broad issue of Anglican identity may lead to two particular areas of disagreement. On the one hand, the men may show less willingness than the women to explore local ecumenical collaboration. On the other hand, the men may show greater enthusiasm than the women to campaign for disestablishment.

Confidence in the future

In order to gauge the level of confidence which committed Anglicans hold in the future of their Church, the *Church Times Survey* asked questions about two main issues: the first issue concerned confidence in the Church's leadership, and the second issue concerned confidence in the future of their own local church.

Once again there are both similarities and dissimilarities regarding the ways in which the men and the women in the pews feel about the leadership experienced by the Church of England. On the one hand, the two sexes hold similar views on the local leadership. Three-quarters of the men (76%) have confidence in the leadership given by their local clergy, and so do 78% of the women. Over two-thirds of the men (69%) have confidence in the leadership given by their diocesan bishop, and so do 70% of the women.

On the other hand, the two sexes adopt significantly different profiles on the national leadership. The women have more confidence than the men in the national leadership. While 45% of the women in the pews have confidence in the leadership given by the General Synod, the proportion falls to 38% among the men. While 42% of the women in the pews have confidence in the leadership given by the Archbishops' Council, the proportion falls to 36% among the men.

There are also both similarities and differences regarding the ways in which the men and the women in the pews feel about their local church. On the one hand, the two sexes hold similar views on the potential for growth in their local church. Two out of every five of the men (39%) believe that the membership of their church will grow in the next 12 months, and so do 38% of the women.

On the other hand, the two sexes adopt significantly different profiles on how such growth can take place. In this regard the women take the more positive and the more proactive view. While 28% of the men in the pews say that they can invite other people to come to their church, a significantly higher proportion of the women take this positive view (32%). While 25% of the men in the pews say that it is not easy for newcomers in their church, a significantly lower proportion of the women take this negative view (21%).

Overall, the fault-line between the men and the women in the pews over the broad issue of confidence in the future shows some significant cracks in the consensus of the laity. Both the Archbishops' Council and the General Synod are likely to be subjected to stronger criticism by the committed laymen than by the committed laywomen.

Sex and family life

The *Church Times Survey* identified four specific areas in which to test the orthodoxy of Anglican views on sex and family life: views on sex and cohabitation before marriage, views on divorce, views on same sex relationships, and views on caring for children and teenagers.

In respect of the majority of issues examined in this section the men and the women in the pews hold very similar or quite similar views. There are, however, three issues concerning which there is considerable disparity between the sexes. The areas of consensus will be reviewed first, followed by the areas of divergence.

Generally the two sexes agree on matters concerned with sex before marriage. A little over two-fifths of the men in the pews (43%) and a little over two-fifths of the women (42%) maintain that it is wrong for men and women to have sex before marriage. Looking at this issue from an opposite perspective, a fifth of the men (20%) and a little under a fifth of the women (18%) maintain that it is a good idea for couples who intend to get married to live together first. Over a quarter of the men (27%) believe that it is all right for a couple to live together without intending to get married. The percentage among the women falls only slightly, but significantly, to 24%.

The two sexes adopt a similar level of acceptance of marriage breakdown. Three-quarters of the women in the pews (75%) believe that marriages can come to a natural end in divorce or separation. The percentage among the men falls only slightly, but significantly, to 72%.

The two sexes are equally reluctant to support the case for same-sex marriages. Just 13% of the men in the pews and 13% of the women believe that homosexual couples should have the right to marry one another.

The two sexes are also in agreement on their evaluation of the case for making contraception available to younger teenagers. A third of the men in the pews (35%) and a third of the women (33%) believe that contraception should be available to teenagers under 16 who want it.

The biggest divergence between the two sexes concerns the case for keeping marriages together for the supposed benefit of the children. While half of the men in the pews (48%) believe that couples should stay together for the sake of the children, the proportion falls among the women to 29%.

The second largest divergence between the two sexes concerns the case for keeping children with their mother rather than with their father. While a quarter of the men in pews (23%) now feel that children thrive equally whether cared for primarily by their father or mother, the proportion increases by half as much again to a third among the women (34%).

The third largest divergence between the two sexes concerns the case for same-sex relationships. While three-fifths of the men in the pews (59%) believe that it is wrong for people of the same gender to have sex together, the proportion is significantly lower among the women at 54%.

Overall, the fault-line between the men and the women in the pews over the broad areas of sex and family life shows further significant cracks in the consensus of the laity. The ethical advice followed and given by committed lay Anglicans may differ on some key issues between committed laymen and committed laywomen.

Social concerns

In order to assess the levels of social concern expressed by committed Anglicans, the *Church Times Survey* included a set of items on global concerns and a set of items on community concerns. The global concerns included environmental and developmental issues, AIDS and genetic research. The more local issues concerned violence on television, paedophiles living in the community, and the effects of the National Lottery.

This section on social concerns reveals some highly significant differences between the levels of priority shaped by the two sexes. Over all the issues of global concerns and over all the issues of community concerns listed in the survey, the women in the pews register a higher level of concern than is the case among the men.

Although very high proportions of the men in the pews are concerned about environmental pollution, the poverty of the developing world, and the spread of AIDS, the proportions are even higher among the women. Thus, 92% of the men and 96% of the women express concern about environmental pollution; 93% of the men and 96% of the women express concern about the poverty of the developing world; 93% of the men and 96% of the women express concern about the spread of AIDS.

Compared with issues like environmental pollution, world poverty, and the spread of AIDS, both sexes register a lower level of concern over research into human genes. At the same time, the gap between the sexes widens over this issue. Thus, 62% of the men in the pews and 71% of the women express concern about research into human genes.

Community concerns are consistently rated more highly by women than by men. While three-quarters of the men in the pews (76%) are concerned about violence on television, the proportion rises to 87% among the women. While half of the men in the pews (51%) are concerned about paedophiles living in the community, the proportion rises to 58% among the women. While two-fifths of the men in the pews (40%) are concerned about the National Lottery, the proportion rises to 48% among the women.

Overall, the fault-line between the men and the women in the pews over the broad areas of social concerns suggests that the women may be more concerned about such issues than the men. These differences in levels of concern and expectations may help to shape very different agenda among men and women for the engagement of the local church in matters of global and community significance.

Social conscience

The *Church Times Survey* assessed social conscience by means of a series of questions exploring the willingness of committed Anglicans to pay more tax in order to fund specific areas of social life. The three broad areas included in the survey concerned health and education, social security and prisons, and defence and development aid.

This section on social conscience reveals some significant differences in the weight given by men and by women in the pews to funding claims made on the public purse. Across a number of areas women are more ready than men to accept a higher level of taxation in order to provide better public funding.

In the area of health care, 83% of the women in the pews would be willing to pay more tax to fund spending on health, compared with 78% of the men. In the area of education, 76% of the women in the pews would be willing to pay more tax to fund spending on schools, compared with 71% of the men. However, there is no significant difference in the proportions of the men and the women in the pews who would be willing to pay more tax to fund spending on universities, 41% and 43% respectively.

In the area of social security, 41% of the women in the pews would be willing to pay more tax to fund spending on social security benefits, compared with 37% of the men. In the area of the prison service, 45% of the women in the pews would pay more tax to fund spending on prisons, compared with 37% of the men.

In the area of international development, 64% of the women in the pews would be willing to pay more taxes to fund spending on overseas aid, compared with 59% of the men. However, there is no significant difference in the proportions of the men and the women in the pews who would be willing to pay more tax to fund spending on security forces, 31% and 29% respectively.

Overall, the fault-line between the men and the women in the pews over the broad areas of social conscience suggests that the women are more likely than the men to support increased spending from the public purse across a number of areas both at home and overseas. Some of the committed laymen may find this attitude more difficult to understand.

Education

The *Church Times Survey* framed questions on three key topics of relevance to the Church of England's concerns with education. These topics related to the debate between the state-funded and the independent sector of schools, the place of religious education and worship in schools, and the future for faith-based schools.

There are no large discrepancies between the ways in which the two sexes view educational matters. To begin with, both sexes hold similar views on state-funded schools. Thus, half of the men sitting in the pews (49%) have confidence in the state-funded education system, and so do half of the women (51%). Among the men in the pews 12% argue that private schools should be abolished. The proportion drops significantly, but only slightly, among the women to 10%.

Second, both sexes hold similar views on the need for religious education lessons and for religious assemblies in schools. Thus, 93% of the men in the pews believe that religious education should be taught in all schools, and so do 94% of the women. Two-thirds of the men in the pews (69%) believe that schools should hold a religious assembly every day, and so do two-thirds of the women (69%).

There is, however, a significant difference between the sexes on their attitude toward teaching world religions in schools. The women are more open than the men to teaching about other faiths. While three-quarters of the men in the pews (75%) believe that religious education in schools should teach about world religions, the proportion rises further to 82% among the women.

Third, both sexes hold similar views on the development of church schools within the state-funded sector. Thus, 85% of the men in the pews are in favour of state-funded church schools, and so are 85% of the women. Three-quarters of the men in the pews (75%) argue that the Church of England should fund more new church primary schools, and so do three-quarters of the women (75%). Three-quarters of the men in the pews (76%) argue that the Church of England should fund more new church secondary schools, and so do three-quarters of the women (78%).

There is, however, a small but significant difference between the sexes on their attitude toward extending the privileges enjoyed by the Christian churches within the state-funded system of schools to other faith communities. The women are less open than the men to such developments. While 41% of the men in the pews are in favour of state-funded Jewish schools, the proportion drops slightly, but significantly, to 38% among the women. While 37% of the men in the pews are in favour of state-funded Islamic schools, the proportion drops slightly, but significantly, to 33% among the women.

Overall, the fault-line between the men and the women in the pews is almost invisible over the broad area of education, except in respect of their attitudes toward world faiths and toward other faith communities. Even here, the fault-line is slight and unlikely to be highly disruptive.

Conclusion

The fault-lines between men and women in the pews identified in the present chapter emerge as the least significant of the fault-lines examined in the whole book. Nonetheless, it would be a mistake to ignore entirely these fault-lines between the sexes. Where the fault-lines emerge most clearly, in areas like paths of spirituality, modern forms of public worship, building a caring and mutually supportive church community, and social concerns, such fault-lines may take the Church of England by surprise and prove themselves to be significantly disruptive.

CHAPTER 6

Young and old in the pews

Introduction

The third of the potential fault-lines within the Church of England to be examined by the present study concerns the ways in which beliefs, attitudes, and values may vary between different generations of the people in the pews. The sample of committed lay Anglicans has been divided for the purposes of this analysis into three discrete age categories. Anglicans in their fifties or sixties are regarded as the largest, most active and most influential group in many congregations. There were 3,006 lay people in this age group included in the analysis. Anglicans under the age of fifty are generally in a minority in church congregations. There were 1,093 lay people in this age group included in the analysis. Anglicans aged seventy and over constitute the second largest age category. There were 1,659 lay people in this age group included in the analysis.

The three age groups will be referred to as young Anglicans (under fifty), middle-aged Anglicans (in their fifties and sixties), and senior Anglicans (aged seventy and over). This odd use of language makes sense within the peculiar age profile of Anglican congregations.

In calculating the statistical significance between the responses of the three age groups, the chi square test has been employed in respect of dichotomised data within each of the three age categories. The division has been made between those who agree or agree strongly with the question on the one hand, and those who check the disagree, disagree strongly, or uncertain categories on the other hand.

Patterns of belief

The *Church Times Survey* identified three doctrinal areas against which to assess the orthodoxy of Anglican belief: beliefs about God, beliefs about Jesus, and beliefs about life after death.

Committed lay Anglicans in all three age groups display a high level of belief in the existence of God: 98% of the young Anglicans say that they believe that God exists, and so do 97% of the middle-aged Anglicans, and 96% of the senior Anglicans. There are, however, some significant differences in the nature of the God in whom the three different age groups believe. The young

Anglicans are significantly more orthodox in their beliefs about God than is the case among the senior Anglicans. While 83% of the young Anglicans believe that God is a personal being, the proportions fall to 79% among the middle-aged Anglicans, and to 76% among the senior Anglicans. Looked at from the opposite perspective, 16% of the senior Anglicans believe that God is an impersonal power, compared with 14% of the middle-aged Anglicans and 12% of the young Anglicans.

The young Anglicans are also the most orthodox of the three age groups in terms of their beliefs about the person of Jesus. Thus, 65% of the young Anglicans believe that Jesus' birth was a virgin birth, compared with 60% of the middle-aged Anglicans. Similarly, 81% of the young Anglicans believe that Jesus rose physically from the dead, compared with 77% of the middle-aged Anglicans. At the same time, 69% of the young Anglicans believe that Jesus really turned water into wine, compared with 64% of the middle-aged Anglicans. The senior Anglicans tend to occupy a middle position between the young Anglicans and the middle-aged Anglicans.

Committed lay Anglicans in all three age groups hold a similar level of belief in the afterlife: 89% of the young Anglicans believe that there is life after death, and so do 87% of the middle-aged Anglicans, and 87% of the senior Anglicans. There are, however, significant differences in the nature of the afterlife in which the three different age groups believe. The young Anglicans are significantly more orthodox in their belief about life after death than is the case among the senior Anglicans. While 82% of the young Anglicans believe that heaven really exists, the proportions fall to 77% among the middle-aged Anglicans, and to 75% among the senior Anglicans. Similarly, while 53% of the young Anglicans believe that hell really exists, the proportions fall to 46% among the middle-aged Anglicans and to 39% among the senior Anglicans.

Overall, the fault-line between different generations of committed lay Anglicans regarding the nature of Christian belief suggests that young committed lay Anglicans may be shaping a Church that is more orthodox and conservative in its fundamental beliefs than the Church shaped by the previous two generations of committed lay Anglicans.

Paths of truth

The *Church Times Survey* identified three means of examining the ways in which truth claims are asserted: beliefs about the bible, beliefs about the exclusivity of Christianity, and beliefs about evolution versus creation.

In their understanding of the nature of scripture the young committed lay Anglicans tend to be more polarised in their opinions than is the case among their older colleagues, especially among the senior Anglicans. Among the senior Anglicans 53% take the view that biblical truths are culturally conditioned and 8% take the contrasting view that the bible is without any errors. Among the young Anglicans larger proportions adopt both positions:

60% take the view that biblical truths are culturally conditioned and 16% take the contrasting view that the bible is without any errors.

In their understanding of the exclusivity claims made for the Christian faith, the young lay Anglicans tend to be more liberal in their beliefs and attitudes than is the case among their older colleagues, especially among the senior Anglicans. Among the senior Anglicans 48% believe that Christianity is the only true religion, but the proportion falls slightly among the young Anglicans to 45%. Among the senior Anglicans 10% believe that all religions are of equal value, but the proportion rises significantly to 17% among the young Anglicans.

The debate about creationism versus evolutionary theory has become slightly more polarised among the young Anglicans, especially in comparison with the senior Anglicans. Among the senior Anglicans 18% take the creationist view that God made the world in six days and rested on the seventh, while 65% take the evolutionist view that all living things evolved. Both percentages increase slightly among the young Anglicans, 20% of whom believe that God made the world in six days and rested on the seventh, and 67% of whom believe that all living things evolved.

Overall, the fault-line between different generations of committed lay Anglicans regarding the sources of religious truth suggests that young committed lay Anglicans may be shaping a Church that is more polarised in its beliefs than the Church shaped by the two previous generations of committed lay Anglicans.

Paths of spirituality

In order to gauge different pathways of spirituality the *Church Times* Survey distinguished between three kinds of issues: personal and private sources of spiritual sustenance, group-based and shared sources of spiritual sustenance, and drawing on wider resources for spiritual sustenance.

Young Anglicans show a slightly higher commitment to personal prayer than that displayed by their older colleagues. While 83% of the senior lay Anglicans feel that they are helped in their faith by praying by themselves, the proportions rise slightly to 85% among the middle-aged Anglicans and to 87% among the young Anglicans.

All three age groups of committed lay Anglicans display a similar level of commitment to reading the bible. Thus, 81% of the senior lay Anglicans feel that they are helped in their faith by reading the bible, and so do 83% of the middle-aged Anglicans and 83% of the young Anglicans.

On the other hand, the young lay Anglicans are much more likely than their older colleagues to derive spiritual sustenance from reading both Christian books and non-religious books. Thus, 80% of the young lay Anglicans feel that they are helped in their faith by reading Christian books, compared with 75% of the senior Anglicans. Similarly, 37% of the young lay Anglicans feel that they are helped in their faith by reading non-religious books, compared with 26% of the senior Anglicans.

All three age groups of committed lay Anglicans show similar levels of commitment to prayer groups as a source of spiritual sustenance. Thus, 49% of the young lay Anglicans feel that they are helped in their faith by prayer groups, and so do 50% of the middle-aged Anglicans, and 49% of the senior Anglicans. By way of comparison, bible study groups are more popular among the middle-aged group, where 57% say that they are helped in their faith by bible study groups, compared with 50% of the young Anglicans and 52% of the senior Anglicans. Discussing their faith with others is of less importance to the senior Anglicans than to their younger colleagues. While 82% of the young lay Anglicans and 81% of the middle-aged Anglicans feel that they are helped in their faith by discussing their faith with others, the proportion drops to 73% among the senior Anglicans.

Moreover, the young committed lay Anglicans have a significantly different perspective regarding the value of wider resources for spirituality in compareson with their older colleagues. The young lay Anglicans are more likely to benefit from going on retreats and from drawing on resources outside the church. Thus, 54% of the young lay Anglicans feel that they are helped in their faith by going on retreat, compared with 51% of the middle-aged Anglicans and 47% of the senior Anglicans. At the same time, 19% of the young lay Anglicans report that they often get more spiritual help outside the church than within it, compared with 15% of the middle-aged Anglicans and 12% of the senior Anglicans.

Overall, the fault-line between the different generations of committed lay Anglicans concerning their paths of spirituality suggests that the young committed lay Anglicans may be embracing a wider view of spirituality than the two previous generations of committed lay Anglicans. This is demonstrated especially by drawing on non-religious books, by seeking spiritual help outside the church, and by going on retreat. The more senior lay Anglicans may be puzzled by these particular emphases in the spiritual quest of their younger colleagues.

Public worship

The *Church Times Survey* included three sets of questions to assess responses to public worship: the first set focused on the debate between traditional and modern forms of public worship, the second set focused on different aspects of the service, and the third set focused on the initiation of children into the worshipping community.

The debate between traditional and modern forms of public worship clearly reveals the different perspectives between the three generations of committed lay Anglicans. The senior lay Anglicans are more likely than the young Anglicans to value the traditional and the young lay Anglicans are more likely than the senior Anglicans to value the modern. Among all three age groups, however, there is more support for the traditional than for the modern. While 78% of the senior lay Anglicans are helped in their faith by traditional forms of service, the proportions fall to 70% among the middle-aged Anglicans and to 66% among the young Anglicans. While 82% of the senior lay Anglicans are helped in their faith by traditional hymns in services, the proportions fall to 75% among the middle-aged Anglicans and to 73% among the young Anglicans.

The opposite trend takes place in respect of modern forms of public worship. While 37% of the senior lay Anglicans are helped in their faith by new forms of service, the proportions rise to 49% among the middle-aged Anglicans and to 55% among the young Anglicans. While 50% of the senior lay Anglicans are helped in their faith by new hymns in services, the proportions rise to 60% among the middle-aged Anglicans and to 61% among the young Anglicans.

There are some significant differences in the value given to different aspects of the services by different generations of committed lay Anglicans. The younger Anglicans are more in favour of silence in worship. Thus, 79% of the young lay Anglicans say that they are helped in their faith by periods of silence in services, compared with 77% of the middle-aged Anglicans and 74% of the senior Anglicans. The younger Anglicans are more in favour of sermons in services. Thus, 78% of the young lay Anglicans say that they are helped in their faith by listening to sermons, compared with 77% of the middle-aged Anglicans and 72% of the senior Anglicans.

On the other hand, the younger Anglicans are less in favour of ritual in worship. Thus, 66% of the young lay Anglicans say that they are helped in their faith by ritual in services, compared with 69% of the middle-aged Anglicans and 71% of the senior Anglicans.

There are some very significant differences in the ways in which the three generations of Anglicans view sacramental initiation into the worshipping community. The younger Anglicans are more likely to support restrictive baptismal policies and to support the admission of children to communion before confirmation. Thus, while only 11% of the senior lay Anglicans take the restrictive view of baptism which maintains that churches should only baptise babies of regular churchgoers, the proportions rise to 12% among the middle-aged Anglicans and to 17% among the young Anglicans. While only 38% of the senior lay Anglicans are in favour of baptised children being admitted to communion before confirmation, the proportions rise to 50% among the middle-aged Anglicans and to 56% among the young Anglicans.

Overall, the fault-line between the different generations of committed lay Anglicans concerning attitudes toward public worship may prove to be surprisingly powerful in fragmenting Anglicanism. The younger generation is more likely not only to apply pressure for modern forms of service and modern hymns, but also to argue for changing theological perspectives which would reduce the emphasis on ritual, raise the threshold for infant baptism, and admit children to communion before confirmation. Some of the more senior lay Anglicans may be discomforted or disturbed by such changes in the landmarks with which they have become so familiar.

Local church life

In order to assess commitment to the local church, the *Church Times Survey* included three groups of questions useful for comparing the responses of different age groups of committed lay Anglicans: questions concerning the cycle of commitment, questions concerning the sense of belonging, and questions concerning the relationship between commitment and power.

There are no significant differences between the three generations of committed lay Anglicans in respect of their position in the cycle of commitment. Young Anglicans were neither more nor less likely than their older colleagues to be in the process of increasing commitment or in the process of disengaging from church life. Thus, 44% of the young lay Anglicans report that they are coming to their church more regularly nowadays, and so do 44% of the middle-aged Anglicans and 41% of the senior Anglicans. Viewed from the opposite perspective, 7% of the young lay Anglicans report that they are coming to church less regularly nowadays, and so do 6% of the middle-aged Anglicans and 5% of the senior Anglicans.

Younger Anglicans express a significantly lower level of commitment and of sense of belonging to their church in comparison with their older colleagues. While 93% of the senior lay Anglicans feel a strong sense of belonging to their church, the proportions fall to 91% among the middle-aged Anglicans and to 85% among the young Anglicans. While three-quarters (75%) of the senior lay Anglicans report that their church is important for their social life, the proportions fall to 71% among the middle-aged Anglicans and to 64% among the young Anglicans. While 62% of the senior lay Anglicans turn to fellow members of their church when they need help, the proportions fall to 61% among the middle-aged Anglicans and to 56% among the young Anglicans.

The middle-aged lay Anglicans emerge as the most powerful group in local church life. For example, 65% of the middle-aged lay Anglicans feel that they can influence their church's decisions, compared with 51% of the senior Anglicans and 61% of the young Anglicans. Looked at from a different perspective, 15% of the middle-aged lay Anglicans feel that they have too little control over the running of their church, but then the proportions rise to 16% among the senior Anglicans and to 19% among the young Anglicans.

All three generations of committed lay Anglicans are content with the demands being made on their money. Only 7% of the young lay Anglicans, 9% of the middle-aged Anglicans, and 8% of the senior Anglicans complain that their church makes too many demands on their money. There is a significant difference, however, in the way in which the three generations of committed lay Anglicans perceive the demands being made on their time. While only 8%

of the senior lay Anglicans complain that their church makes too many demands on their time, the proportions rise to 15% among the middle-aged Anglicans and to 15% among the young Anglicans.

Overall, the fault-line between the different generations of committed lay Anglicans concerning local church life raises several warning signs. The first warning sign concerns the marginalisation of the senior lay Anglicans who derive so much of their personal and social identity from their church, but who have now handed over leadership and decision making to the next generation, the middle-aged lay Anglicans. The second warning sign concerns the growing pressures being placed on the time commitment of the young Anglicans. Those who feel that the church is making too many demands on their time are the most likely to burn out or to disengage. The third warning sign concerns the way in which the young lay Anglicans are identifying less strongly with their local church compared with older members. This may indicate that the younger generation of lay Anglicans experiences less need to identify with their local church in this way. If this is so, young lay Anglicans may be building a church which has less social significance for its members in the future.

Ordained ministry

The *Church Times Survey* included questions about four issues which divide opinion in the Church of England: the ordination of women, the ordination of individuals who are divorced, the ordination of individuals who are divorced and remarried, and the ordination of practising homosexuals. In respect of each of these issues the survey distinguished between ordination as priest and ordination as bishop.

The younger generation of committed lay Anglicans holds a much more inclusive view of the ordained ministry in comparison with their older colleagues. To begin with, the younger generation of Anglicans displays more sympathy for the ordination of women, both to the priesthood and to the episcopacy. While 72% of the senior lay Anglicans are in favour of the ordination of women as priests, the proportions rise to 78% among the middle-aged Anglicans and to 80% among the young Anglicans. While 53% of the senior lay Anglicans are in favour of the ordination of women as bishops, the proportions rise to 66% among the middle-aged Anglicans and to 71% among the young Anglicans.

The younger generation of committed lay Anglicans displays more sympathy for the ordination of individuals who have experienced divorce, both to the priesthood and to the episcopacy. While 38% of the senior lay Anglicans are in favour of divorced people as priests, the proportions rise to 54% among the middle-aged Anglicans and to 63% among the young Anglicans. While 29% of the senior lay Anglicans are in favour of divorced people as bishops, the proportions rise to 45% among the middle-aged Anglicans and to 57% among the young Anglicans. A similar pattern appertains to the ordination of individuals who have remarried after divorce. Thus, 57% of the young lay Anglicans are in favour of divorced and remarried priests, compared with 49% of the middle-aged Anglicans and 35% of the senior Anglicans. Similarly, 52% of the young lay Anglicans are in favour of divorced and remarried bishops, compared with 41% of the middle-aged Anglican and 27% of the senior Anglicans.

Consistent with these patterns, the younger generation of committed lay Anglicans also displays more sympathy for the ordination of practising homosexuals, both to the priesthood and to the episcopacy. While just 15% of the senior lay Anglicans are in favour of the ordination of practising homo-sexuals as priests, the proportions rise to 23% among the middle-aged Angli-cans and to 34% among the young Anglicans. While just 11% of the senior lay Anglicans are in favour of the ordination of practising homosexuals as bishops, the proportions rise to 19% among the middle-aged Anglicans and to 32% among the young Anglicans.

Overall, the fault-line between the different generations of committed lay Anglicans concerning who is and who is not fit to be ordained to the priesthood or ordained to the episcopacy raises some interesting warning signs for the Church of England. The debate about the ordination of women to the priesthood has been won across the three age groups, and the debate about the ordination of women to the episcopacy has been won not only among the young lay Anglicans, but also among the middle-aged lay Anglicans. While the young Anglicans find considerable support for the ordination of those who are divorced or divorced and remarried, there is significantly less support among older lay Anglicans, and it is these older people who still represent a very large proportion of the body of committed lay Anglicans. None of the three age groups appears ready as yet, however, to accept the ordination of practising homosexuals as priests or as bishops.

Church leadership

In order to assess attitudes toward two major areas of change in church leadership, the *Church Times Survey* included a section on the development of ordained ministry and a section on the development of lay ministry.

The generation of committed lay Anglicans with the most radical views on the development of the clerical profession is not the young Anglicans, but the middle-aged Anglicans. This is the age group which is most likely to advocate the abolition of clergy freehold, most likely to argue that clergy should be employed on short-term renewable contracts, and most likely to support the view that clergy should live in their own houses rather than in parsonages provided by the church.

Thus, 43% of middle-aged lay Anglicans maintain that clergy freehold should be abolished, compared with 34% of young Anglicans and 37% of senior Anglicans. Following the same trend, 33% of middle-aged lay Anglicans argue that clergy should be employed on short-term renewable contracts, compared with 24% of young Anglicans and 27% of senior Anglicans. The view that clergy should live in their own houses is supported by 28% of middle-aged lay Anglicans, compared with 20% of young Anglicans and 25% of senior Anglicans.

Concerning views on lay ministry, the major division in the opinion of committed lay Anglicans comes between the middle-aged Anglicans and the senior Anglicans. Both the young lay Anglicans and the middle-aged lay Anglicans are significantly more in favour of lay ministry than is the case among senior lay Anglicans. Thus, 88% of the young lay Anglicans and 87% of the middle-aged lay Anglicans are in favour of lay people leading morning and evening prayer, compared with 80% of the senior Anglicans. Similarly, 85% of the young lay Anglicans and 83% of the middle-aged lay Anglicans are in favour of lay people preaching at morning and evening prayer, compared with 74% of the senior Anglicans.

This pattern is reproduced in terms of attitudes toward lay leadership in the communion service. Four-fifths (80%) of the young lay Anglicans and 75% of the middle-aged lay Anglicans are in favour of lay people preaching at communion services, compared with 61% of the senior Anglicans. Similarly, 71% of the young Anglicans and 72% of the middle-aged Anglicans are in favour of lay people leading the first part of the communion service, compared with 59% of the senior Anglicans. The pattern even extends to the question of lay presidency at the eucharist. A quarter (24%) of the young lay Anglicans and 22% of the middle-aged lay Anglicans are in favour of lay people taking the whole communion service, compared with 13% of the senior Anglicans. Committed lay Anglicans of all three generations seem far from ready to accept lay eucharistic presidency.

Overall, the fault-line between different generations of committed lay Anglicans concerning the ways in which clergy are employed suggests that the voice of the most powerful group of committed lay people, the middle-aged Anglicans, is representative neither of their more senior colleagues nor of their younger colleagues. Pressures for changes in the method of clergy deployment are unlikely to be given momentum by the young lay Anglicans. The parallel fault-line between different generations of committed lay Anglicans concerning the development of lay ministries raises a warning about the situation of the senior Anglicans. Developments encouraged by their younger colleagues may leave some senior Anglicans feeling isolated and let down.

Churches and cathedrals

The *Church Times Survey* included two sets of questions to assess attitudes toward churches and cathedrals, the buildings used for worship. The first set of questions focused on attitudes toward the individual respondent's local church, while the second set of questions focused on wider issues of policy.

The three generations of committed lay Anglicans have slight, but statistically significant, differences in their perceptions of their own church buildings. It is the middle-aged lay Anglicans (the group generally most closely involved in running the local church) who are most anxious about the future of their local church. Thus, 33% of the middle-aged lay Anglicans consider that in order to survive their church building needs more grants from the state, compared with 30% of the young Anglicans and 27% of the senior Anglicans. Similarly, 26% of the middle-aged lay Anglicans consider that in order to survive their church building needs more money from tourists and visitors, compared with 22% of the young Anglicans and 24% of the senior Anglicans.

The young and the middle-aged committed lay Anglicans see a somewhat more desperate future for their local church than is the case among the senior Anglicans. Thus, 22% of the young lay Anglicans and 21% of the middle-aged lay Anglicans believe that their congregation can no longer afford to pay for its church building, compared with 17% of the senior Anglicans.

A similar pattern emerges in respect of the wider issues of maintaining churches and cathedrals in general. It is the middle-aged lay Anglicans who tend to take the toughest line on keeping churches open. Thus, 14% of the middle-aged lay Anglicans take the view that many rural churches should be closed, compared with 11% of the young Anglicans and 10% of the senior Anglicans. One-third of the middle-aged lay Anglicans (34%) take the view that more church buildings should be taken over by the state, compared with 29% of the young Anglicans and 22% of the senior Anglicans. One-third of the young lay Anglicans (33%) and of the middle-aged lay Anglicans (34%) maintain that too much money is spent on keeping old churches, compared with 23% of the senior Anglicans.

A different pattern emerges, however, in respect of the maintenance of cathedrals. This time it is the senior lay Anglicans who are most likely to argue that cathedrals should charge visitors for entry (31%), compared with 24% of the middle-aged Anglicans and 16% of the young Anglicans.

Overall, the fault-line between different generations of committed lay Anglicans suggests that there may be some conflict between the middle-aged lay Anglicans and the senior lay Anglicans regarding the future of their church buildings. It is the middle-aged lay Anglicans, the people who may be taking much of the responsibility for maintaining the infrastructure and the fabric of their church, who are most likely to concede that the maintenance of the building is no longer financially viable. It is the senior lay Anglicans, the people who are more likely to have retired from taking the lead role in their local church, who are most likely either to resist or to be hurt and confused by threats to the continuing viability of their church.

Money and policy

In order to gauge the priorities of committed Anglicans, the *Church Times*

Survey posed a series of questions about how they envisaged the use of their church funds. Four specific areas were identified: central church structures, the clergy, development and mission, and community regeneration.

Comparison between the young committed lay Anglicans and the senior committed lay Anglicans shows a significant shift in the way in which different generations view the central church structures. Overall the young lay Anglicans hold a more positive view of the ways in which their local church is called on to support the central church structures, in comparison with the view of the senior Anglicans. Thus, over half (53%) of the young lay Anglicans are happy for some money given to their church to go to church central funds, compared with under half (48%) of the senior Anglicans. Looked at from the opposite perspective, 32% of the senior lay Anglicans complain that their parish pays too much for its parish share (quota), compared with 28% of the young Anglicans.

In comparison with senior lay Anglicans, young lay Anglicans show a significantly higher level of commitment to paying for the clergy. Thus 90% of the young lay Anglicans are happy for some money given to their church to go to training new priests, compared with 85% of the senior Anglicans. At the same time, 82% of the young lay Anglicans are happy for some money given to their church to go to clergy pensions, compared with 79% of the senior Anglicans.

The differences in perspective held by young lay Anglicans and by senior lay Anglicans is even more pronounced in respect of commitment to development and mission and in respect of commitment to community regeneration. While 89% of the young lay Anglicans are happy for some money given to their church to go to struggling parishes, the proportion falls to 79% among the senior Anglicans. While 87% of the young lay Anglicans are happy for some money given to their church to go to churches in developing countries, the proportion falls to 75% among the senior Anglicans. While two-thirds (68%) of the young lay Anglicans are happy for some money given to their church to go to urban regeneration, the proportion falls to half (51%) among the senior Anglicans.

The comparative commitment shown by different generations of Anglicans to urban issues and to rural issues may be very instructive regarding perceived emphases within the Church of England. Among senior lay Anglicans the levels of commitment to rural issues and to urban issues is quite close, but weighted marginally toward the countryside. Half of the senior lay Anglicans (51%) are happy for some money given to their church to go to urban regeneration, and slightly more (54%) are happy for some money given to their church to go to the farming community. The level of commitment to the farming community remains stable across the three generations, with 54% of the senior lay Anglicans, 54% of the middle-aged lay Anglicans, and 54% of the young lay Anglicans being willing for their church to use some of its income in this way. The level of commitment to urban regeneration, however, shows a significant rise across the age group, with 51% of the senior lay

Anglicans, 61% of the middle-aged lay Anglicans and 68% of the young lay Anglicans being willing for their church to use some of its income in this way.

Overall, the fault-line between different generations of committed lay Anglicans suggests that there may be some conflict between the young Anglicans and the senior Anglicans regarding the ways in which their church income is used. Some senior Anglicans may resent the willingness with which young Anglicans vote for their church income to be spent on the needs of the central church structures, on support for the clergy, on development and mission, and on urban regeneration projects. The fault-line between the different generations of committed lay Anglicans also suggests that young Anglicans are wanting to emphasise the Church of England's commitment to the urban agenda more actively than commitment to the rural agenda.

Anglican identity

The *Church Times Survey* focused two kinds of questions on Anglican identity: the first concentrated on willingness to merge Anglican identity with other denominations, and the second concentrated on the future of establishment for the Church of England.

Comparison between young committed lay Anglicans and senior committed lay Anglicans reveals a highly significant shift in the extent to which lay Anglicans perceive permeable boundaries between their own denomination and other Christian denominations. While nearly half of the senior lay Anglicans (46%) say that they would never become a member of another denomination, the proportion falls to a third among the middle-aged Anglicans (33%) and to just over a quarter among the young Anglicans (27%). While 31% of the senior lay Anglicans say that they would not want to be a member of an ecumenical church or local ecumenical project, the proportion falls to 23% among the middle-aged Anglicans and to 20% among the young Anglicans. While a quarter of the senior lay Anglicans (25%) would not want their denomination to merge with another, the proportions fall to 20% among the middle-aged Anglicans and to 19% among the young Anglicans.

This greater openness among young committed lay Anglicans to permeable boundaries between the denominations does not, however, extend to a greater willingness to see Anglicanism brought under closer papal control. One in four of each of the three generational groups would be prepared to accept the Pope as their church leader in some situations: 26% of the young Anglicans, 26% of the middle-aged Anglicans, and 27% of the senior Anglicans.

Comparison between young committed lay Anglicans and senior committed lay Anglicans also reveals a highly significant shift in attitude toward establishment. This shift is seen most clearly in respect of the role of the monarch as head of the Church of England. While 62% of the senior lay Anglicans maintain that the monarch should continue to be the Supreme Governor of the Church of England, the proportions fall to 50% among the middle-aged Anglicans, and to 39% among the young Anglicans. There is also a significant, but much less dramatic, shift in attitude toward the role of bishops in the House of Lords. While 86% of the senior lay Anglicans maintain that senior bishops should continue to sit in the reformed House of Lords, the proportions fall to 82% among the middle-aged Anglicans and to 78% among the young Anglicans.

The cry in support of disestablishment is significantly stronger among young committed lay Anglicans, but still represents a minority perspective. While 22% of the senior lay Anglicans maintain that the Church of England should be disestablished, the proportions rise to 29% among both the middle-aged Anglicans and the young Anglicans.

In spite of being less in favour of disestablishment, the senior committed lay Anglicans show little support for the state retaining control over key areas of church life. Just 5% of all three generational groups hold to the view that diocesan bishops should be appointed by the state. Just 15% of the senior lay Anglicans, 13% of the middle-aged lay Anglicans, and 11% of the young Anglicans hold the view that Parliament should retain control of Church of England legislation.

Overall, the fault-line between different generations of committed lay Anglicans suggests that senior Anglicans may well be puzzled by the future which young Anglicans are beginning to shape for the Church of England. This future is likely to be more ecumenical in emphasis, less closely identified with the monarchy, and more likely to question the future of establishment.

Confidence and the future

In order to gauge the level of confidence which committed Anglicans hold in the future of their Church, the *Church Times Survey* asked questions about two main issues: the first issue concerned confidence in the Church's leadership, and the second issue concerned confidence in the future of their own local church.

Comparison between young committed lay Anglicans and senior committed lay Anglicans highlight the way in which confidence in the Archbishops' Council is so much less secure among the young lay people. While nearly half of the senior lay Anglicans (46%) report that they have confidence in the leadership given by the Archbishops' Council, the proportion falls to 38% among the middle-aged Anglicans and then it falls further to 32% among the young Anglicans. There is a similar, but less pronounced, decline in confidence in the bishops. While 72% of the senior lay Anglicans report that they have confidence in the leadership given by their diocesan bishop, the proportion falls to 70% among the middle-aged Anglicans and then it falls further to 67% among the young Anglicans.

On the other hand, levels of confidence shown in local clergy and in the General Synod do not fluctuate significantly with age. Over three-quarters

(77%) of the senior lay Anglicans have confidence in the leadership given by their local clergy, and so do 77% of the middle-aged Anglicans and 80% of the young Anglicans. Two-fifths (40%) of the young lay Anglicans have confidence in the leadership given by the General Synod, and so do 41% of the middle-aged Anglicans and 44% of the senior Anglicans.

Comparison between young committed lay Anglicans and senior committed lay Anglicans also highlight the ways in which young Anglicans both have more confidence in the future of their local church and more awareness of the difficulties their local church faces. On the one hand, 42% of the young lay Anglicans believe that the membership of their church will grow in the next twelve months, compared with 40% of the middle-aged Anglicans and 32% of the senior Anglicans. The young lay Anglicans are also more inclined to make this happen by inviting others to their church. Thus, 32% of the young lay Anglicans and 32% of the middle-aged Anglicans feel that they can invite other people to come to their church, compared with 27% of the senior Anglicans.

On the other hand, twice as many young lay Anglicans recognise that it is not easy for newcomers to find their way into membership of the local church. Thus, 31% of the young lay Anglicans feel that it is not easy for newcomers in their church, compared with 23% of the middle-aged Anglicans and 15% of the senior Anglicans.

Overall, the fault-line between different generations of committed lay Anglicans suggests that young lay Anglicans feel some discontent with what they may perceive as complacency among senior Anglicans about the future of the Church of England. At a national level the young lay Anglicans are more likely to press for more effective and more efficient leadership from the centre. At a local level the young lay Anglicans are more likely to press for their own church to become more welcoming and more accessible to newcomers.

Sex and family life

The *Church Times Survey* identified four specific areas in which to test the orthodoxy of Anglican views on sex and family life: views on sex and cohabitation before marriage, views on divorce, views on same sex relationships, and views on caring for children and teenagers.

Comparison between young committed lay Anglicans and senior committed lay Anglicans highlights just how much successive generations of Anglicans have been adopting more liberal attitudes toward sex and family life, on issues like sex before marriage, separation and divorce, same sex relationships, and children and teenagers.

On the issue of sex before marriage, over half of the senior lay Anglicans (54%) take the view that it is wrong for men and women to have sex before marriage. The proportion falls to 41% among the middle-aged Anglicans and then further to 31% among the young Anglicans. Just 17% of the senior lay Anglicans feel that it is all right for a couple to live together without intending to get married. The proportion rises to 27% among the middle-aged Anglicans and then further to 34% among the young Anglicans. Just 15% of the senior lay Anglicans feel that it is a good idea for couples who intend to get married to live together first. The proportion rises to 19% among the middle-aged Anglicans and then further to 25% among the young Anglicans.

On the issue of separation and divorce, over half of the senior lay Anglicans (52%) take the view that couples should stay together for the sake of the children. The proportion falls to 33% among the middle-aged Anglicans and then further to 26% among the young Anglicans. The view that some marriages can come to a natural end in divorce is supported by 69% of the senior lay Anglicans, 77% of the middle-aged Anglicans, and 73% of the young Anglicans.

On the issue of same sex relationships, two-thirds of the senior lay Anglicans (66%) take the view that it is wrong for people of the same gender to have sex together. The proportion falls to 56% among the middle-aged Anglicans, and then further to 42% among the young Anglicans. Just 8% of the senior lay Anglicans believe that homosexual couples should have the right to marry one another. The proportion rises to 13% among the middle-aged Anglicans and then further to 23% among the young Anglicans.

On the issue of children and teenagers, one in five of the senior lay Anglicans (19%) argue that children thrive equally whether cared for primarily by their father or mother. The proportion rises to 31% among the middle-aged Anglicans and then further to 43% among the young Anglicans. One in four (24%) of the senior lay Anglicans argue that contraception should be available to teenagers under sixteen who want it. The proportion rises to 36% among the middle-aged Anglicans and then further to 44% among the young Anglicans.

Overall, the marked fault-line between different generations of committed lay Anglicans over the issues of sex and family life suggests that the values system espoused by Anglicans is in a state of considerable flux, and that there is considerable room for misunderstanding and conflict between young Anglicans and senior Anglicans in this area. Young Anglicans may tend to feel that senior Anglicans are too staid and conservative in their values system. Senior Anglicans may tend to feel that young Anglicans are too progressive and liberal in their values system.

Social concerns

In order to assess the levels of social concern expressed by committed Anglicans, the *Church Times Survey* included a set of items on global concerns and a set of items on community concerns. The global concerns included environmental and developmental issues, AIDS and genetic research. The community concerns included violence on television, paedophiles living in the community, and the effects of the National Lottery.

Comparison between young committed lay Anglicans and senior committed lay Anglicans demonstrates that young Anglicans register even *higher* levels of concern about global issues than is the case among senior Anglicans. While 91% of the senior lay Anglicans are concerned about environmental pollution, the proportion rises even higher to 95% among both the middle-aged Anglicans and the young Anglicans. While 93% of the senior lay Anglicans are concerned about the poverty of the developing world, the proportion rises even higher to 95% among the middle-aged Anglicans and to 96% among the young Anglicans. Between 94% and 95% of all three generational groups of committed lay Anglicans are concerned about the spread of AIDS.

Comparison between young committed lay Anglicans and senior committed lay Anglicans also demonstrates that young lay Anglicans register *lower* levels of concern about community issues than is the case among senior lay Anglicans. While 88% of the senior lay Anglicans are concerned about violence on television, the proportions drop to 84% among the middle-aged Anglicans and to 70% among the young Anglicans. While 58% of the senior lay Anglicans are concerned about paedophiles living in the community, the proportions drop a little to 54% among the middle-aged Anglicans and to 53% among the young Anglicans. While 48% of the senior lay Anglicans are concerned about the National Lottery, the proportions drop a little to 45% among the middle-aged Anglicans and to 40% among the young Anglicans.

Overall, the fault-line between three different generations of committed lay Anglicans over social concerns suggests that senior Anglicans may sometimes be frustrated that young Anglicans fail to share their own perceptions of priorities on such issues as protesting about violence on television or about the evils of the National Lottery.

Social conscience

The *Church Times Survey* assessed social conscience by means of a series of questions exploring the willingness of committed lay Anglicans to pay more tax in order to fund specific areas of social life. The three broad areas included in the survey concerned health and education, social security and prisons, and defence and development aid.

Comparison between young committed lay Anglicans and senior committed lay Anglicans reveals some key differences in the social conscience shaped by different generations of Anglicans. In particular, young Anglicans are more committed to supporting health and education, and the senior Anglicans are more committed to supporting the defence budget.

First, young committed lay Anglicans are slightly more likely to express a willingness to pay more tax to fund spending on health. This is the case for 83% of the young lay Anglicans, 81% of the middle-aged Anglicans, and 78% of the senior Anglicans.

Second, young committed lay Anglicans are much more likely to express willingness to fund education. Four-fifths of the young lay Anglicans (79%)

would pay more tax to fund spending on schools, compared with 75% of the middle-aged Anglicans and 68% of the senior Anglicans. Half of the young lay Anglicans (51%) would pay more tax to fund spending on universities, compared with 42% of the middle-aged Anglicans and 37% of the senior Anglicans.

Third, young committed lay Anglicans are much less likely to express willingness to fund defence. While two in five (41%) of the senior lay Anglicans would pay more tax to fund spending on security forces, the proportion more than halves to 18% among the young Anglicans. The middle-aged lay Anglicans occupy the midway position between the senior Anglicans and the young Anglicans: 28% of the middle-aged Anglicans would pay more tax to fund spending on security forces.

On other areas of social conscience, however, there is little disagreement between the three generations of committed lay Anglicans. Between 60% and 64% of all three age groups would pay more tax to fund spending on overseas aid. Between 38% and 40% of all three age groups would pay more tax to fund spending on social security benefits. Between 38% and 41% of all three age groups would pay more tax to fund spending on prisons.

Overall, the fault-line between different generations of committed lay Anglicans suggests that it is issues like the education budget and the defence budget which are most likely to divide the Anglican sense of social conscience across the generations.

Education

The *Church Times Survey* framed questions on three key topics of relevance to the Church of England's concerns with education. These topics related to the debate between the state-funded sector of schools and the independent sector of schools, the place of religious education and worship in schools, and the future of faith-based schools.

Comparison between young committed lay Anglicans and senior committed lay Anglicans reveals some key differences regarding the ways in which these different generations of Anglicans view the educational agenda, as well as some key points of agreement.

Regarding the debate between the state-funded sector of schools and the independent sector schools, there is no significant variation in the proportions of the three age groups who have confidence in the state-funded system. Thus, 50% of the senior lay Anglicans express confidence in the state-funded education system and so do 50% of the middle-aged Anglicans and 50% of the young Anglicans. Nevertheless, there is significantly less sympathy for the independent sector of schools among the young Anglicans. Just 7% of the senior lay Anglicans argue that private schools should be abolished. The proportions rise to 11% among the middle-aged Anglicans and to 14% among the young Anglicans.

Regarding the place of religious education and worship in schools, there are some very significant differences in the perceptions of the young committed lay Anglicans and the senior committed lay Anglicans. Between 92% and 94% of all three age groups believe that religious education should be taught in all schools. However, their understanding of the nature of this religious education is not necessarily the same. While 71% of the senior lay Anglicans believe that religious education in schools should teach about world religions, the proportions who take this view rise to 81% among the middle-aged Anglicans and 87% among the young Anglicans. The young Anglicans are also less likely to believe that schools should hold a religious assembly every day. This view is taken by 58% of the young lay Anglicans, compared with 68% of the middle-aged Anglicans and 77% of the senior Anglicans.

Regarding the future for faith-based schools, there are further significant differences in the perspectives adopted by the three generations of committed lay Anglicans. On the one hand, the young Anglicans are more open than the senior Anglicans to the participation of other faiths within the state-funded system of schools. While 36% of the senior lay Anglicans are in favour of state-funded Jewish schools, the proportions rise to 41% among the middle-aged Anglicans and to 42% among the young Anglicans. While 30% of the senior lay Anglicans are in favour of state-funded Islamic schools, the proportions rise to 36% among the middle-aged Anglicans and to 38% among the young Anglicans.

On the other hand, the young committed lay Anglicans are less convinced than the senior committed lay Anglicans about the desirability of expanding some aspects of the Church of England's own involvement within the state-funded system of schools. While 78% of the senior lay Anglicans argue that the Church of England should fund more new church primary schools, the proportions fall to 75% among the middle-aged Anglicans and to 70% among the young Anglicans. All three generations, however, share a similar level of enthusiasm for expanding the Church of England's stake in secondary education. Thus, 78% of the senior lay Anglicans, 78% of the middle-aged Anglicans, and 75% of the young Anglicans support the view that the Church of England should fund more new church secondary schools.

Overall, the fault-line between different generations of committed lay Anglicans over educational issues suggests that it is attitudes toward other world faiths which may prove to be most divisive. Young lay Anglicans may tend to interpret the views of senior lay Anglicans on teaching world faiths in religious education and on the provision of state-funded schools for other faith traditions as far too anachronistic and conservative. Senior lay Anglicans, on the other hand, may tend to interpret the views of young lay Anglicans on these issues as too liberal and as undermining their Anglican roots.

Conclusion

There is significant evidence in the present analysis to alert the Church of England to the wisdom of taking seriously the fault-line between different generations of committed Anglicans in the pews. Decisions made on the basis of accommodating and welcoming the perspectives of those younger committed lay Anglicans under the age of fifty may well be uncomfortable or incomprehensible to some of the older committed lay Anglicans who continue to be the backbone of the Church of England.

CHAPTER 7

Catholics and Evangelicals in the pulpit

Introduction

The fourth of the potential fault-lines within the Church of England to be examined by the present study concerns the ways in which beliefs, attitudes and values may vary between clergy who have been shaped in the Catholic tradition of the Church of England and by clergy who have been shaped in the Evangelical tradition of the Church of England. The division between Catholic clergy and Evangelical clergy has been made on the basis of responses to the seven-point semantic differential scale included in the survey. Clergy who checked the two values closest to the Catholic end of the continuum have been regarded as Catholics. A total of 846 clergy came into this category. Clergy who checked the two values closest to the Evangelical end of the continuum have been regarded as Evangelicals. A total of 366 clergy came into this category. The remaining clergy who either checked the three middle values on the scale or omitted the question have been excluded from the analysis.

In calculating the statistical significance between the responses of the two groups of clergy, the chi square test has been employed in respect of dichotomised data within each of the two groups. The division has been made between those who agree or agree strongly with the question on the one hand, and those who check the disagree, disagree strongly or uncertain categories on the other hand.

Patterns of belief

The *Church Times Survey* identified three doctrinal areas against which to assess the orthodoxy of Anglican belief: beliefs about God, beliefs about Jesus, and beliefs about life after death.

Comparison between the pattern of beliefs held by Catholics and the pattern of beliefs held by Evangelicals clearly illustrates the diversity of religious believing among Anglican clergy. In this sense the Church of England is a very broad church.

The majority of clergy on both wings of the Anglican Church clearly claim to believe that God exists: 99% of the Evangelicals and 97% of the Catholics. There are significant differences, however, in the nature of the God in whom Evangelicals believe and in whom Catholics believe. While 98% of

Evangelicals clearly believe that God is a personal being, the proportion drops significantly to 89% among Catholic clergy. Looked at from a different perspective, one in ten Catholic clergy (10%) believe that God is an impersonal power, compared with just 4% of Evangelical clergy.

If Catholic and Evangelical clergy differ a little in their understanding of the nature of God, they differ much more widely in their understanding of the nature of Jesus. Catholics are less committed to belief in the physical resurrection. While 98% of Evangelical clergy believe that Jesus rose physically from the dead, the proportion falls to 73% among Catholic clergy. Catholics are less committed to belief in the virgin birth. While 93% of Evangelical clergy believe that Jesus' birth was a virgin birth, the proportion plummets to 54% among Catholic clergy. There is a similarly wide gap between Catholics and Evangelicals concerning belief in some of the miracles of Jesus. While 92% of Evangelical clergy believe that Jesus really turned water into wine, the proportion again plummets to 53% among Catholic clergy.

The differences between the ways in which Evangelical and Catholic clergy understand and express the Church's teaching on life after death are very illuminating. Regarding basic belief in life after death, the two groups stand just eight percentage points apart. Thus, 90% of Catholic clergy believe that there is life after death, compared with 98% of Evangelical clergy. Regarding belief in heaven, the gap between the two groups widens to 16 percentage points. Thus, 82% of Catholic clergy believe that heaven really exists, compared with 98% of Evangelical clergy. Regarding belief in hell, the gap between the two groups widens even further to 42 percentage points. Thus, 41% of Catholic clergy believe that hell really exists, compared with 83% of Evangelical clergy.

Overall, the fault-line between Catholic and Evangelical clergy concerning their basic patterns of beliefs is strongly developed and very pronounced. The kind of Jesus in whom the two groups believe is defined in very different terms. The doctrine of the afterlife espoused by the two groups is defined in very different terms. The scope for theological disagreement between the two groups is far from insignificant.

Paths of truth

The *Church Times Survey* identified three means of examining the ways in which truth claims are asserted: beliefs about the bible, beliefs about the exclusivity of Christianity, and beliefs about evolution versus creation.

Comparison between the paths of truth pursued by Catholic clergy and the paths of truth pursued by Evangelical clergy clearly illustrates the very different perspectives held by the two groups. In this sense, too, the Church of England is a very broad church.

To begin with, Catholics and Evangelicals hold quite different views on the authority of scripture. Catholic clergy are much less likely to maintain the inerrancy of scripture. While two in every five Evangelical clergy (42%)

believe that the bible is without any errors, the proportion falls to just 4% of Catholic clergy who take this view. Looking at the matter from the opposite perspective, while 49% of Evangelical clergy believe that biblical truths are culturally conditioned, the proportion rises to 78% of Catholic clergy who take this view.

Second, Catholics and Evangelicals hold quite different views on the exclusivity of the Christian faith. The Catholic clergy are less likely to maintain that there is only one path to salvation. While 85% of Evangelical clergy believe that Christianity is the only true religion, the proportion falls to 40% of Catholic clergy who take this view. Even the very radical item which asserts the equality of all religions draws a significant difference between Catholics and Evangelicals. While only 10% of Catholic clergy take the view that all religions are of equal value, the proportion falls even further to 3% among Evangelical clergy.

Third, Catholics and Evangelicals hold quite different positions on the debate between creationism and evolutionary theory. While nearly half of the Evangelical clergy (47%) accept the view that all living things evolved, the proportion rises to 82% among Catholic clergy. While between a quarter and a third of Evangelical clergy (29%) accept the view that God made the world in six days and rested on the seventh, the proportion drops to 4% among Catholic clergy.

Overall, the fault-line between Catholic and Evangelical clergy concerning the grounds of theological truth is strongly developed and very pronounced. The kind of bible in which the two groups believe is defined in very different terms. The kind of world in which the two groups live was created in very different ways. The scope for disagreement between the two groups on the nature of theological truth is far from insignificant.

Paths of spirituality

In order to gauge different pathways of spirituality the *Church Times Survey* distinguished between three kinds of issues: personal and private sources of spiritual sustenance, group-based and shared sources of spiritual sustenance, and drawing on wider resources for spiritual sustenance.

There are some ways in which Catholic and Evangelical clergy share very similar perspectives on the value of certain personal spiritual practices. Both groups give equal weight to personal prayer and to reading Christian books. For example, 92% of Catholic clergy feel that they are helped in their faith by praying by themselves, and so do 93% of Evangelical clergy. Similarly, 89% of Catholic clergy feel that they are helped in their faith by reading Christian books, and so do 91% of Evangelical clergy.

In other ways, however, Catholic and Evangelical clergy begin to part company in their differing perspectives on the value of certain personal spiritual practices. The two groups give significantly different weight to reading the bible and to reading non-Christian books. For example, while 98% of Evangelical clergy feel that they are helped in their faith by reading the bible, the proportion drops by seven percentage points to 91% among Catholic clergy. At the same time, while 34% of Evangelical clergy feel that they are helped in their faith by reading non-religious books, the proportion rises by 27 percentage points among Catholic clergy to 61%.

The gap between the preferred spirituality of Catholic and Evangelical clergy widens in a much more dramatic way when their attitudes on group spiritual practices are taken into account. Catholic clergy are much less attracted to bible study groups and to prayer groups and are somewhat less attracted to discussing their faith more generally. For example, while 83% of Evangelical clergy feel that they are helped in their faith by bible study groups, the proportion nearly halves among Catholic clergy to 45%. Similarly, while 80% of Evangelical clergy feel that they are helped in their faith by prayer groups, the proportion nearly halves among Catholic clergy to 44%. Indeed, while 96% of Evangelical clergy feel that they are helped in their faith by discussing their faith with others, the proportion drops significantly to 86% among Catholic clergy.

While, in comparison with Evangelical clergy, the spirituality of Catholic clergy is less likely to be supported by group activities, it is more likely to be supported by a wider perspective. The Catholic spirituality is more likely to be rooted in the natural world, in going on retreat, and in secular resources. Thus, 71% of Catholic clergy feel that they are helped in their faith by considering the natural world, compared with 56% of Evangelical clergy. Four out of every five Catholic clergy (81%) feel that they are helped in their faith by going on retreat, compared with three out of every five Evangelical clergy (60%). Two out of every ten Catholic clergy (20%) feel that they often get more spiritual help outside the church than within it, compared with fewer than one out of every ten Evangelical clergy (8%).

Overall, the fault-line between Catholic and Evangelical clergy concerning their preferred paths of spirituality is significant and wide. At times, the two groups may find it quite difficult to believe that they are really part of the same Anglican Church.

Public worship

The *Church Times Survey* included three sets of questions to assess responses to public worship: the first set focused on the debate between traditional and modern forms of public worship, the second set focused on different aspects of the service, and the third set focused on the initiation of children into the worshipping community.

Catholic and Evangelical clergy hold significantly different perspectives on the debate between traditional and modern forms of worship. Catholic clergy place greater weight than Evangelical clergy on the traditional forms of worship. For example, while 70% of Catholic clergy feel that they are helped in their faith by traditional forms of service, the proportion almost halves among Evangelical clergy to 39%. While 77% of Catholic clergy feel that they are helped in their faith by traditional hymns in services, the proportion drops significantly among Evangelical clergy to 65%.

Looked at from the opposite perspective, Evangelicals place greater weight than Catholics on the modern forms of worship. For example, while 59% of Catholic clergy feel that they are helped in their faith by modern forms of service, the proportion rises to 72% among Evangelical clergy. While 57% of Catholic clergy feel that they are helped in their faith by new hymns in services, the proportion rises to 85% among Evangelical clergy.

Catholic and Evangelical clergy also hold significantly different perspectives on the debate between different styles of worship. Catholic clergy place greater weight than Evangelical clergy on silence and on ritual in worship. Evangelical clergy place greater weight than Catholic clergy on preaching in worship. For example, while 86% of Catholic clergy feel that they are helped in their faith by periods of silence in services, the proportion falls to 68% among Evangelical clergy. While 94% of Catholic clergy feel that they are helped in their faith by ritual in services, the proportion plummets to 29% among Evangelical clergy. On the other hand, while 73% of Catholic clergy feel that they are helped in their faith by listening to sermons, the proportion rises further to 86% among Evangelical clergy.

The two questions included in the survey on children and church reveal some further important differences between the perspectives taken by Evangelical clergy and by Catholic clergy. In some senses Catholic clergy espouse a more inclusive model of what it is to be church. In some senses Evangelical clergy espouse a model of church which is more likely to emphasise the boundaries between the church and the world. The Catholic preference for a more inclusive model of church is illustrated by their overwhelming rejection of placing stringent criteria on infant baptism. Just 6% of Catholic clergy are in favour of churches baptising only babies of regular churchgoers, compared with one in every three Evangelical clergy (34%).

There is no significant difference, however, in the proportions of Catholic clergy (68%) and Evangelical clergy (63%) who are in favour of baptised children being admitted to communion before confirmation.

Overall, the fault-line between Catholic and Evangelical clergy concerning public worship is deep and highly visible. This long-established and well-recognised division has not been healed. Catholics continue to feel out of place in evangelical congregations, while Evangelicals continue to feel out of place in Catholic congregations.

Local church life

In order to assess commitment to the local church, the *Church Times Survey* included three groups of questions: questions concerning the cycle of commitment, questions concerning the sense of belonging, and questions concerning the relationship between commitment and power.

Catholic and Evangelical clergy occupy similar positions on the cycle of commitment. A third (33%) of Catholic clergy are coming to their local church more regularly nowadays, and so are 37% of Evangelical clergy. Looked at from the opposite perspective, just 4% of Catholic clergy and 5% of Evangelical clergy are coming to their church less regularly nowadays.

Compared with Catholic clergy, Evangelical clergy experience a higher sense of commitment and belonging to their church. Although 92% of Catholic clergy and 89% of Evangelical clergy say that they feel a strong sense of belonging to their church, significant differences appear in the ways in which they express and experience that sense of belonging. Three-quarters (73%) of Evangelical clergy say that their church is important for their social life, compared with two-thirds (64%) of Catholic clergy. Similarly, 66% of Evangelical clergy turn to fellow members of their church when they need help, compared with 57% of Catholic clergy.

Compared with Catholic clergy, Evangelical clergy experience a higher sense of active control over their church. Thus, 78% of Evangelical clergy say that they can influence their church's decisions, compared with 69% of Catholic clergy. On the other hand, the same low proportions of Catholic clergy (11%) and Evangelical clergy (11%) feel that they have too little control over the running of their church.

Similar proportions of Catholic clergy and Evangelical clergy feel that the work-related demands of their church are excessive. Just under a quarter (23%) of Catholic clergy complain that their church makes too many demands on their time, and so do 24% of Evangelical clergy. On the other hand, Catholic clergy are slightly more likely than Evangelical clergy to complain that their church makes too many demands on their money (8% compared with 4%).

Overall, the most significant aspect of the fault-line between Evangelical and Catholic clergy in respect of local church life concerns their *personal* commitment to the local congregation. Evangelical clergy are more inclined to make the local church their life.

Ordained ministry

The *Church Times Survey* included questions about four issues which divide opinion in the Church of England on the question of ordained ministry: the ordination of women, the ordination of individuals who are divorced, the ordination of individuals who are divorced and remarried, and the ordination of practising homosexuals. In respect of each of these issues the survey distinguished between ordination as priest and ordination as bishop.

Opinion between Catholic clergy and Evangelical clergy is quite clearly divided on the categories of people who qualify and who do not qualify for ordination as priests and for ordination as bishops. To begin with Evangelicals are more liberal than Catholics on the question of the ordination of women as priests. While 81% of Evangelical clergy are in favour of the ordination of women as priests, the proportion falls to 73% among Catholic clergy. Nonetheless, the two groups adopt very similar profiles on the question of the ordination of women as bishops. Three-fifths of Catholic clergy (60%) are in favour of the ordination of women as bishops, and so are 59% of Evangelical clergy.

While Evangelicals are more inclusive than Catholics regarding the ordination of women, Catholics are more liberal than Evangelicals regarding the ordination of divorced people. While two-thirds of Catholic clergy (66%) are in favour of divorced people as priests, the proportion drops to 52% among Evangelical clergy. While three-fifths of Catholic clergy (58%) are in favour of divorced people as bishops, the proportion drops to 43% among Evangelical clergy.

The divide between Catholics and Evangelicals widens even further over the question of ordination of divorced and re-married people. While three-fifths of Catholic clergy (60%) are in favour of divorced and remarried priests, the proportion drops to 43% among Evangelical clergy. While half of the Catholic clergy (51%) are in favour of divorced and remarried bishops, the proportion drops to 35% among Evangelical clergy.

The widest division between Catholics and Evangelicals, however, occurs over the question of the ordination of practising homosexuals. Although between two-fifths and half of the Catholic clergy (44%) are in favour of the ordination of practising homosexuals as priests, only a very small minority of Evangelical clergy agree with this view (5%). Although two-fifths of Catholic clergy (39%) are in favour of the ordination of practising homosexuals as bishops, an even smaller minority of Evangelical clergy agree with this view (3%).

Overall, the fault-line between Evangelical and Catholic clergy over the ordination of practising homosexuals is almost insuperable. While a significant group of Catholic priests is willing to approve the ordination of practising homosexuals, the Evangelical clergy stand solidly against the possibility.

Church leadership

In order to assess attitudes toward two major areas of change in church leadership, the *Church Times Survey* included a section on the development of ordained ministry and a section on the development of lay ministry.

On the questions concerning the development of ordained ministry, Catholic and Evangelical clergy speak as if with one voice. To begin with, similar proportions of Catholic clergy (58%) and of Evangelical clergy (53%) argue that clergy should be paid a better wage. Just over a third of both groups argue that clergy freehold should be abolished. This view is espoused by 35% of

Catholic clergy and by 36% of Evangelical clergy. A quarter of both groups argue that clergy should be employed on short-term renewable contracts. This view is espoused by 24% of Catholic clergy and by 24% of Evangelical clergy. A quarter of both groups argue that clergy should live in their own houses rather than in church-owned parsonages. This view is espoused by 25% of Catholic clergy and by 23% of Evangelical clergy.

On the questions concerning the development of lay ministry, however, Catholic and Evangelical clergy speak with diverging voices. The Catholic clergy are significantly more conscious of the distinctiveness of ordained ministry and are significantly more cautious about recognising the liturgical ministry of the laity.

Although the vast majority of all clergy are already in favour of lay people leading morning and evening prayer, even on this relatively uncontroversial issue Catholic clergy are significantly more cautious than Evangelical clergy. While 97% of Evangelical clergy are in favour of lay people leading morning and evening prayer, the proportion drops significantly to 92% among Catholic clergy.

The gap between Catholic and Evangelical clergy widens further when the issue at stake moves from lay people leading morning and evening prayer to lay people preaching at morning and evening prayer. Among Evangelical clergy, while 97% are in favour of lay people leading morning and evening prayer, the proportion drops only marginally to 94% who are in favour of lay people preaching at morning and evening prayer. Among Catholic clergy the distinction between leading the service and preaching is more strongly marked. In this case the proportion drops from 92% who are in favour of lay people leading morning and evening prayer to 78% who are in favour of lay people preaching at morning and evening prayer.

The gap between Catholic and Evangelical clergy widens even further when the issues at stake move to the involvement of lay leadership at the communion service. While 91% of Evangelical clergy are in favour of lay people preaching at communion services, the proportion falls to 70% among Catholic clergy. While 93% of Evangelical clergy are in favour of lay people leading the first part of the communion, the proportion falls to 56% among Catholic clergy.

The biggest divide between Catholic and Evangelical clergy over lay leadership concerns lay presidency at the eucharist. Nearly two out of every five Evangelical clergy (37%) are in favour of lay people taking the whole communion service. For Catholic clergy, however, such departure from the traditional Anglican view on ordained eucharistic presidency is almost unthinkable. Just 2% of Catholic clergy are in favour of lay people taking the whole communion service.

Overall, the fault-line between Evangelical and Catholic clergy on lay liturgical leadership is deeply ingrained and highly significant. Evangelical clergy are much more comfortable with sharing eucharistic leadership with lay people, up to and including lay people taking the whole communion service.

For Catholic clergy the traditional requirement for ordained presidency at the eucharist is non-negotiable.

Churches and cathedrals

The *Church Times Survey* included two sets of questions to assess attitudes toward churches and cathedrals, the buildings used for worship. The first set of questions focused on attitudes toward the individual respondent's local church, while the second set of questions focused on wider issues of policy.

Catholic and Evangelical clergy hold similar perceptions regarding the difficulties faced by their local congregation to maintain its church building. Thus, 22% of Catholic clergy feel that their congregation can no longer afford to pay for its church building, and so do 18% of Evangelical clergy.

Although Catholic and Evangelical clergy hold similar perceptions regarding the financial burden of maintaining their local churches, these two groups hold significantly different views on how such difficulties should be overcome. Evangelical theology tends to see a sharper divide between the church and the secular world and consequently is more reluctant to draw on secular resources to pay for church-related concerns. While 38% of Catholic clergy argue that their church building needs more grants from the state in order to survive, the proportion drops by a third among Evangelical clergy to 25%. While 27% of Catholic clergy argue that their church building needs more money from tourists and from visitors in order to survive, the proportion drops by a half among Evangelical clergy to 14%.

The priorities adopted by Evangelical clergy tend to place less importance on church buildings than is the case among Catholic clergy. For example, Evangelical clergy are less inclined than Catholic clergy to support the value of spending significant sums on church buildings. While two in every five Catholic clergy (41%) feel that too much money is spent on keeping old churches, the proportion rises to three in every five Evangelical clergy (61%). Consistent with this view Evangelical clergy are more likely than Catholic clergy to press for the closure of what they may perceive as surplus churches. Thus, 28% of Evangelical clergy take the view that many rural churches should be closed, compared with 19% of Catholic clergy.

While Evangelical clergy are more reluctant than Catholic clergy to accept state aid for keeping churches open, they are less reluctant than Catholic clergy to see churches closed and handed over to the state. Thus, 53% of Evangelical clergy believe that more church buildings should be taken over by the state, compared with 46% of Catholic clergy.

Finally in this section, Catholic and Evangelical clergy hold similar perceptions on the responsibility of visitors and tourists for helping to maintain historic cathedrals. Thus, 23% of Catholic clergy believe that cathedrals should charge visitors for entry, and so do 20% of Evangelical clergy.

Overall, the fault-line between Catholic and Evangelical clergy on the future of church buildings touches some key issues regarding the acceptance of secular funding to keep churches open and regarding the closure of churches which may seem surplus to requirements or too expensive to maintain. Evangelical clergy may fail to appreciate the symbolic and sacramental value which Catholic clergy perceive in these buildings. Catholic clergy may fail to appreciate the reluctance of Evangelical clergy to seek and to accept secular funding to keep more churches open.

Money and policy

In order to gauge the priorities of committed Anglicans, the *Church Times Survey* posed a series of questions about how they envisaged the use of their church funds. Four specific areas were identified: central church structures, the clergy, development and mission, and community regeneration.

Catholic and Evangelical clergy hold similar perspectives on financing church structures. Both groups place higher value on diocesan structures than on central church structures. Thus, three-quarters of Catholic clergy (75%) are happy for some money given to their church to go to diocesan funds, and so are 71% of Evangelical clergy. Lower in their priorities, just over three-fifths (63%) of Catholic clergy are happy for some money given to their church to go to church central funds, and so are 60% of Evangelical clergy.

Catholic and Evangelical clergy also hold similar perspectives on the fairness and realism of the charges levied by the parish share or quota system. Around a fifth of both Catholic clergy (22%) and Evangelical clergy (19%) maintain that their parish pays too much for its parish share (quota).

Catholic and Evangelical clergy share similar perceptions of the financial priority which should be given to training new priests. Evangelical clergy, however, give slightly lower priority than Catholic clergy to finance which should be given to clergy pensions. Thus, 92% of Catholic clergy are happy for some money given to their church to go to training new priests, and so are 90% of Evangelical clergy. At the same time, 91% of Catholic clergy are happy for some money given to their church to go to clergy pensions, but the proportion falls to 85% among Evangelical clergy.

Evangelical clergy are more inclined than Catholic clergy to take a congregational view of local church life, according to which local congregations should be able to resource their own needs. While 93% of Catholic clergy are happy for some money given to their church to go to struggling parishes, the proportion falls to 86% among Evangelical clergy.

Catholic and Evangelical clergy take similar views on the financial priority which should be given to supporting churches in developing countries. Nearly nine out of ten Catholic clergy (87%) are happy for some money given to their church to go to churches in developing countries, and so are nine out of ten Evangelical clergy (89%).

Evangelical clergy give a slightly lower financial priority than Catholic clergy to supporting urban regeneration. While two-thirds of Catholic clergy (67%) are happy for some money given to their church to go to urban regeneration, the proportion falls to 60% among Evangelical clergy. On the other hand, Catholic and Evangelical clergy give similar levels of financial priority to supporting the farming community. Thus, 57% of Catholic clergy and 54% of Evangelical clergy are happy for some money given to their church to go to the farming community.

Overall, there are few significant fault-lines between Catholic and Evangelical clergy revealed by this discussion of money and policy. The one fault-line to be revealed concerns the greater reluctance of Evangelical clergy to subsidise struggling parishes. Behind this simple statistic may stand a much more significant fault-line concerning basic ecclesiology and the fundamental relationship between local congregations within the overall structure of the Church of England.

Anglican identity

The *Church Times Survey* focused two kinds of questions on Anglican identity: the first concentrated on willingness to merge Anglican identity with other denominations, and the second concentrated on the future of establishment for the Church of England.

Evangelical and Catholic clergy hold significantly different perspectives on what it means to be an Anglican in the age of ecumenism. The Catholic clergy are much more protective of the boundaries around their denominational identity. This is demonstrated in a variety of ways.

A quarter of the Evangelical clergy (26%) say that they would never become a member of another denomination. The proportion rises, however, to 42% among Catholic clergy. One in ten Evangelical clergy (11%) say that they would not want their denomination to merge with another. The proportion rises, however, to one in five among Catholic clergy (19%). One in seven Evangelical clergy (15%) say that they would not want to be a member of an ecumenical church or local ecumenical project. The proportion rises, however, to one in four among Catholic clergy (24%).

The sharpest and clearest divide between Catholic and Evangelical clergy occurs in respect of their views on the papacy. Nearly three-fifths of Catholic clergy (57%) say that they would be prepared to accept the Pope as their church leader in some situations. The proportion falls, however, to one in ten among Evangelical clergy (9%).

Catholic and Evangelical clergy are not significantly divided in their views on disestablishment. Around a third of both groups believe that the Church of England should be disestablished. This is the case for 32% of Catholic clergy and for 37% of Evangelical clergy.

There is a small but statistically significant difference in the proportions of Catholic and Evangelical clergy who continue to support the role of the Queen as head of the Church of England. There is significantly less support among the Evangelical clergy. While 46% of Catholic clergy believe that the monarch should continue to be the Supreme Governor of the Church of England, the proportion falls to 40% among Evangelical clergy.

Evangelical and Catholic clergy are equal in their support for what they might regard as some of the positive aspects of establishment. For example, 74% of Catholic clergy and 77% of Evangelical clergy maintain that senior bishops should continue to sit in the reformed House of Lords.

At the same time, Evangelical and Catholic clergy are equal in their criticism of what they might regard as some of the negative aspects of establishment. For example, only 7% of Catholic clergy and 6% of Evangelical clergy are in favour of diocesan bishops being appointed by the state. Only 15% of Catholic clergy and 15% of Evangelical clergy are in favour of Parliament retaining control of Church of England legislation.

Overall, the fault-line between Catholic and Evangelical clergy on the nature of Anglican identity impacts some of the scenarios for the future of the Church of England. While Catholic clergy are generally more resistant than Evangelical clergy to seeing the boundaries of Anglicanism blurred by merging with other denominations, Evangelical clergy remain adamant that ecumenical developments will never affirm notions of papal supremacy.

Confidence in the future

In order to gauge the level of confidence which committed Anglicans hold in the future of their Church, the *Church Times Survey* asked questions about two main issues: the first issue concerned confidence in the Church's leadership, and the second issue concerned confidence in the future of their local church.

Evangelical clergy display a significantly higher level of confidence in the leadership given to the Church of England by diocesan bishops, by the General Synod, and by the Archbishops' Council. This is demonstrated by the following sets of statistics.

While 72% of Catholic clergy have confidence in the leadership given by their diocesan bishop, the proportion rises by six percentage points to 78% among Evangelical clergy. While 35% of Catholic clergy have confidence in the leadership given by the General Synod, the proportion rises by nine percentage points to 44% among Evangelical clergy. While 28% of Catholic clergy have confidence in the leadership given by the Archbishops' Council, the proportion rises by 21 percentage points to 49% among Evangelical clergy.

Although Evangelical clergy record significantly higher levels of confidence than Catholic clergy in diocesan bishops, in the General Synod and in the Archbishops' Council, there is no significant difference between the two groups in levels of confidence in local clergy. Thus, 66% of Catholic clergy and 69% of Evangelical clergy say that they have confidence in the leadership given by their local clergy.

Evangelical clergy are significantly more confident than Catholic clergy about the future growth potential of their churches. Three-fifths of Evangelical clergy (62%) believe that the membership of their church will grow in the next 12 months, compared with 45% of Catholic clergy. Related to this greater confidence in church growth among Evangelical clergy is their greater commitment to inviting others to join their congregation. Two-thirds of Evangelical clergy (66%) feel that they can invite other people to come to their church, compared with 55% of Catholic clergy.

Although Evangelical clergy record significantly higher levels of confidence than Catholic clergy in being able to invite other people to come to their church, there is no significant difference between the two groups in their perception of the difficulties faced by newcomers to their congregations. About a quarter of Catholic clergy (23%) say that it is not easy for newcomers in their church, and so do 24% of Evangelical clergy.

Overall, the fault-line between Catholic and Evangelical clergy concerning their levels of confidence in the future demonstrates further just how much these two groups seem to belong to two rather different Anglican Churches in England running side-by-side. Evangelical clergy are much more confident in the leadership of the Church of England and in the potential for growth in the future. Evangelical clergy may at times find it difficult to understand the dissatisfaction with the leadership expressed more frequently by their Catholic colleagues. Catholic clergy may find it difficult to understand the grounds for optimism expressed more frequently by their Evangelical colleagues.

Sex and family life

The *Church Times Survey* identified four specific areas in which to test the orthodoxy of Anglican views on sex and family life: views on sex and cohabitation before marriage, views on divorce, views on same sex relationships, and views on caring for children and teenagers.

Catholic and Evangelical clergy are very seriously divided in their views on sex and family life. Catholic clergy tend to favour a more liberal view. Evangelical clergy tend to favour a more conservative view. This significant difference is maintained consistently throughout the four areas discussed in this section.

First, Evangelical clergy take a consistently more conservative view on sex before marriage. For example, four-fifths of Evangelical clergy (82%) believe that it is wrong for men and women to have sex before marriage, compared with a third of Catholic clergy (33%). Only 4% of Evangelical clergy believe that it is all right for a couple to live together without intending to get married, compared with 36% of Catholic clergy. Only 3% of Evangelical clergy believe that it is a good idea for couples who intend to get married to live together first, compared with 21% of Catholic clergy.

Second, Evangelical clergy take a consistently more conservative view on separation and divorce. While 83% of Catholic clergy believe that some marriages can come to a natural end in divorce or separation, the proportion falls to 68% among Evangelical clergy. Looking at this issue from a different perspective, 53% of Evangelical clergy believe that couples should stay together for the sake of the children, compared with 37% of Catholic clergy.

Third, Evangelical clergy take a consistently more conservative view on same sex relationships. For example, 85% of Evangelical clergy believe that it is wrong for people of the same gender to have sex together, compared with 36% of Catholic clergy. Looking at this issue from a different perspective, only 3% of Evangelical clergy believe that homosexual couples should have the right to marry one another, compared with 23% of Catholic clergy.

Fourth, Evangelical clergy take a consistently more conservative view on caring for children and teenagers. While a third of Catholic clergy (33%) believe that children thrive equally whether cared for primarily by their father or mother, the proportion falls to a quarter among Evangelical clergy (23%). While 41% of Catholic clergy believe that contraception should be available to teenagers under 16 who want it, the proportion almost halves to 23% among Evangelical clergy.

Overall, the fault-line between Catholic and Evangelical clergy regarding issues of sex and family life reveals just how much these two church traditions inhabit startlingly different moral universes. The disagreements that Catholic and Evangelical clergy may experience over matters of doctrine and worship may be less significant than the disagreements they experience over issues of human sexuality. As a consequence of such a pronounced fault-line it may be very difficult to find these two wings of the church agreeing common statements on matters to do with sex and family life.

Social concerns

In order to assess the levels of social concern expressed by committed Anglicans, the *Church Times Survey* included a set of items on global concerns and a set of items on community concerns. The global concerns included environmental and developmental issues, AIDS and genetic research. The community concerns included violence on television, paedophiles living in the community, and the effects of the National Lottery.

Catholic and Evangelical clergy have shaped very similar agendas on matters of global concern. For both groups environmental pollution, the poverty of the developing world and the spread of AIDS stand at the top of the list, and research into human genes comes somewhat lower on the list. Thus, 95% of Catholic clergy are concerned about environmental pollution and so are 93% of Evangelical clergy. Similarly, 97% of Catholic clergy are concerned about the poverty of the developing world, and so are 95% of Evangelical clergy. Concern about the spread of AIDS is expressed by 96% of Catholic clergy and by 95% of Evangelical clergy.

Lower down the list of priorities, 69% of Catholic clergy and 74% of Evangelical clergy are concerned about research into human genes. The difference between the two groups is not statistically significant.

Although Catholic and Evangelical clergy have shaped very similar agendas on matters of global concern, these two groups adopt significantly different perspectives on matters of community concern. On all three issues within this category listed in the survey, Evangelical clergy register a significantly higher level of concern compared with Catholic clergy.

Seven out of every ten Catholic clergy (71%) register concern about violence on television, but the proportion rises to 85% among Evangelical clergy. A third of Catholic clergy (36%) register concern about paedophiles living in the community, but the proportion rises to 53% among Evangelical clergy. Two out of every five Catholic clergy (40%) register concern about the National Lottery, but the proportion rises to 71% among Evangelical clergy.

Overall, the fault-line between Catholic and Evangelical clergy regarding social concerns reveals just how much these two groups may view some issues through different lenses. The clearest example of these different lenses concerns their attitude toward the National Lottery. Catholic clergy may be more inclined than Evangelical clergy to welcome support from the Lottery Fund for developing an ancient Cathedral or for funding a church-sponsored community project. On the other hand, Evangelical clergy may be more inclined than Catholic clergy to preach against the corrupting influences of the lottery culture and to campaign against churches accepting lottery funding. Here is very fruitful ground for conflict between Catholic and Evangelical members of the Cathedral Chapter contemplating renovation and development programmes.

Social conscience

The *Church Times Survey* assessed social conscience by means of a series of questions exploring the willingness of committed Anglicans to pay more tax in order to fund specific areas of social life. The three broad areas included in the survey concerned health and education, social security and prisons, and defence and development aid.

Catholic and Evangelical clergy have shaped very similar perspectives on the priority they give to health and to education. On these issues they speak with one voice. Both groups of clergy place health at the top of their spending priorities. Thus, 86% of Catholic clergy say that they would pay more tax to fund spending on health, and so do 84% of Evangelical clergy.

Both groups of clergy place schools second on their list of spending priorities, not far behind health. Thus, 79% of Catholic clergy say that they would pay more tax to fund spending on schools, and so do 81% of Evangelical clergy.

Both groups of clergy place universities much lower on their spending priorities, well below schools. Thus, 49% of Catholic clergy say that they would pay more tax to fund spending on universities, and so do 44% of Evangelical clergy.

Although there are no significant differences between Catholic clergy and Evangelical clergy in the priority which they give to health-related issues and education-related issues, the gap between the two groups begins to open up in respect of issues concerned with defence and development aid. On the one hand, Catholic clergy give greater priority than Evangelical clergy to defence. While 20% of Evangelical clergy say that they would pay more tax to fund spending on security forces, the proportion rises to 25% among Catholic clergy. On the other hand, Evangelical clergy give greater priority than Catholic clergy to development aid. While 74% of Catholic clergy say that they would pay more tax to fund spending on overseas aid, the proportion rises to 79% among Evangelical clergy.

The gap between Catholic and Evangelical clergy opens up more dramatically in respect of issues concerned with social security and prisons. On both of these fronts Catholic clergy register a significantly higher level of social concern in comparison with Evangelical clergy. Half of the Catholic clergy (51%) say that they would pay more tax to fund spending on prisons, compared with 38% of Evangelical clergy. Half of the Catholic clergy (51%) say that they would pay more tax to fund spending on social security, compared with 40% of Evangelical clergy.

Overall, the fault-line between Catholic and Evangelical clergy comes into prominence in respect of some aspects of the Christian social conscience. There are a number of ways of explaining this. Perhaps Catholic theology may be more inclined to promote a gospel concerned with community and social coherence. Such a gospel would promote concern for the communal responsibility to care for the poor and disadvantaged through social security benefits and to provide adequate funding for the prison service. By contrast, Evangelical theology may be said to be more inclined to promote a gospel concerned with individual responsibility and personal salvation. Such a gospel would be more inclined to promote the view that individuals should make proper provision for themselves rather than relying on state aid and community intervention.

Education

The *Church Times Survey* framed questions on three key topics of relevance to the Church of England's concerns with education. These topics related to the debate between the state-funded and the independent sector of schools, the place of religious education and worship in schools, and the future for faith-based schools.

Catholic and Evangelical clergy are not sharply divided in their attitudes toward the state-maintained sector of education. Three-fifths of both groups have confidence in the state-funded education system: this is the case for 60% of Catholic clergy and for 61% of Evangelical clergy. Nonetheless, Catholic clergy are slightly, but significantly, more hostile to the independent sector of schools. While 12% of Evangelical clergy consider that private schools should be abolished, the proportion rises to 16% among Catholic clergy.

Similarly, Catholic and Evangelical clergy are not sharply divided in their attitude toward religious education in schools, although there are some small but telling differences in perspectives between the two groups. On the one hand, Evangelical clergy are even more committed than Catholic clergy to the provision of religious education in schools. Nine out of ten Catholic clergy (89%) argue that religious education should be taught in all schools, and the proportion rises even further to 93% among Evangelical clergy. On the other hand, Evangelical clergy are somewhat more cautious than Catholic clergy about teaching world faiths in religious education classes. Six out of seven Catholic clergy (86%) argue that religious education in schools should teach about world religions, and the proportion drops a little to 80% among Evangelical clergy.

On the issue of school worship, however, there is no significant difference between the perception of Catholic clergy and the perception of Evangelical clergy. Thus, 61% of Catholic clergy argue that schools should hold a religious assembly every day, and so do 65% of Evangelical clergy.

Catholic and Evangelical clergy hold similar views on the continuing involvement of the Church of England within the state-maintained sector of education. Nearly nine out of every ten Evangelical clergy (89%) are in favour of state-funded church schools, and so are 87% of Catholic clergy. Eight out of every ten Evangelical clergy (80%) argue that the Church of England should fund more new church secondary schools, and so do 78% of Catholic clergy. Just over seven out of every ten Evangelical clergy (72%) argue that the Church of England should fund more new church primary schools, and so do 69% of Catholic clergy.

The real difference between Catholic and Evangelical clergy opens up, however, on the issue of extending the privileges enjoyed by the Christian Churches in respect of church schools to other faith communities. In comparison with Evangelical clergy, Catholic clergy hold a much more inclusive view of the relationship between Christianity and other world faiths. While 58% of Catholic clergy are in favour of state-funded Jewish schools, the proportion falls to 35% among Evangelical clergy. While 54% of Catholic clergy are in favour of state-funded Islamic schools, the proportion falls to 32% among Evangelical clergy.

Overall, the fault-line between Catholic and Evangelical clergy really comes to the surface in educational debate over issues concerned with other world faiths. Evangelical clergy are slightly less supportive than Catholic clergy regarding teaching about other world faiths in religious education classes. Evangelical clergy are much less supportive than Catholic clergy regarding providing faith-based schools for the Jewish community and for the Islamic community. When Catholic and Evangelical clergy are invited to present an Anglican voice on religious education syllabuses to local SACREs, or on faith school provision to local education planning committees, they may be unlikely to speak with one voice.

Conclusion

There is sufficient evidence in the present analysis to alert the Church of England to the wisdom of taking seriously the fault-line between Catholics and Evangelicals in the pulpit. This fault-line, ostensibly theological in origin, pervades much of the worldview of these two very different groups of clergy. Inhabiting such different worldviews, it is not surprising that tensions arise between Catholics and Evangelicals and that consensus between the two groups on key matters of doctrine, church practice, and personal and social values remains difficult to achieve.

CHAPTER 8

Charismatics and non-charismatics in the pulpit

Introduction

The fifth of the potential fault-lines within the Church of England to be examined by the present study concerns the ways in which beliefs, attitudes, and values may vary between clergy who are clear that they have been influenced by the charismatic movement and clergy who are clear that they have not been influenced by the charismatic movement. The division between these two groups of clergy has been made on the basis of responses to the seven-point semantic differential scale included in the survey. Clergy who checked the two values closest to the charismatic end of the continuum have been regarded as those most clearly influenced by the charismatic movement. A total of 193 clergy came into this category. Clergy who checked the two values closest to the non-charismatic end of the continuum have been regarded as those most clearly resistant to influence from the charismatic movement. A total of 818 clergy came into this category. The remaining clergy who either checked the three middle values on the scale or omitted the question have been excluded from the analysis.

In calculating the significance between the responses of the two groups of clergy, the chi square test has been employed in respect of dichotomised data within each of the two groups. The division has been made between those who agree or agree strongly with the question on the one hand, and those who check the disagree, disagree strongly, or uncertain categories on the other hand.

Patterns of belief

The *Church Times Survey* identified three doctrinal areas against which to assess the orthodoxy of Anglican belief: beliefs about God, beliefs about Jesus, and beliefs about life after death.

Identification with the charismatic movement is a clear indicator of strong doctrinal orthodoxy within all three of the areas of belief included in the survey. To begin with, among the charismatic clergy there is no shadow of doubt about the existence of God. All of the clergy influenced by the charismatic movement (100%) are solid in their conviction that God exists. Among those clergy who are clear that they have not been influenced by the charismatic movement, the proportion falls slightly but significantly to 97%.

The God in whom the charismatic clergy believe is first and foremost a personal God. Thus, 99% of the charismatic clergy are solid in their conviction that God is a personal being, compared with 88% of the non-charismatic clergy. Just a handful of the charismatic clergy are willing to use impersonal language of their God. Thus, 5% of the clergy influenced by the charismatic movement believe that God is an impersonal power, compared with twice that number (9%) of the clergy who are clear that they have not been influenced by the charismatic movement.

Second, among the charismatic clergy there is little shadow of doubt about the physical resurrection of Jesus. Nearly all of the clergy influenced by the charismatic movement (97%) believe that Jesus rose physically from the dead. Among those clergy who are clear that they have not been influenced by the charismatic movement, the proportion drops considerably to 71%.

Similarly, among the charismatic clergy there is comparatively little doubt about the truth claims regarding the virgin birth. Thus, 88% of the charismatic clergy sign up to the belief that Jesus' birth was a virgin birth, compared with just half of the non-charismatic clergy (49%). The Jesus in whom the charismatic clergy believe clearly possesses divine or supernatural power reflected in the literal truth of the actions attributed to him in the gospel narratives. Thus, 89% of the charismatic clergy sign up to the belief that Jesus really turned water into wine, compared with just half of the non-charismatic clergy (51%).

Third, among the charismatic clergy there is no shadow of doubt about the reality of the afterlife. All of the clergy influenced by the charismatic movement (100%) are solid in their conviction that there is life after death. Among those clergy who are clear that they have not been influenced by the charismatic movement, the proportion drops to 87%.

The afterlife in which the charismatic clergy believe is first and foremost one shaped by the traditional language and images of the Christian scriptures, in which heaven and hell figure large. Thus, 98% of the charismatic clergy sign up to the belief that heaven really exists, compared with 78% of the non-charismatic clergy. Even the charismatic clergy, however, find the doctrine of hell somewhat less credible than the doctrine of heaven. While 98% of the clergy influenced by the charismatic movement believe that heaven really exists, the proportion falls to 80% who believe that hell really exists. Among the non-charismatic clergy the gap between heaven and hell is even more pronounced. While 78% of the clergy who are clear that they have not been influenced by the charismatic movement believe that heaven really exists, the proportion falls to 36% who believe that hell really exists.

Overall, the fault-line between the basic Christian beliefs of charismatic clergy and non-charismatic clergy is significant and profound. The charismatic clergy hold fast to much more traditionally shaped beliefs about the nature of God, the person of Jesus, and the Christian hope concerning life after death. Shaping doctrinal statements to which charismatic clergy and non-charismatic clergy can give wholehearted and unequivocal agreement will prove no easy matter for the fragmenting Anglican Church.

Paths of truth

The *Church Times Survey* identified three means of examining the ways in which truth claims are asserted: beliefs about the bible, beliefs about the exclusivity of Christianity, and beliefs about evolution versus creation.

Relationship with the charismatic movement is reflected in some very clear differences in the ways in which clergy assess and ground the truth claims of their faith. Clergy influenced by the charismatic movement are rooted in a significantly more conservative account of their Christian faith as demonstrated by all three components of this aspect of the survey.

First, the charismatic clergy take a significantly more conservative approach to the nature of the bible. While 8% of the non-charismatic clergy take the view that the bible is without any errors, the proportion more than quadruples to 35% among the charismatic clergy. While four out of every five of the non-charismatic clergy maintain that biblical truths are culturally conditioned (80%), the proportion drops to two-thirds among the charismatic clergy (65%).

Second, the charismatic clergy take a significantly more conservative approach to the exclusivity claims made by the Christian creeds. While two-fifths of the non-charismatic clergy (39%) maintain that Christianity is the only true religion, the proportion doubles among the charismatic clergy to four-fifths (81%). Those clergy influenced by the charismatic movement stand almost unanimously against the notion that Christianity can be placed on an equal footing with other faiths. Just 1% of the charismatic clergy believe that all religions are of equal value, compared with 8% of the non-charismatic clergy.

Third, the charismatic clergy take a significantly more conservative approach to the debate between creationism and evolution. While four-fifths of the non-charismatic clergy (80%) take the view that all living things evolved, the proportion drops to just over half of the charismatic clergy (54%). Clergy influenced by the charismatic movement are, nonetheless, still likely to veer away from a fully literalistic view of biblical creationism. Just 6% of the non-charismatic clergy take the view that God made the world in six days and rested on the seventh. The proportion who take this view rises significantly among the charismatic clergy, but still remains less than one in five (18%).

Overall, the fault-line between charismatic clergy and non-charismatic clergy concerning the grounds of theological truth is quite well established. The two groups of clergy are likely to come into conflict over debates on the authority of scripture. They are likely to come into conflict over debates on evolutionary theory and on the interface between science and religion. Most fundamentally, however, they are likely to come into conflict over the ways in which they see the ultimate salvific value of other faiths.

Paths of spirituality

In order to gauge different pathways of spirituality the *Church Times Survey* distinguished between three kinds of issues: personal and private sources of spiritual sustenance, group-based and shared sources of spiritual sustenance, and drawing on wider resources for spiritual sustenance.

Charismatic and non-charismatic clergy demonstrate some highly significant differences in their preferred paths of spirituality. These differences are revealed in all three areas explored by this part of the survey.

First, charismatic and non-charismatic clergy differ significantly in the nature and content of their personal spiritual practices. In their personal spiritual life the clergy influenced by the charismatic movement place heavier weight on inspiration which comes from the bible, while the clergy who are clear that they have not been influenced by the charismatic movement place heavier weight on inspiration which comes from secular sources. Thus, while nine out of ten of the non-charismatic clergy (91%) say that they are helped in their faith by reading the bible, the proportion rises even higher to 99% of the charismatic clergy. Looking at matters from the opposite perspective, however, while three-fifths of the non-charismatic clergy (61%) say that they are helped in their faith by reading non-religious books, the proportion falls to two-fifths (39%) among the charismatic clergy.

On the other hand, charismatic and non-charismatic clergy draw equally in their personal spiritual life on the sustenance derived from prayer and from Christian literature. Thus, 91% of the charismatic clergy say that they are helped in their faith by praying by themselves, and so do 91% of the non-charismatic clergy. Similarly, 92% of the charismatic clergy say that they are helped in their faith by reading Christian books, and so do 91% of the non-charismatic clergy.

Second, charismatic and non-charismatic clergy differ significantly in the emphasis which they place on group-based spiritual practices. Clergy who have been influenced by the charismatic movement place more emphasis than other clergy on the group experience. Thus, while 89% of the non-charismatic clergy say that they are helped in their faith by discussing their faith with others, the proportion is even higher among the charismatic clergy (96%). Four-fifths of the charismatic clergy (81%) say that they are helped in their faith by bible study groups, compared with half of the non-charismatic clergy (48%). Four-fifths of the charismatic clergy (83%) say that they are helped in their faith by prayer groups, compared with two-fifths of the non-charismatic clergy (41%).

Third, charismatic and non-charismatic clergy differ significantly in the extent to which they draw on spiritual resources outside the church. Just 7% of the charismatic clergy say that they often get more spiritual help outside the church than within it. By way of comparison three times that proportion of non-charismatic clergy (22%) say that they often get more spiritual help outside the church than within it.

On the other hand, charismatic and non-charismatic clergy draw equally on wider spiritual resources like the wonder of the natural world and like spiritual retreats. Thus, two-thirds of the charismatic clergy (66%) say that they are helped in their faith by considering the natural world, and so do 71% of the non-charismatic clergy. Three-quarters of the charismatic clergy (74%) say that they are helped in their faith by going on retreat, and so do 73% of the non-charismatic clergy.

Overall, the fault-line between charismatic clergy and non-charismatic clergy concerning their preferred paths of spirituality is quite well established. The two groups of clergy are likely to find it quite difficult to agree on a common programme of spiritual development, either for themselves, or for the churches they serve. The charismatic clergy are likely to press for more group-based, shared spiritual experience, while the non-charismatic clergy are likely to resist such activities. The non-charismatic clergy are likely to press for more emphasis to be placed on secular, non-religious sources of spiritual inspiration, while the charismatic clergy are likely to resist such openness to secular sources.

Public worship

The *Church Times Survey* included three sets of questions to assess responses to public worship: the first set focused on the debate between traditional and modern forms of public worship, the second set focused on different aspects of the service, and the third set focused on the initiation of children into the worshipping community.

Charismatic and non-charismatic clergy demonstrate some highly significant differences in their attitudes toward public worship. These differences are revealed clearly in all three areas explored by this part of the survey.

First, charismatic and non-charismatic clergy differ significantly in their attachment to traditional forms of worship. Those clergy who have been influenced by the charismatic movement are significantly less sympathetic to the traditional forms of Anglican worship. While two-thirds of the non-charismatic clergy (67%) feel that they are helped in their faith by traditional forms of service, the proportion halves among the charismatic clergy to one-third (32%). While three-quarters of the non-charismatic clergy (75%) feel that they are helped in their faith by traditional hymns in services, the proportion drops among the charismatic clergy to three-fifths (60%).

Looked at from the opposite perspective, those clergy who have not been influenced by the charismatic movement are significantly less sympathetic to new forms of worship. While three-quarters of the charismatic clergy (77%) feel that they are helped in their faith by new forms of service, the proportion drops among the non-charismatic clergy to two-thirds (58%). While 86% of the charismatic clergy feel that they are helped in their faith by new hymns in services, the proportion drops among the non-charismatic clergy to 59%.

Second, charismatic clergy and non-charismatic clergy differ significantly in their attachment to some styles of worship. Those clergy who have been influenced by the charismatic movement are significantly less sympathetic to ritual in services. While four-fifths of the non-charismatic clergy (82%) feel that they are helped in their faith by ritual in services, the proportion falls to under half of the charismatic clergy (47%).

On the other hand, there are other aspects of worship which fail to distinguish between the preferences of charismatics and of non-charismatics, including the use of silence in worship and the use of sermons. Thus, 81% of the charismatic clergy say that they are helped in their faith by periods of silence in services, and so do 81% of the non-charismatic clergy. Four out of every five charismatic clergy (80%) say that they are helped in their faith by listening to sermons. Although the proportion drops to 73% among the non-charismatic clergy, this difference does not reach the threshold of statistical significance.

Third, charismatic and non-charismatic clergy differ significantly in their attachment to traditional Anglican models of Christian initiation. Those clergy who have been influenced by the charismatic movement are significantly more willing to depart from traditional Anglican thinking. While the traditional Anglican position was to offer infant baptism to most parents who are seeking it for their offspring, charismatic clergy are now leading the way in pressing for a more restrictive view of infant baptism. Thus, almost one in three of the charismatic clergy (31%) are in favour of churches baptising only babies of regular churchgoers, compared with 8% of non-charismatic clergy. While the traditional Anglican practice was generally to withhold admission to communion until after confirmation, charismatic clergy now lead the way in pressing for communion before confirmation. Thus, three-quarters of the charismatic clergy (75%) are in favour of baptised children being admitted to communion before confirmation, compared with 65% of the non-charismatic clergy.

Overall, the fault-line between charismatic clergy and non-charismatic clergy concerning the shape and form of public worship is quite well established. The two groups of clergy are likely to experience considerable difficulty in shaping forms of public worship in which they can both feel at home. While the non-charismatic clergy are likely to be pushing for well-known traditional forms of liturgy and for well-known traditional hymns, the charismatic clergy are likely to be pushing for innovation and for change. This difference in perspective may well prove to be highly disruptive to many occasions when Anglicans wish to portray a united front through the shop window of special and high profile services.

Local church life

In order to assess commitment to the local church, the *Church Times Survey* included three groups of questions: questions concerning the cycle of commitment, questions concerning the sense of belonging, and questions concerning the relationship between commitment and power.

The experience which charismatic clergy have of local church life differs significantly from the experience of non-charismatic clergy in three interesting and important ways. First, the charismatic tradition by its very nature continually encourages its followers to renew their energies and redouble their commitment to the faith. This is reflected in the way in which the charismatic clergy locate themselves on the cycle of commitment. Thus, two-fifths of the charismatic clergy (42%) report that they are coming to their church more regularly nowadays, compared with a third of the non-charismatic clergy (32%). Looked at from the opposite perspective, just 3% of the charismatic clergy and 6% of the non-charismatic clergy report that they are coming to church less regularly nowadays.

Second, the charismatic tradition by its very nature encourages its followers to share their experiences of faith and to support each other in their spiritual pilgrimage. This is reflected in the way in which the charismatic clergy see themselves as turning to fellow members of their congregation for support. Thus, 64% of the charismatic clergy say that they turn to fellow members of their church when they need help, compared with 55% of the non-charismatic clergy.

In other ways, however, charismatic and non-charismatic clergy share similar perceptions of their sense of commitment and belonging to the local church. Thus, 92% of the charismatic clergy feel a strong sense of belonging to their church, and so do 89% of the non-charismatic clergy. Similarly, 68% of the charismatic clergy feel that their church is important to their social life, and so do 63% of the non-charismatic clergy.

Third, the charismatic tradition by its very nature tends to make all-enveloping claims on its followers. The diary can become tightly packed with prayer meetings, bible study groups, service preparation groups, and many other core and essential activities. This is reflected in the way in which the charismatic clergy are more likely to see the demands of ministry taking over their lives. Thus, 29% of the charismatic clergy feel that their church makes too many demands on their time, compared with 22% of the non-charismatic clergy.

In other ways, however, charismatic and non-charismatic clergy share similar perceptions of their role in the local church. Thus, 71% of the charismatic clergy feel that they can influence their church's decisions, and so do 77% of the non-charismatic clergy. Just 12% of the charismatic clergy feel that they have too little control over the running of their church, and so do 12% of the non-charismatic clergy. Just 6% of the charismatic clergy feel that their church makes too many demands on their money and so do 7% of the non-charismatic clergy.

Overall, the fault-line between charismatic clergy and non-charismatic clergy concerning local church life, although not profound, reveals some key underlying differences between the two groups. The charismatic tradition generates a higher sense of commitment to the local church and also a higher sense of frustration with the demands made by such commitment. Clergy who have remained uninfluenced by the charismatic movement may be puzzled by the willingness of their charismatic colleagues to accept such demands and may remain unwilling themselves to follow in the charismatic footsteps.

Ordained ministry

The *Church Times Survey* included questions about four issues which divide opinion in the Church of England on the question of ordained ministry: the ordination of women, the ordination of individuals who are divorced, the ordination of individuals who are divorced and remarried, and the ordination of practising homosexuals. In respect of each of these issues the survey distinguished between ordination as priest and ordination as bishop.

There is no great divide between the views of charismatic clergy and the views of non-charismatic clergy over the ordination of women, over the ordination of individuals who have been divorced, and over the ordination of individuals who have been divorced and remarried. On all three of these major areas of debate charismatic clergy and non-charismatic clergy occupy similar positions.

On the question of the ordination of women, 85% of the charismatic clergy are in favour of the ordination of women as priests. The proportion drops significantly but only slightly among the non-charismatic clergy to 78%. There is no significant difference in the proportions of charismatic clergy and non-charismatic clergy who are in favour of the ordination of women as bishops (69% and 64% respectively).

On the question of the ordination of individuals who have been divorced, 67% of the charismatic clergy are in favour of divorced people as priests. The proportion remains roughly the same among non-charismatic clergy at 68%. There is no significant difference in the proportions of charismatic clergy and non-charismatic clergy who are in favour of divorced people as bishops (58% and 59% respectively).

On the question of the ordination of individuals who have been divorced and remarried, 57% of the charismatic clergy are in favour of divorced and remarried priests. The proportion is not significantly different among non-charismatic clergy at 63%. There is no significant difference in the proportions of charismatic clergy and non-charismatic clergy who are in favour of divorced and remarried bishops (47% and 53% respectively).

Although charismatic clergy and non-charismatic clergy are in basic agreement over the ordination of women, over the ordination of individuals who have been divorced, and over the ordination of individuals who have been divorced and remarried, all possibility of agreement fragments over the ordination of practising homosexuals. While 40% of non-charismatic clergy are in favour of the ordination of practising homosexuals as priests, the proportion falls to just 8% among the charismatic clergy. While 36% of the non-charismatic clergy are in favour of the ordination of practising homosexuals as bishops, the proportion falls to just 7% of the charismatic clergy.

Overall, the fault-line between charismatic clergy and non-charismatic clergy is insignificant in respect of some contentious issues concerning the church's ministry, like the ordination of women, like the ordination of individuals who have been divorced, and like the ordination of individuals who have been divorced and remarried. Over the issue of the ordination of practising homosexuals the fault-line is very well defined and highly significant. Debate on this issue clearly forces a wedge between the charismatic lobby and the rest of the Anglican Church.

Church leadership

In order to assess attitudes toward two major areas of change in church leadership, the *Church Times Survey* included a section on the development of ordained ministry and a section on the development of lay ministry.

This part of the survey demonstrates that charismatic clergy and non-charismatic clergy share highly similar perceptions regarding the development of ordained ministry. There is very little room for dissension between the two groups in this area. To begin with, the same proportions of charismatic clergy (57%) and non-charismatic clergy (57%) argue that clergy should be paid a better wage. There is no significant difference in the proportions of charismatic clergy and non-charismatic clergy who argue that clergy freehold should be abolished (43% and 36% respectively). A quarter of both groups argue that clergy should be employed on short-term renewable contracts. This view is espoused by 27% of the charismatic clergy and by 24% of the non-charismatic clergy. A quarter of both groups argue that clergy should live in their own houses. This view is espoused by 27% of the charismatic clergy and by 25% of the non-charismatic clergy.

Although charismatic clergy and non-charismatic clergy share highly similar perceptions regarding the development of ordained ministry (within the areas examined by the survey), these two groups hold significantly different perspectives on the development of lay ministry. The charismatic clergy are significantly more supportive of expanding a wide range of ministries among the laity.

To begin with the charismatic clergy show greater commitment to expanding the preaching ministry of lay people in the context both of the offices and of the eucharist. Thus, 92% of the charismatic clergy are in favour of lay people preaching at morning and evening prayer, compared with 81% of the non-charismatic clergy. Similarly, 91% of the charismatic clergy are in favour of lay people preaching at communion services, compared with 75% of non-charismatic clergy.

The charismatic clergy also show greater commitment to expanding the liturgical ministry of lay people in the sense of acting as worship leaders. Thus, 99% of the charismatic clergy are in favour of lay people leading morning and evening prayer, compared with 92% of the non-charismatic clergy. The difference in perspective between the two groups of clergy is even greater when it comes to leading the ministry of the word at communion services. While 99% of the charismatic clergy are in favour of lay people leading morning and evening prayer, the proportion drops by 12 percentage points to 87% of the charismatic clergy who are in favour of lay people leading the first part of the communion service. While 92% of the non-charismatic clergy are in favour of lay people leading morning and evening prayer, the proportion drops by 27 percentage points to 65% of the non-charismatic clergy who are in favour of lay people leading the first part of the communion service.

The charismatic clergy are more than four times as likely as the non-charismatic clergy to want to expand the liturgical ministry of lay people to include eucharistic presidency. While just 7% of the non-charismatic clergy are in favour of lay people taking the whole communion service, the proportion rises to 31% among the charismatic clergy.

Overall, the fault-line between charismatic clergy and non-charismatic clergy comes into considerable prominence over the issue of the development of lay ministries. The church of the future envisaged by the charismatic clergy may well be led by lay preachers, by lay worship leaders, and, in some cases, by lay eucharistic presidents. The non-charismatic clergy may well find it difficult to identify with a church which has so radically departed from the more traditional Anglican view of valuing the distinctiveness of ordained ministry. The thin end of the wedge which will separate the church of the future envisaged by the charismatic clergy from the rest of the Anglican Church concerns lay eucharistic presidency.

Churches and cathedrals

The *Church Times Survey* included two sets of questions to assess attitudes toward churches and cathedrals, the buildings used for worship. The first set of questions focused on attitudes toward the individual respondent's local church, while the second set of questions focused on wider issues of policy.

This part of the survey demonstrates that the charismatic clergy hold quite a different view from the non-charismatic clergy on the future of the Church of England's stock of historic churches. For the charismatic tradition the emphasis is less on church buildings and more on the gifts of the spirit employed by the people who are God's church in the world. This distinctive doctrinal emphasis is seen very clearly in the ways in which the two groups of clergy view the maintenance of historic church buildings.

To begin with, two-thirds of the charismatic clergy (68%) argue that too much money is spent on keeping old churches, compared with two-fifths of the non-charismatic clergy (41%). Consistent with the view that the maintenance of church buildings is an inappropriate drain on parish resources is the greater emphasis placed by the charismatic clergy on closing churches and on handing historic buildings over to the state. Thus, 29% of charismatic clergy argue that many rural churches should be closed, compared with 20% of non-charismatic clergy. Similarly, 57% of charismatic clergy argue that more church buildings should be taken over by the state, compared with 48% of non-charismatic clergy.

The different perspectives taken by charismatic clergy and by non-charismatic clergy on the maintenance of church buildings does not carry over to shaping different perspectives on the vexed issue of charging visitors an entry fee to cathedrals. There is no significant difference in the proportions of charismatic clergy and of non-charismatic clergy who maintain that cathedrals should charge visitors for entry (19% and 23% respectively).

Charismatic clergy and non-charismatic clergy share similar perceptions regarding the ability of their local congregation to maintain its own church buildings. Between a fifth and a quarter of the charismatic clergy (23%) argue that their congregation can no longer afford to pay for its church building, and so do 22% of the non-charismatic clergy.

While charismatic and non-charismatic clergy share similar perceptions regarding the inability of their local congregation to afford the upkeep of their church building, they have somewhat different perspectives on whose responsibility it is to keep the walls standing and the roof watertight. Charismatic clergy may hold a more sectarian view of the church and be less happy about collecting secular funding to keep the show on the road. Thus, while 27% of non-charismatic clergy argue that in order to survive, their church building needs more money from tourists and visitors, the proportion falls by a third among charismatic clergy to 17%. While 38% of non-charismatic clergy argue that in order to survive, their church building needs more grants from the state, the proportion falls to 31% among charismatic clergy.

Overall, the fault-line between charismatic clergy and non-charismatic clergy comes into considerable prominence over the future of church buildings. The church of the future envisaged by the charismatic clergy may well be moving out of the medieval or Victorian gothic church into a purpose-built worship centre next door, just as the previous generation of clergy moved out of the Georgian parsonage into the purpose-built vicarage erected on the old parsonage tennis courts. The non-charismatic clergy may well find it difficult to identify with a church which has so radically abandoned its heritage of fine buildings.

Money and policy

In order to gauge the priorities of committed Anglicans, the *Church Times Survey* posed a series of questions about how they envisaged the use of their church funds. Four specific areas were identified: central church structures, the clergy, development and mission, and community regeneration.

Charismatic and non-charismatic clergy hold similar perspectives on the financial relationship between their own church and the wider church structures. Both groups of clergy show greater sympathy toward their own diocese than toward the London headquarters. Just over a quarter of the charismatic clergy (78%) are happy for some money given to their church to go to diocesan funds, and so are 74% of the non-charismatic clergy. While 78% of the charismatic clergy are happy for some money given to their church to go to diocesan funds, the proportion falls to 67% who are happy for some money given to their church to go to church central funds. While 74% of the non-charismatic clergy are happy for some money given to their church to go to diocesan funds, the proportion drops to 62% who are happy for some money given to their church to go to church central funds.

Both groups of clergy show a broad acceptance of the parish share or quota system. Just one in five of the charismatic clergy (19%) feel that their parish pays too much for its parish share or quota, and so do 21% of the non-charismatic clergy.

Both groups of clergy show the same high level of support for parish income contributing to the costs of clergy training. Nine out of every ten charismatic clergy (93%) are happy for some money given to their church to go to training new priests, and so are nine out of every ten non-charismatic clergy (91%). The charismatic clergy are, however, significantly less sympathetic toward supporting clergy pensions. While 90% of non-charismatic clergy are happy for some money given to their church to go to clergy pensions, the proportion drops slightly, but significantly, to 83% among charismatic clergy.

Both groups of clergy show the same high level of support for parish income helping other parishes that are less financially viable. Nine out of every ten charismatic clergy (93%) are happy for some money given to their church to go to struggling parishes, and so are nine out of every ten non-charismatic clergy (90%). The charismatic clergy are, however, significantly more sympathetic toward supporting churches overseas. While 86% of the non-charismatic clergy are happy for some money given to their church to go to churches in developing countries, the proportion rises significantly to 96% among charismatic clergy.

Both groups of clergy show the same level of support for parish income helping with community regeneration projects. Nearly two-thirds of the charismatic clergy (65%) are happy for some money given to their church to go to urban regeneration, and so are 64% of the non-charismatic clergy. Nearly three-fifths of the charismatic clergy (58%) are happy for some money given to their church to go to the farming community, and so are 55% of the non-charismatic clergy.

Overall, the fault-line between charismatic and non-charismatic clergy revealed by this discussion of money and policy may not seem pronounced.

What has been revealed is a slightly greater commitment on the part of the charismatic clergy for supporting churches in developing countries and a slightly lower level of commitment for supporting clergy pensions. Behind these simple statistics, however, may stand a more significant fault-line concerning the kind of church to which these two groups of clergy belong. For the charismatic clergy domestic issues may be of lower importance and issues of worldwide church growth of greater importance than is the case for non-charismatic clergy.

Anglican identity

The *Church Times Survey* focused two kinds of questions on Anglican identity: the first concentrated on willingness to merge Anglican identity with other denominations, and the second concentrated on the future of establishment for the Church of England.

The charismatic clergy are less committed than the non-charismatic clergy to protecting their identity as Anglicans. There is a sense in which the charismatic movement transcends denominational boundaries, and this feature is well represented in the statistical data in a variety of ways. While only two-fifths of the non-charismatic clergy (38%) take the view that they would never become a member of another denomination, the proportion drops even further to 30% among the charismatic clergy. Only 12% of the charismatic clergy and 16% of the non-charismatic clergy take the view that they would not want their denomination to merge with another.

The charismatic clergy are more open than the non-charismatic clergy to working and worshipping in an ecumenical context. While only one-fifth of the non-charismatic clergy (21%) say that they would not want to be a member of an ecumenical church or local ecumenical project, the proportion drops even further to 10% among the charismatic movement.

Although more ecumenically-minded in a broad sense, the charismatic clergy also remain more hostile to aspects of the Roman Catholic tradition. While between two-fifths and one half of the non-charismatic clergy (44%) say that they would be prepared to accept the Pope as their church leader in some situations, the proportion halves among the charismatic clergy to 24%.

The charismatic clergy have less sympathy than the non-charismatic clergy with the established status of the Church of England. While less than a third of the non-charismatic clergy (29%) argue that the Church of England should be disestablished, the proportion of charismatic clergy who take this view rises to nearly half (46%). While 45% of the non-charismatic clergy believe that the monarch should continue to be the Supreme Governor of the Church of England, the proportion drops to 37% among the charismatic clergy.

Just 2% of the charismatic clergy and 7% of the non-charismatic clergy believe that diocesan bishops should be appointed by the state. Just 10% of the charismatic clergy and 14% of the non-charismatic clergy believe that

Parliament should retain control of Church of England legislation. In spite of such clear views about the need to disentangle church affairs from the affairs of the state, the clear majority of both groups of clergy continue to support the place of Anglican bishops in the House of Lords. Indeed, it is the charismatic clergy who are most in favour of the Church of England's continued presence in the parliamentary procedures, in spite of their greater enthusiasm for disestablishment. Thus, 82% of the charismatic clergy believe that senior bishops should continue to sit in the reformed House of Lords, and so do 75% of the non-charismatic clergy.

Overall, this section of the survey draws attention to two aspects of the fault-line between the charismatic clergy and non-charismatic clergy as they model the future of the Church of England. The first aspect concerns ecumenical collaboration. Charismatic clergy may be surprised by the greater reluctance of some of their non-charismatic colleagues to submerge their Anglican identity within an ecumenical venture. The second aspect concerns disestablishment. Non-charismatic clergy may be surprised by the weight of support for disestablishment among their charismatic colleagues.

Confidence in the future

In order to gauge the level of confidence which committed Anglicans hold in the future of their Church, the *Church Times Survey* asked questions about two main issues: the first issue concerned confidence in the Church's leadership, and the second issue concerned confidence in the future of their own local church.

The charismatic clergy show a significantly higher level of confidence in the future for the Church of England, when compared with the non-charismatic clergy. This higher level of confidence is reflected in their attitudes both toward the leadership of the church and toward the local church.

Confidence in the leadership of the Church of England is provided by the following statistics. While 70% of non-charismatic clergy have confidence in the leadership given by their diocesan bishop, the proportion rises by 11 percentage points to 81% among the charismatic clergy. While 37% of the non-charismatic clergy have confidence in the leadership given by the General Synod, the proportion rises by 12 percentage points to 49% among the charismatic clergy. While 29% of the non-charismatic clergy have confidence in the leadership given by the Archbishops' Council, the proportion rises by 14 percentage points to 53% among the charismatic clergy.

Although charismatic clergy record significantly higher levels of confidence than non-charismatic clergy in the diocesan bishops, in the General Synod, and in the Archbishops' Council, there is no significant difference between the two groups in levels of confidence in local clergy. Thus, 66% of non-charismatic clergy and 73% of charismatic clergy say that they have confidence in the leadership given by their local clergy.

Confidence in the local church is provided by the following statistics. Charismatic clergy are more likely to envisage growth in their local church. While two-fifths of the non-charismatic clergy (40%) say that the membership of their church will grow in the next 12 months, the proportion rises to two-thirds among the charismatic clergy (65%). Charismatic clergy are more likely to feel confident about inviting newcomers to their church. While half of the non-charismatic clergy (52%) say that they can invite other people to come to their church, the proportion rises to 63% among charismatic clergy.

Although charismatic clergy record significantly higher levels of confidence than non-charismatic clergy in being able to invite other people to come to their church, there is no significant difference between the two groups in their perception of the difficulties faced by newcomers to their congregations. A quarter of charismatic clergy (26%) say that it is not easy for newcomers in their church, and so do 28% of non-charismatic clergy.

Overall, the fault-line between charismatic clergy and non-charismatic clergy regarding confidence and the future is quite clear. The charismatic clergy have more confidence in the leadership of the Church of England and are more confident about planning for growth. The optimism of the charismatic clergy may, at times, be difficult for the non-charismatic clergy to comprehend. It may seem as if the two groups are part of two very different Anglican Churches.

Sex and family life

The *Church Times Survey* identified four specific areas in which to test the orthodoxy of Anglican views on sex and family life: views on sex and cohabitation before marriage, views on divorce, views on same sex relationships, and views on caring for children and teenagers.

Charismatic clergy and non-charismatic clergy hold fundamentally different ideas about sex. The charismatic clergy are much clearer about when it is wrong to have sex and with whom it is wrong to have sex.

According to the majority of charismatic clergy, heterosexual sex is to be confined to the marriage relationship. The non-charismatic clergy tend to be less restrictive in their view of heterosexual activity. Thus, three-quarters of the charismatic clergy (73%) take the view that it is wrong for men and women to have sex together before marriage. Among non-charismatic clergy the proportion falls to one-third (36%) who take this view. Just 9% of charismatic clergy consider that it is all right for a couple to live together without intending to get married, compared with 34% of non-charismatic clergy. Just 5% of charismatic clergy consider that it is a good idea for couples who intend to get married to live together first, compared with 19% of non-charismatic clergy.

According to the majority of charismatic clergy, homosexual sex is to be avoided. The non-charismatic clergy tend to be less prohibitive in their view of homosexual activity. Thus, three-quarters of the charismatic clergy (76%) take the view that it is wrong for people of the same gender to have sex together. Among non-charismatic clergy the proportion falls to two-fifths (41%) who take this view. Just 5% of charismatic clergy consider that homosexual couples should have the right to marry one another, compared with 21% of non-charismatic clergy.

On matters concerned with some other aspects of family life, however, charismatic clergy and non-charismatic clergy are in much closer agreement with each other. The two groups of clergy are in quite close agreement in their views on divorce. While two-fifths of the non-charismatic clergy (39%) believe that couples should stay together for the sake of the children, the proportion rises only slightly and not significantly among the charismatic clergy to 45%. While four-fifths of the non-charismatic clergy (81%) believe that some marriages can come to a natural end in divorce or separation, the proportion drops only slightly, but significantly, among the charismatic clergy to 73%.

The two groups of clergy are also in quite close agreement in their views on children and teenagers. Between a quarter and a third of the charismatic clergy (28%) believe that children thrive equally whether cared for primarily by their father or mother. Between a quarter and a third of the non-charismatic clergy (30%) take the same view. A third of the charismatic clergy (33%) believe that contraception should be available to teenagers under 16 who want it. A third of non-charismatic clergy (37%) take the same view.

Overall, the fault-line between charismatic clergy and non-charismatic clergy regarding their attitudes toward sex is clear and stark. Many charismatic clergy may well wonder whether their non-charismatic colleagues who condone sex before marriage or who condone homosexual relationships are really part of the Christian Church at all. Many non-charismatic clergy may be surprised by the strength of conviction with which their charismatic colleagues stand out against sex before marriage and against homosexual practices.

Social concerns

In order to assess the levels of social concern expressed by committed Anglicans, the *Church Times Survey* included a set of items on global concerns and a set of items on community concerns. The global concerns included environmental and developmental issues, AIDS and genetic research. The community concerns included violence on television, paedophiles living in the community, and the effects of the National Lottery.

Charismatic clergy and non-charismatic clergy share the same high levels of concern for global issues like environmental pollution, the poverty of the developing world, and the spread of AIDS. The vast majority of the charismatic clergy (96%) are concerned about environmental pollution, and so are 95% of the non-charismatic clergy. The vast majority of the charismatic clergy (97%) are concerned about the poverty of the developing world, and so are 97% of the non-charismatic clergy. The vast majority of the charismatic clergy (95%) are concerned about the spread of AIDS, and so are 96% of the non-charismatic clergy.

The issue of research into human genes is lower down the list of priorities of both charismatic and non-charismatic clergy, some way after issues like pollution, poverty, and AIDS. On this issue, however, the charismatic clergy register a significantly higher level of concern than is the case among non-charismatic clergy. Thus, three-quarters of the charismatic clergy (77%) say that they are concerned about research into human genes, compared with 67% of the non-charismatic clergy.

On matters of community concern, the charismatic clergy consistently register a higher level of concern than is the case among the non-charismatic clergy. Nearly three-quarters of the non-charismatic clergy (72%) voice concern about violence on television, but the proportion increases further to 88% among the charismatic clergy. Two-fifths of the non-charismatic clergy (41%) voice concern about paedophiles living in the community, but the proportion increases further to 49% among the charismatic clergy. Nearly half of the non-charismatic clergy (47%) voice concern about the National Lottery, but the proportion increases further to 59% among the charismatic clergy.

Overall, the fault-line between charismatic clergy and non-charismatic clergy comes into prominence over issues on which there can be moral debate. Charismatic clergy are more likely to take the higher moral ground on issues like violence on television, paedophiles living in the community, and the evils of the National Lottery. Non-charismatic clergy may be surprised by the strength of feeling associated with these issues by their charismatic colleagues.

Social conscience

The *Church Times Survey* assessed social conscience by means of a series of questions exploring the willingness of committed Anglicans to pay more tax in order to fund specific areas of social life. The three broad areas included in the survey concerned health and education, social security and prisons, and defence and development aid.

The social conscience of charismatic clergy and the social conscience of non-charismatic clergy reflect very similar priorities. There are hardly any significant differences between the responses of the two groups of clergy to this part of the survey.

First, charismatic clergy and non-charismatic clergy hold similar views on the priority which should be given to health and education. Thus, 86% of the charismatic clergy say that they would pay more tax to fund spending on health, and so do 85% of the non-charismatic clergy. Four-fifths of the charismatic clergy (82%) say that they would pay more tax to fund spending on schools and so do 80% of the non-charismatic clergy. Under half of the charismatic clergy (45%) say that they would pay more tax to fund spending on universities, and so do 48% of the non-charismatic clergy.

Second, charismatic clergy and non-charismatic clergy hold similar views on the priority which should be given to social security and to prisons. Under half of the charismatic clergy (44%) say that they would pay more tax to fund spending on prisons, and so do 50% of the non-charismatic clergy. Under half of the charismatic clergy (47%) say that they would pay more tax to fund spending on social security benefits, and so do 49% of the non-charismatic clergy.

Third, charismatic clergy and non-charismatic clergy hold similar views on the priority which should be given to defence. Just 21% of the charismatic clergy say that they would pay more tax to fund spending on security forces. Just 25% of the non-charismatic clergy take the same position.

However, there is a small but significant difference in the level of priority given by the two groups of clergy to the issue of overseas aid. While three-quarters of the non-charismatic clergy (75%) say that they would pay more tax to fund spending on overseas aid, the proportion is even higher among charismatic clergy (82%).

Overall, the fault-line between charismatic clergy and non-charismatic clergy is hardly visible in respect of the Christian social conscience. Both follow highly similar agendas and share a high level of agreement over such issues.

Education

The *Church Times Survey* framed questions on three key topics of relevance to the Church of England's concerns with education. These topics related to the debate between the state-funded and the independent sector of schools, the place of religious education and worship in schools, and the future for faith-based schools.

Charismatic clergy and non-charismatic clergy share the same basic views on the state-maintained provision of schools and on the place of religious education within these schools. On the issue of state provision, three-fifths of the charismatic clergy (61%) and three-fifths of the non-charismatic clergy (63%) express confidence in the state-funded education system. Looking at the issue from the opposite perspective, 15% of the charismatic clergy and 18% of the non-charismatic clergy take the strong line that private schools should be abolished.

On the issue of religious education, the same high proportions of charismatic clergy and of non-charismatic clergy support the case that religious education should be taught in all schools (90% and 92% respectively). Moreover, the two groups of clergy are also in basic agreement about the emphasis that should be given to non-Christian faiths within schools. Thus, 82% of the charismatic clergy and 86% of the non-charismatic clergy support the case that religious education in schools should teach about world religions. Charismatic clergy and non-charismatic clergy are also in basic agreement about the importance that should be given to school worship. Both groups are less likely to support the case for a daily religious assembly than the case for religious education lessons. While 90% of the charismatic clergy agree that religious education should be taught in all schools, the proportion falls to 64% who agree that schools should hold a religious assembly every day. While 92% of the non-charismatic clergy agree that religious education should be taught in all schools, the proportion falls to 57% who agree that schools should hold a religious assembly every day.

It is over the issue of faith schools, however, that the views of charismatic clergy and the views of non-charismatic clergy begin to part company. Both groups are clearly in favour of the state supporting faith schools in principle, with 89% of the charismatic clergy and 86% of the non-charismatic clergy speaking in favour of state-funded church schools. It is after this basic level of agreement that the cracks begin to appear. The charismatic clergy show greater support for the expansion of Christian church schools and greater caution regarding the expansion of such provision for other faith communities.

Looking at the Church of England's agenda for church schools, the charismatic clergy are more likely than the non-charismatic clergy to vote for expansion in both the primary sector and the secondary sector. While 63% of the non-charismatic clergy argue that the Church of England should fund more new church primary schools, the proportion rises to 77% among the charismatic clergy. While 72% of the non-charismatic clergy argue that the Church of England should fund more new church secondary schools, the proportion rises to 81% among the charismatic clergy.

Looking at the agenda of other faith communities for the development of schools within the state-maintained sector, the charismatic clergy are less likely than the non-charismatic clergy to vote for the development of Jewish schools or for the development of Islamic schools. While 57% of the non-charismatic clergy are in favour of state-funded Jewish schools, the proportion falls to 40% among the charismatic clergy. While 53% of the non-charismatic clergy are in favour of state-funded Islamic schools, the proportion falls to 36% among the charismatic clergy.

Overall, the fault-line between charismatic clergy and non-charismatic clergy really comes to the surface in educational debate over the provision of state-funded schools for non-Christian faith communities. This is indicative of the ways in which non-charismatic clergy may find interfaith dialogue more comfortable than is the case among charismatic clergy. Charismatic clergy may remain puzzled by their non-charismatic colleagues' willingness to support the cause of other world faiths.

Conclusion

There is sufficient evidence in the present analysis to alert the Church of England to the wisdom of taking seriously the fault-line between charismatics and non-charismatics in the pulpit. This fault-line is theological in origin, and shapes different views of God, different notions of religious truth, and different attitudes toward worship. Equally important, however, is the way in which such a theologically-based fault-line shapes different views of the world, different personal, social and political priorities, and different attitudes toward morality. Inhabiting such different worldviews, it is not surprising that tensions arise between charismatics and non-charismatics and that consensus between the two groups on key matters of doctrine, church practice, and personal and social values remains difficult to achieve.

CHAPTER 9

Conclusion

The *Church Times Survey* has taken the lid off the Church of England today, revealed the rich diversity of beliefs, opinions and attitudes among the clergy and the committed laity, and drawn attention to the major fault-lines which divide Anglican opinion. Just suppose that in the summer of 2003 the Bishop of Oxford had had access to the *Church Times Survey* to test Anglican opinion before nominating the Reverend Canon Jeffrey John for the post of Bishop of Reading. What would the Bishop of Oxford have discovered?

He would have discovered that, if the *Church Times Survey* can be trusted, current opinion in the Church of England is still basically against the ordination of homosexuals. According to chapter three, over half (53%) of the respondents to the *Church Times Survey* expressed themselves as against the ordination of practising homosexuals as priests, compared with just a quarter (25%) who expressed themselves as in favour of the ordination of practising homosexuals as priests. In the case of ordination to the episcopacy, the weight of opinion was even more strongly divided. Nearly three-fifths (58%) of the respondents to the *Church Times Survey* expressed themselves as against the ordination of practising homosexuals as bishops, compared with just one-fifth (21%) who expressed themselves in favour. In each case the remaining 22% and 21% were undecided.

As the analysis of the data provided by the *Church Times Survey* unfolded, it became clear that opposition to the ordination of homosexuals was stronger among the laity than among the clergy. While 29% of the clergy expressed themselves as in favour of the ordination of practising homosexuals as bishops, the proportion fell to 19% among the laity.

Looking more closely at the laity, it became clear that opposition to the ordination of homosexuals was equally strong among the women as among the men in the pews. Just 19% of the men were in favour of the ordination of practising homosexuals as bishops and so were just 20% of the women. There were, however, some important differences in the attitudes of the different age groups of the laity. While only 11% of the lay people aged seventy and over were in favour of the ordination of practising homosexuals as bishops, the proportions rose to 19% among those in their fifties and sixties, and to 32% among those aged under fifty. As the senior lay Anglicans give way to a younger generation of Anglicans the acceptability of homosexual bishops is likely to increase. The summer of 2003 may just have been too early to go public on such a proposal.

Looking more closely at the clergy, it became clear that the ordination of homosexuals was much less acceptable among the Evangelicals than among the Catholics. While 39% of the Catholic clergy were in favour of the ordination of practising homosexuals as bishops, the proportion plummeted to just 3% among the Evangelical clergy. Such strong opposition among the Evangelical clergy might have been likely to sound a warning that Evangelical groups might orchestrate significant and influential protest against the nomination of a homosexual priest to the post of Bishop of Reading in the summer of 2003.

Had these statistics been available to the Bishop of Oxford at that time, there would have been a number of serious questions raised about their usefulness. The first two questions concern the validity of the information derived from the survey. First, it could be objected that the *Church Times* readership fails to produce an accurate picture of the Church of England as a whole. This objection is well placed since we have no real way to test the representativeness of the sample without somehow surveying the opinions of other groups within the Church of England. Second, it could be objected that the precise question formulated in the *Church Times Survey* focused specifically on the ordination of *practising* homosexuals. Such a precise question could be irrelevant to gauging the reaction of, say, Evangelical clergy to the ordination of non-practising homosexuals. However, as events turned out the strong reaction across the Church of England to the nomination of Canon Jeffrey John to the post of Bishop of Reading suggested that the validity of the findings of the *Church Times Survey* was robust. After all, it is only in the context of such public behaviour that the predictive power of attitude surveys can be properly examined. It seems, then, that the *Church Times Survey* passed this critical test.

There is, however, a stronger objection against using empirical data from studies like the *Church Times Survey* to shape Christian doctrine and practice. This objection begins from the view that studies of this nature may define what *is* the case, but they cannot progress into discussion of what *should be* the case. According to this objection statistical norms cannot lead into moral or theological normativity. Such an objection, however, may undervalue the ways in which God continues to speak in and through the community of believers. Is there no way in which the voice of God may be heard to speak to the Church through studies like the *Church Times Survey*?

This is the *theological* problem addressed by Jeff Astley in his book, *Ordinary Theology: looking, listening and learning in theology.* Here Astley (2002) stresses the importance of a form of what may be called 'theological listening', in which we listen out for the non-scholarly, non-technical and unsystematic, but nonetheless properly reflective, God-talk of the 'ordinary theologians' who make up the great majority of the lay members of every church. At the same time, in his analysis of the concept of ordinary theology, Astley (2002) recognises the proper constraints on such an activity. Anyone who takes the expression of such ordinary religious beliefs seriously, as *theology*, must face some important questions about theological and moral normativity.

The claim that is key here is that the non-academic theology of most believers 'can furnish us with a wider understanding of doctrinal norms, by providing a wider concept of what the church believes as a norm for doctrine' (Astley, 2002:154). However, this suggestion remains highly contentious. Surely any claim to theological truth must be tested against the classic threefold criteria of conformity to scripture, tradition and reason? We do not deny this. Yet some accounts of rationality already allow a reference to what is 'very widely and consistently taken for granted in our society' (Hudson, 1980:84), and many theologians and religious believers are sympathetic to increasingly democratic accounts of tradition. For this latter group, tradition does not just reside in an official magisterium or teaching office of the church, expressed in the decisions of its councils, doctors and bishops. It is also to be found in a *consensus fidelium* (consensus of the faithful) that embraces the whole church.

We would certainly wish to argue that a church that is open to the ordinary theology of those who sit in its pews (and the more developed and theologically educated views of those who preach from its pulpits) needs to acknowledge that there is something unstable, at the very least, about any account of Christian beliefs and practice that ignores their voices while mapping the acceptable limits of Christian doctrine. Hans van der Ven (1993) has cautiously expressed the relevance of empirical research that reveals the contours of the *consensus fidelium*.

> Empirical methodology provides practical theology with the techniques and instruments to order, analyze, interpret and evaluate the religious convictions, beliefs, images and feelings of men and women. If the *sensus fidei* [understanding of the faith] and *consensus fidelium* are not to degenerate into mere rhetoric, they must be conscientiously investigated. Only then can the dialectic, or the discrepancy, between the teaching of the church and the faith of its members . . . be clearly brought to light and explicitly presented as an inevitable subject for ecclesiastical and pastoral considerations (van der Ven, 1993:109).

While this sort of research cannot and should not *determine* the prescribed standards of Christian belief and practice, understood in terms of orthodox 'right opinions', 'social norms' or ideals; it does describe the 'statistical' or 'descriptive' norms of the thought and behaviour of real Christians. It is simply naive to pretend that these two species of norm do not interact. There is little doubt that what Christians really think and how they really behave does in fact *influence* the claims that we are able honestly and consistently to make about the proper nature of Christian truth and practice. And whatever we make of it theologically (and different theological traditions will make different things of it), 'speaking statistically ordinary theology is the theology of God's church' (Astley, 2002:162).

In particular, we would wish to argue that, taken seriously, looking for and listening to ordinary theology (properly informed by the best methodology of the empirical social sciences and the best theory of empirical theology) may prove to be a God-given tool to enable the people of God to hear the voice of God. Considered in this way, the voice of God may call the church of God in two very different directions at two very different times. At times the voice of God, heard and articulated through the proper empirical investigation of the *consensus fidelium*, may call the people of God on to new, deeper and richer theological insights that will radically disturb the views shaped by an earlier generation of Christian believers, church leaders and professional theologians. Equally, at other times, the voice of God, heard and articulated in precisely the same way, may call the people of God to conserve traditions, expectations and understanding that have been adequately shaped by an earlier generation. Thus, ordinary theology, which in so many ways stimulates radical and progressive reinterpretations of core components of the Christian tradition, may in other ways stimulate a perspective of prudent caution and even conservatism. Both perspectives demand proper respect and theological critique.

The fundamental thesis of the present book concerning the fragmented nature of Anglican faith and Anglican belief is unlikely to have taken many by surprise. The starkness and the clarity of the evidence supporting the thesis may, however, be more surprising. Moreover, having been revealed with such clarity, the fragmentation may be considerably less easy to ignore, to deny or to conceal.

Such rich diversity of views reveals what may prove to be very fragile fault-lines along which the Church of England could be torn apart. Or they may prove to be expressive of the enduring strength of a multifaceted and inclusive church within which the people of God cannot merely embrace and sustain diversity, but positively celebrate the infinite resourcefulness of a creator God. Such celebration embraces a view of God who created human beings not only with rich potential for individuality and characteristic distinctiveness in their personal development and interpersonal relationship, but also with equally rich diversity in their experience of God, in their relationship with God and in the reflective formulation of their understanding of God.

Living with diversity, however, requires high levels of special human qualities. These are not always widely represented, even among the people of God. They include such qualities as love, joy, peace, patience, kindness, goodness, faithfulness, humility and self-control. In another context such qualities may seem very Pauline and soundly biblical.

References

Archbishop of Canterbury=s Commission On Urban Priority Areas (1985), *Faith in the City*, London, Church House Publishing.

Astley, J. (2002), *Ordinary Theology: looking, listening and learning in theology*, Aldershot, Ashgate.

Bax, J. (1986), *The Good Wine: spiritual renewal in the Church of England*, London, Church House Publishing.

Bibby, R.W. (1986), *Anglitrends: a profile and prognosis,* Lethbridge, Alberta, University of Lethbridge.

Cartledge, M.J. (1999), Empirical theology: inter- or intra- disciplinary? *Journal of Beliefs and Values*, 20, 98-104.

Dearing Report (2001), *The Way Ahead: Church of England schools in the new millennium*, London, Church House Publishing.

Francis, L.J. (1984), *Teenagers and the Church: a profile of church-going youth in the 1980s*, London, Collins Liturgical Publications.

Francis, L.J. (1985), *Rural Anglicanism: a future for young Christians?* London, Collins Liturgical Publications.

Francis, L.J. (1986), *Partnership in Rural Education: church schools and teacher attitudes*, London, Collins Liturgical Publications.

Francis, L.J. (1987), *Religion in the Primary School: partnership between church and state?* London, Collins Liturgical Publications.

Francis, L.J. (1996), *Church Watch: Christianity in the countryside*, London, SPCK.

Francis, L.J. (2000), The pews talk back: the church congregation survey, in J. Astley (ed.), *Learning in the Way: research and reflection on adult Christian education*, pp 161-186, Leominster, Gracewing.

Francis, L.J. (2001), *The Values Debate: a voice from the pupils*, London, Woburn Press.

Francis, L.J., Brown, L.B. and Philipchalk, R. (1992), The development of an abbreviated form of the Revised Eysenck Personality Questionnaire (EPQR-A): its use among students in England, Canada, the USA and Australia, *Personality and Individual Differences*, 13, 443-449.

Francis, L.J. and Kay, W.K. (1995), *Teenage Religion and Values*, Leominster, Gracewing.

Francis, L.J. and Lankshear, D.W. (1990), The impact of church schools on village church life, *Educational Studies*, 16, 117-129.

Francis, L.J. and Lankshear, D.W. (1991), *Continuing in the Way: children, young people and the church*, London, National Society.

Francis, L.J. and Lankshear, D.W. (1992a), The impact of children=s work on church life in hamlets and small villages, *Journal of Christian Education*, 35, 57-63.

Francis, L.J. and Lankshear, D.W. (1992b), The rural rectory: the impact of a resident priest on local church life, *Journal of Rural Studies*, 8, 97-103.

Francis, L.J. and Lankshear, D.W. (1993), Ageing Anglican clergy and performance indicators in the rural church, compared with the suburban church, *Ageing and Society*, 13, 339-363.

Francis, L.J. and Lankshear, D.W. (1995a), *In the Catholic Way: children, young people and the church*, London, National Society.

Francis, L.J. and Lankshear, D.W. (1995b), *In the Evangelical Way: children, young people and the church*, London, National Society.

Francis, L.J., Littler, K. and Martineau, J. (2000), *Rural Ministry*, Stoneleigh Park, Acora Publishing.

Francis, L.J. and Martineau, J. (1996), *Rural Praise,* Leominster, Gracewing.

Francis, L.J. and Martineau, J. (2001a), *Rural Youth*, Stoneleigh Park, Acora Publishing.

Francis, L.J. and Martineau, J. (2001b), *Rural Visitors*, Stoneleigh Park, Acora Publishing.

Francis, L.J. and Martineau, J. (2002), *Rural Mission*, Stoneleigh Park, Acora Publishing.

Francis, L.J. and Robbins, M. (1999), *The Long Diaconate: 1987-1994*, Leominster, Gracewing.

Francis, L.J., Robbins, M., Louden, S.H. and Haley, J.M. (2001), A revised psychoticism scale for the Revised Eysenck Personality Questionnaire: a study among clergy, *Psychological Report,* 88, 1131-1134.

Gill, R. (1975), *Social Context of Theology*, London, Mowbray.

Gill, R. (1999), *Churchgoing and Christian Ethics*, Cambridge, Cambridge University Press.

Gill, R. (2003), *The 'Empty' Church Revisited*, Aldershot, Ashgate.

Hudson, W.D. (1980), The rational system of beliefs, in D. Martin, J.O. Mills and W.S.F. Pickering (eds), *Sociology and Theology: alliance and conflict*, pp. 80-101, Brighton, Harvester.

Kaldor, P., Bellamy, J., Correy, M. and Powell, R. (1992), *First Look in the Mirror: initial findings of the 1991 National Church Life Survey*, Australia, Anzea Publishers.

Kaldor, P., Dixon, R. and Powell, R. (1999), *Taking Stock: a profile of Australian church attenders*, Adelaide, South Australia, Openbook Publishers.

Kaldor, P., Powell, R., Bellamy, J., Castle, K., Correy, M. and Moore, S. (1995), *Views from the Pews: Australian church attenders speak out*, Adelaide, South Australia, Openbook Publishers.

Kay, W.K. and Francis, L.J. (1996), *Drift from the Churches: attitude toward Christianity during childhood and adolescence*, Cardiff, University of Wales Press.

Likert, R. (1932), A technique for the measurement of attitudes, *Archives of Psychology*, 140, 1-55.

Louden, S.H. and Francis, L.J. (2003), *The Naked Parish Priest: what priests really think they're doing*, London, Continuum.

Osgood, C.E., Suci, G.J. and Tannenbaum, P.H. (1957), *The Measurement of Meaning*, Urbana, Illinois, University of Illinois Press.

Park, A., Curtice, J., Thomson, K., Jarvis, L. and Bromley, C. (eds) (2001), *British Social Attitudes: the eighteenth report*, London, Sage.

Penhale, F. (1986), *Catholics in Crisis*, London, Mowbray.

Richter, P. and Francis, L.J. (1998), *Gone but not Forgotten: church leaving and returning*, London, Darton, Longman and Todd.

Russell, A. (1986), *The Country Parish*, London, SPCK.

Saward, M. (1987), *Evangelicals on the Move*, London, Mowbray.

van der Ven, J. A. (1993), *Practical Theology: an empirical approach*, Kampen, Kok Pharos.

van der Ven, J. A. (1998), *Education for Reflective Ministry*, Louvain, Peeters.

Appendix

Statistical tables

Table 3.1   Patterns of belief: overview

	Yes %	? %	No %
God			
I believe that God exists	97	2	0
I believe that God is a personal being	82	13	5
I believe that God is an impersonal power	13	18	70
Jesus			
I believe that Jesus' birth was a virgin birth	62	26	12
I believe that Jesus rose physically from the dead	78	16	6
Jesus really turned water into wine	64	27	9
Life after death			
I believe that there is life after death	88	10	2
I believe that heaven really exists	79	17	4
I believe that hell really exists	46	34	20

Table 3.2   Paths of truth: overview

	Yes %	? %	No %
Bible			
The bible is without any errors	12	18	70
Biblical truths are culturally conditioned	62	23	15
Exclusivity			
I believe that Christianity is the only true religion	46	22	32
I believe that all religions are of equal value	11	22	67
Evolution			
God made the world in six days and rested on the seventh	16	23	62
I believe that all living things evolved	69	21	11

Table 3.3   Paths of spirituality: overview

	Yes %	? %	No %
Personal practices			
I am helped in my faith by praying by myself	87	11	3
I am helped in my faith by reading the bible	85	10	5
I am helped in my faith by reading Christian books	82	14	5
I am helped in my faith by reading non-religious books	36	36	28
Group activities			
I am helped in my faith by discussing my faith with others	82	12	6
I am helped in my faith by bible study groups	55	26	19
I am helped in my faith by prayer groups	50	30	20
Wider activities			
I am helped in my faith by considering the natural world	69	22	10
I am helped in my faith by going on retreat	56	29	15
Often I get more spiritual help outside the church than within it	15	19	66

Table 3.4   Public worship: overview

	Yes %	? %	No %
Ancient and modern			
I am helped in my faith by traditional forms of service	68	18	14
I am helped in my faith by new forms of service	51	30	19
I am helped in my faith by traditional hymns in services	76	16	8
I am helped in my faith by new hymns in services	60	25	15
Styles of worship			
I am helped in my faith by periods of silence in services	78	16	7
I am helped in my faith by listening to sermons	76	18	6
I am helped in my faith by ritual in services	70	17	13
Children and church			
I am in favour of churches baptising only babies of regular churchgoers	13	15	72
I am in favour of baptised children being admitted to communion before confirmation	53	21	27

Table 3.5   Local church life: overview

	Yes %	? %	No %
Cycle of commitment			
I am coming to my church more regularly nowadays	41	20	39
I am coming to my church less regularly nowadays	6	16	78
Commitment and belonging			
I feel a strong sense of belonging to my church	90	6	4
My church is important for my social life	70	12	18
I turn to fellow members of my church when I need help	60	18	22
Commitment and power			
I can influence my church's decisions	63	21	17
I have too little control over the running of my church	15	20	65
My church makes too many demands on my time	16	15	69
My church makes too many demands on my money	8	13	79

Table 3.6   Ordained ministry: overview

	Yes %	? %	No %
Women			
I am in favour of the ordination of women as priests	77	8	15
I am in favour of the ordination of women as bishops	64	15	21
Divorced			
I am in favour of divorced people as priests	55	27	18
I am in favour of divorced people as bishops	47	27	27
Divorced and remarried			
I am in favour of divorced and remarried priests	50	28	22
I am in favour of divorced and remarried bishops	42	29	29
Practising homosexuals			
I am in favour of the ordination of practising homosexuals as priests	25	22	53
I am in favour of the ordination of practising homosexuals as bishops	21	21	58

Table 3.7   Church leadership: overview

	Yes %	? %	No %
Clergy			
Clergy should be paid a better wage	62	26	12
Clergy freehold should be abolished	39	32	29
Clergy should be employed on short-term renewable contracts	29	23	48
Clergy should live in their own houses	25	32	43
Laity			
I am in favour of lay people leading morning and evening prayer	88	7	6
I am in favour of lay people preaching at morning and evening prayer	82	10	9
I am in favour of lay people preaching at communion services	74	12	15
I am in favour of lay people leading the first part of the communion services	69	12	19
I am in favour of lay people taking the whole communion service	18	15	67

Table 3.8   Churches and cathedrals: overview

	Yes %	? %	No %
My church			
My congregation can no longer afford to pay for its church building	20	18	61
In order to survive my church building needs more grants from the state	32	21	47
In order to survive my church building needs more money from tourists and visitors	24	20	56
Wider issues			
Too much money is spent on keeping old churches	35	23	42
More church buildings should be taken over by the state	34	24	42
Many rural churches should be closed	15	21	65
Cathedrals should charge visitors for entry	24	21	55

Table 3.9   Money and policy: overview

	Yes %	? %	No %
Church structures			
My parish pays too much for its parish share (quota)	29	32	40
I am happy for some money given to my church to go to diocesan funds	71	18	12
I am happy for some money given to my church to go to church central funds	55	27	19
Clergy support			
I am happy for some money given to my church to go to training new priests	89	9	2
I am happy for some money given to my church to go to clergy pensions	82	12	5
Development and mission			
I am happy for some money given to my church to go to struggling parishes	86	10	4
I am happy for some money given to my church to go to churches in developing countries	83	13	4
Community regeneration			
I am happy for some money given to my church to go to urban regeneration	61	26	13
I am happy for some money given to my church to go to the farming community	55	29	16

Table 3.10   Anglican identity: overview

	Yes %	? %	No %
Ecumenism			
I would never become a member of another denomination	36	30	35
I would not want my denomination to merge with another	20	27	53
I would not want to be a member of an ecumenical church or local ecumenical project	23	24	53
I would be prepared to accept the Pope as my church leader in some situations	29	22	48
Establishment			
The Church of England should be disestablished	28	30	42
Senior bishops should continue to sit in the reformed House of Lords	81	12	7
The monarch should continue to be the Supreme Governor of the Church of England	49	25	26
Diocesan bishops should be appointed by the state	5	13	82
Parliament should retain control of Church of England legislation	14	24	63

Table 3.11   Confidence in the future: overview

	Yes %	? %	No %
Leadership			
I have confidence in the leadership given by my local clergy	75	18	7
I have confidence in the leadership given by my diocesan bishop	71	20	9
I have confidence in the leadership given by the General Synod	41	40	19
I have confidence in the leadership given by the Archbishops' Council	38	47	15
Local church			
The membership of my church will grow in the next 12 months	40	47	13
I can invite other people to come to my church	37	19	44
It is not easy for newcomers in my church	23	23	54

Table 3.12   Sex and family life: overview

	Yes %	? %	No %
Sex before marriage			
It is wrong for men and women to have sex before marriage	43	23	34
It is all right for a couple to live together without intending to get married	26	24	50
It is a good idea for couples who intend to get married to live together first	18	32	50
Separation and divorce			
Some marriages can come to a natural end in divorce or separation	75	16	10
Couples should stay together for the sake of the children	38	32	31
Same sex relationships			
It is wrong for people of the same gender to have sex together	54	18	27
Homosexual couples should have the right to marry one another	14	17	69
Children and teenagers			
Children thrive equally whether cared for primarily by their father or mother	30	33	38
Contraception should be available to teenagers under 16 who want it	35	23	42

Table 3.13   Social concerns: overview

	Yes	?	No
	%	%	%
Global concerns			
I am concerned about environmental pollution	94	4	2
I am concerned about the poverty of the developing world	95	4	1
I am concerned about the spread of AIDS	95	4	1
I am concerned about research into human genes	68	15	17
Community concerns			
I am concerned about violence on television	81	13	7
I am concerned about paedophiles living in the community	52	32	16
I am concerned about the National Lottery	47	27	27

Table 3.14   Social conscience: overview

	Yes	?	No
	%	%	%
Health and education			
I would pay more tax to fund spending on health	82	12	7
I would pay more tax to fund spending on schools	75	16	9
I would pay more tax to fund spending on universities	44	36	21
Social security and prisons			
I would pay more tax to fund spending on prisons	43	36	21
I would pay more tax to fund spending on social security benefits	42	35	23
Defence and development aid			
I would pay more tax to fund spending on security forces	29	36	35
I would pay more tax to fund spending on overseas aid	66	22	12

Table 3.15   Education: overview

	Yes	?	No
	%	%	%
State provision			
Private schools should be abolished	12	14	74
I have confidence in the state-funded education system	53	28	20
Religious education			
Religious education should be taught in all schools	93	5	3
Religious education in schools should teach about world religions	81	13	6
Schools should hold a religious assembly every day	66	22	12
Faith schools			
I am in favour of state-funded church schools	85	11	4
The Church of England should fund more new church primary schools	73	21	6
The Church of England should fund more new church secondary schools	77	18	6
I am in favour of state-funded Jewish schools	42	32	26
I am in favour of state-funded Islamic schools	38	32	30

Table 4.1   Patterns of belief: clergy and laity

	laity %	clergy %	χ^2	p<
God				
I believe that God exists	97	97	0.5	NS
I believe that God is a personal being	79	90	118.7	.001
I believe that God is an impersonal power	14	9	36.9	.001
Jesus				
I believe that Jesus' birth was a virgin birth	62	60	2.9	NS
I believe that Jesus rose physically from the dead	78	78	0.0	NS
Jesus really turned water into wine	65	61	9.3	.01
Life after death				
I believe that there is life after death	87	91	20.1	.001
I believe that heaven really exists	78	84	30.1	.001
I believe that hell really exists	46	48	4.0	.05

Table 4.2   Paths of truth: clergy and laity

	laity %	clergy %	χ^2	p<
Bible				
The bible is without any errors	11	13	4.9	.05
Biblical truths are culturally conditioned	58	74	144.2	.001
Exclusivity				
I believe that Christianity is the only true religion	46	48	4.0	.05
I believe that all religions are of equal value	12	7	32.7	.001
Evolution				
God made the world in six days and rested on the seventh	17	10	60.5	.001
I believe that all living things evolved	67	74	29.4	.001

Table 4.3   Paths of spirituality: clergy and laity

	laity %	clergy %	χ^2	p<
Personal practices				
I am helped in my faith by praying by myself	85	92	52.4	.001
I am helped in my faith by reading the bible	82	94	140.1	.001
I am helped in my faith by reading Christian books	79	90	125.6	.001
I am helped in my faith by reading non-religious books	30	55	374.2	.001
Group activities				
I am helped in my faith by discussing my faith with others	79	90	109.8	.001
I am helped in my faith by bible study groups	54	58	8.3	.01
I am helped in my faith by prayer groups	49	54	15.5	.001
Wider activities				
I am helped in my faith by considering the natural world	68	69	0.6	NS
I am helped in my faith by going on retreat	51	74	306.9	.001
Often I get more spiritual help outside the church than within it	15	18	10.7	.01

Table 4.4   Public worship: clergy and laity

	laity %	clergy %	χ^2	p<
Ancient and modern				
I am helped in my faith by traditional forms of service	71	59	98.4	.001
I am helped in my faith by new forms of service	47	65	184.9	.001
I am helped in my faith by traditional hymns in services	77	72	18.1	.001
I am helped in my faith by new hymns in services	58	67	52.1	.001
Styles of worship				
I am helped in my faith by periods of silence in services	77	81	15.5	.001
I am helped in my faith by listening to sermons	76	75	0.7	NS
I am helped in my faith by ritual in services	69	73	7.6	.01
Children and church				
I am in favour of churches baptising only babies of regular churchgoers	13	13	0.1	NS
I am in favour of baptised children being admitted to communion before confirmation	48	68	229.9	.001

Table 4.5   Local church life: clergy and laity

	laity %	clergy %	χ^2	p<
Cycle of commitment				
I am coming to my church more regularly nowadays	43	34	45.4	.001
I am coming to my church less regularly nowadays	6	5	3.7	NS
Commitment and belonging				
I feel a strong sense of belonging to my church	91	90	0.8	NS
My church is important for my social life	71	65	21.8	.001
I turn to fellow members of my church when I need help	60	60	0.2	NS
Commitment and power				
I can influence my church's decisions	60	72	85.7	.001
I have too little control over the running of my church	16	11	22.8	.001
My church makes too many demands on my time	13	24	126.7	.001
My church makes too many demands on my money	8	7	3.4	NS

Table 4.6   Ordained ministry: clergy and laity

	laity %	clergy %	χ^2	p<
Women				
I am in favour of the ordination of women as priests	77	80	10.5	.01
I am in favour of the ordination of women as bishops	63	66	3.2	NS
Divorced				
I am in favour of divorced people as priests	51	66	133.5	.001
I am in favour of divorced people as bishops	43	58	124.6	.001
Divorced and remarried				
I am in favour of divorced and remarried priests	46	60	104.7	.001
I am in favour of divorced and remarried bishops	39	51	79.4	.001
Practising homosexuals				
I am in favour of the ordination of practising homosexuals as priests	23	33	75.0	.001
I am in favour of the ordination of practising homosexuals as bishops	19	29	75.1	.001

Table 4.7   Church leadership: clergy and laity

	laity %	*clergy* %	χ^2	*p*<
Clergy				
Clergy should be paid a better wage	64	56	31.7	.001
Clergy freehold should be abolished	40	38	1.0	NS
Clergy should be employed on short-term renewable contracts	30	26	9.8	.01
Clergy should live in their own houses	26	25	0.8	NS
Laity				
I am in favour of:				
lay people leading morning and evening prayer	85	94	95.1	.001
lay people preaching at morning and evening prayer	81	85	18.3	.001
lay people preaching at communion services	72	79	39.9	.001
lay people leading the first part of the communion service	68	72	7.8	.01
lay people taking the whole communion service	20	12	53.4	.001

Table 4.8   Churches and cathedrals: clergy and laity

	laity %	*clergy* %	χ^2	*p*<
My church				
My congregation can no longer afford to pay for its church building	20	21	1.0	NS
In order to survive my church building:				
needs more grants from the state	31	35	14.0	.001
needs more money from tourists and visitors	25	23	1.5	NS
Wider issues				
Too much money is spent on keeping old churches	30	47	178.6	.001
More church buildings should be taken over by the state	29	48	220.1	.001
Many rural churches should be closed	12	22	108.4	.001
Cathedrals should charge visitors for entry	25	22	3.2	NS

Table 4.9   Money and policy: clergy and laity

	laity %	*clergy* %	χ^2	*p*<
Church structures				
My parish pays too much for its parish share (quota)	32	20	90.8	.001
I am happy for some money given to my church to go to diocesan funds	69	75	27.9	.001
I am happy for some money given to my church to go to church central funds	52	64	90.9	.001
Clergy support				
I am happy for some money given to my church:				
to go to training new priests	88	92	16.9	.001
to go to clergy pensions	81	89	61.2	.001
Development and mission				
I am happy for some money given to my church:				
to go to struggling parishes	85	90	35.4	.001
to go to churches in developing countries	81	88	51.5	.001
Community regeneration				
I am happy for some money given to my church:				
to go to urban regeneration	59	67	29.5	.001
to go to the farming community	54	58	9.0	.01

Table 4.10   Anglican identity: clergy and laity

	laity %	clergy %	χ^2	p<
Ecumenism				
I would never become a member of another denomination	35	37	1.3	NS
I would not want my denomination to merge with another	21	15	41.2	.001
I would not want to be a member of an ecumenical church or local ecumenical project	25	17	43.7	.001
I would be prepared to accept the Pope as my church leader in some situations	26	38	92.6	.001
Establishment				
The Church of England should be disestablished	27	32	17.6	.001
Senior bishops should continue to sit in the reformed House of Lords	82	76	33.8	.001
The monarch should continue to be the Supreme Governor of the Church of England	51	43	33.2	.001
Diocesan bishops should be appointed by the state	5	6	4.2	.05
Parliament should retain control of Church of England legislation	13	14	0.4	NS

Table 4.11   Confidence in the future: clergy and laity

	laity %	clergy %	χ^2	p<
Leadership				
I have confidence in the leadership given by my local clergy	77	68	64.7	.001
I have confidence in the leadership given by my diocesan bishop	70	74	11.2	.001
I have confidence in the leadership given by the General Synod	42	40	1.9	NS
I have confidence in the leadership given by the Archbishops' Council	39	35	10.0	.01
Local church				
The membership of my church will grow in the next 12 months	38	47	45.6	.001
I can invite other people to come to my church	30	57	420.8	.001
It is not easy for newcomers in my church	23	25	5.3	.05

Table 4.12   Sex and family life: clergy and laity

	laity %	clergy %	χ^2	p<
Sex before marriage				
It is wrong for men and women to have sex before marriage	43	45	2.2	NS
It is all right for a couple to live together without intending to get married	25	27	3.1	NS
It is a good idea for couples who intend to get married to live together first	19	15	12.0	.001
Separation and divorce				
Some marriages can come to a natural end in divorce or separation	74	80	28.1	.001
Couples should stay together for the sake of the children	37	39	2.1	NS
Same sex relationships				
It is wrong for people of the same gender to have sex together	56	48	35.5	.001
Homosexual couples should have the right to marry one another	13	18	24.7	.001
Children and teenagers				
Children thrive equally whether cared for primarily by their father or mother	30	30	0.0	NS
Contraception should be available to teenagers under 16 who want it	34	37	7.2	.01

Table 4.13   Social concerns: clergy and laity

	laity %	clergy %	χ^2	p<
Global concerns				
I am concerned about environmental pollution	94	95	2.5	NS
I am concerned about the poverty of the developing world	95	97	12.9	.001
I am concerned about the spread of AIDS	95	96	3.7	NS
I am concerned about research into human genes	67	70	5.4	.05
Community concerns				
I am concerned about violence on television	82	76	33.1	.001
I am concerned about paedophiles living in the community	55	43	83.2	.001
I am concerned about the National Lottery	45	51	22.4	.001

Table 4.14   Social conscience: clergy and laity

	laity %	clergy %	χ^2	p<
Health and education				
I would pay more tax to fund spending on health	80	85	23.1	.001
I would pay more tax to fund spending on schools	74	81	34.1	.001
I would pay more tax to fund spending on universities	42	47	13.2	.001
Social security and prisons				
I would pay more tax to fund spending on prisons	42	48	20.8	.001
I would pay more tax to fund spending on social security benefits	39	49	57.9	.001
Defence and development aid				
I would pay more tax to fund spending on security forces	30	24	21.7	.001
I would pay more tax to fund spending on overseas aid	62	77	144.1	.001

Table 4.15   Education: clergy and laity

	laity %	clergy %	χ^2	p<
State provision				
Private schools should be abolished	10	16	41.0	.001
I have confidence in the state-funded education system	50	62	79.0	.001
Religious education				
Religious education should be taught in all schools	93	91	10.1	.01
Religious education in schools should teach about world religions	79	85	28.6	.001
Schools should hold a religious assembly every day	69	59	58.1	.001
Faith schools				
I am in favour of state-funded church schools	85	86	2.7	NS
The Church of England should fund more new church primary schools	75	68	39.1	.001
The Church of England should fund more new church secondary schools	77	75	3.0	NS
I am in favour of state-funded Jewish schools	39	51	81.9	.001
I am in favour of state-funded Islamic schools	35	47	84.3	.001

Table 5.1   Patterns of belief: men and women in the pews

	men %	women %	χ^2	p<
God				
I believe that God exists	97	97	0.0	NS
I believe that God is a personal being	78	80	3.8	NS
I believe that God is an impersonal power	17	12	26.4	.001
Jesus				
I believe that Jesus' birth was a virgin birth	63	61	3.6	NS
I believe that Jesus rose physically from the dead	80	76	9.4	.01
Jesus really turned water into wine	66	65	1.0	NS
Life after death				
I believe that there is life after death	87	88	1.6	NS
I believe that heaven really exists	78	77	0.5	NS
I believe that hell really exists	48	43	13.6	.001

Table 5.2   Paths of truth: men and women in the pews

	men %	women %	χ^2	p<
Bible				
The bible is without any errors	13	10	18.6	.001
Biblical truths are culturally conditioned	60	57	3.7	NS
Exclusivity				
I believe that Christianity is the only true religion	47	44	6.4	.05
I believe that all religions are of equal value	12	12	0.7	NS
Evolution				
God made the world in six days and rested on the seventh	17	18	0.1	NS
I believe that all living things evolved	68	67	1.7	NS

Table 5.3   Paths of spirituality: men and women in the pews

	men %	women %	χ^2	p<
Personal practices				
I am helped in my faith by praying by myself	83	86	11.7	.001
I am helped in my faith by reading the bible	81	84	8.9	.01
I am helped in my faith by reading Christian books	76	81	20.7	.001
I am helped in my faith by reading non-religious books	29	31	2.3	NS
Group activities				
I am helped in my faith by discussing my faith with others	75	82	44.5	.001
I am helped in my faith by bible study groups	46	60	100.6	.001
I am helped in my faith by prayer groups	39	56	149.0	.001
Wider activities				
I am helped in my faith by considering the natural world	60	74	122.4	.001
I am helped in my faith by going on retreat	43	57	112.9	.001
Often I get more spiritual help outside the church than within it	15	15	0.0	NS

Table 5.4   Public worship: men and women in the pews

	men	women		
	%	*%*	χ^2	*p<*
Ancient and modern				
I am helped in my faith by traditional forms of service	73	70	5.1	.05
I am helped in my faith by new forms of service	42	51	47.3	.001
I am helped in my faith by traditional hymns in services	78	76	2.3	NS
I am helped in my faith by new hymns in services	50	63	111.5	.001
Styles of worship				
I am helped in my faith by periods of silence in services	72	80	59.1	.001
I am helped in my faith by listening to sermons	76	76	0.1	NS
I am helped in my faith by ritual in services	68	70	1.7	NS
Children and church				
I am in favour of churches baptising only babies of regular churchgoers	15	11	13.7	.001
I am in favour of baptised children being admitted to communion before confirmation	46	49	4.8	.05

Table 5.5   Local church life: men and women in the pews

	men	women		
	%	*%*	χ^2	*p<*
Cycle of commitment				
I am coming to my church more regularly nowadays	42	45	5.2	.05
I am coming to my church less regularly nowadays	6	6	0.1	NS
Commitment and belonging				
I feel a strong sense of belonging to my church	90	91	1.1	NS
My church is important for my social life	69	72	5.2	.05
I turn to fellow members of my church when I need help	49	68	217.1	.001
Commitment and power				
I can influence my church=s decisions	64	56	37.3	.001
I have too little control over the running of my church	17	16	1.4	NS
My church makes too many demands on my time	14	13	3.7	NS
My church makes too many demands on my money	9	8	1.2	NS

Table 5.6   Ordained ministry: men and women in the pews

	men	women		
	%	*%*	χ^2	*p<*
Women				
I am in favour of the ordination of women as priests	73	80	39.8	.001
I am in favour of the ordination of women as bishops	59	67	38.7	.001
Divorced				
I am in favour of divorced people as priests	49	52	4.7	.05
I am in favour of divorced people as bishops	43	43	0.1	NS
Divorced and remarried				
I am in favour of divorced and remarried priests	47	46	1.2	NS
I am in favour of divorced and remarried bishops	40	38	2.0	NS
Practising homosexuals				
I am in favour of the ordination of practising homosexuals as priests	22	23	2.9	NS
I am in favour of the ordination of practising homosexuals as bishops	19	20	0.8	NS

Table 5.7   Church leadership: men and women in the pews

	men %	women %	χ^2	p<
Clergy				
Clergy should be paid a better wage	63	64	1.8	NS
Clergy freehold should be abolished	42	38	13.5	.001
Clergy should be employed on short-term renewable contracts	28	31	5.4	.05
Clergy should live in their own houses	26	26	0.1	NS
Laity				
I am in favour of:				
lay people leading morning and evening prayer	85	86	1.3	NS
lay people preaching at morning and evening prayer	81	81	0.0	NS
lay people preaching at communion services	73	72	0.9	NS
lay people leading the first part of the communion service	69	68	0.2	NS
lay people taking the whole communion service	22	18	13.6	.001

Table 5.8   Churches and cathedrals: men and women in the pews

	men %	women %	χ^2	p<
My church				
My congregation can no longer afford to pay for its church building	20	20	0.1	NS
In order to survive my church building:				
needs more grants from the state	31	30	0.6	NS
needs more money from tourists and visitors	25	25	0.0	NS
Wider issues				
Too much money is spent on keeping old churches	32	29	4.8	.05
More church buildings should be taken over by the state	33	26	34.4	.001
Many rural churches should be closed	15	10	24.3	.001
Cathedrals should charge visitors for entry	26	23	5.1	.05

Table 5.9   Money and policy: men and women in the pews

	men %	women %	χ^2	p<
Church structures				
My parish pays too much for its parish share (quota)	31	32	0.4	NS
I am happy for some money given to my church to go to diocesan funds	69	69	0.3	NS
I am happy for some money given to my church to go to church central funds	54	50	6.7	.01
Clergy support				
I am happy for some money given to my church:				
to go to training new priests	90	87	13.4	.001
to go to clergy pensions	80	81	0.5	NS
Development and mission				
I am happy for some money given to my church:				
to go to struggling parishes	87	83	15.8	.001
to go to churches in developing countries	79	82	8.2	.01
Community regeneration				
I am happy for some money given to my church:				
to go to urban regeneration	56	62	26.5	.001
to go to the farming community	45	60	132.3	.001

Table 5.10   Anglican identity: men and women in the pews

	men %	women %	χ^2	$p<$
Ecumenism				
I would never become a member of another denomination	36	34	2.4	NS
I would not want my denomination to merge with another	21	21	0.0	NS
I would not want to be a member of an ecumenical church or local ecumenical project	28	22	21.9	.001
I would be prepared to accept the Pope as my church leader in some situations	34	21	127.5	.001
Establishment				
The Church of England should be disestablished	33	23	69.5	.001
Senior bishops should continue to sit in the reformed House of Lords	82	83	0.9	NS
The monarch should continue to be the Supreme Governor of the Church of England	52	50	1.6	NS
Diocesan bishops should be appointed by the state	7	4	32.8	.001
Parliament should retain control of Church of England legislation	17	10	60.0	.001

Table 5.11   Confidence in the future: men and women in the pews

	men %	women %	χ^2	$p<$
Leadership				
I have confidence in the leadership given by my local clergy	76	78	2.1	NS
I have confidence in the leadership given by my diocesan bishop	69	70	1.7	NS
I have confidence in the leadership given by the General Synod	38	45	30.3	.001
I have confidence in the leadership given by the Archbishops' Council	36	42	20.7	.001
Local church				
The membership of my church will grow in the next 12 months	39	38	1.1	NS
I can invite other people to come to my church	28	32	13.3	.001
It is not easy for newcomers in my church	25	21	13.8	.001

Table 5.12   Sex and family life: men and women in the pews

	men %	women %	χ^2	$p<$
Sex before marriage				
It is wrong for men and women to have sex before marriage	43	42	0.0	NS
It is all right for a couple to live together without intending to get married	27	24	5.3	.05
It is a good idea for couples who intend to get married to live together first	20	18	3.4	NS
Separation and divorce				
Some marriages can come to a natural end in divorce or separation	72	75	5.0	.05
Couples should stay together for the sake of the children	48	29	208.2	.001
Same sex relationships				
It is wrong for people of the same gender to have sex together	59	54	11.1	.001
Homosexual couples should have the right to marry one another	13	13	0.1	NS
Children and teenagers				
Children thrive equally whether cared for primarily by their father or mother	23	34	90.5	.001
Contraception should be available to teenagers under 16 who want it	35	33	1.8	NS

Table 5.13   Social concerns: men and women in the pews

	men	women		
	%	%	χ^2	p<
Global concerns				
I am concerned about environmental pollution	92	96	30.6	.001
I am concerned about the poverty of the developing world	93	96	26.4	.001
I am concerned about the spread of AIDS	93	96	25.8	.001
I am concerned about research into human genes	62	71	57.1	.001
Community concerns				
I am concerned about violence on television	76	87	112.6	.001
I am concerned about paedophiles living in the community	51	58	30.8	.001
I am concerned about the National Lottery	40	48	36.9	.001

Table 5.14   Social conscience: men and women in the pews

	men	women		
	%	%	χ^2	p<
Health and education				
I would pay more tax to fund spending on health	78	83	21.1	.001
I would pay more tax to fund spending on schools	71	76	16.3	.001
I would pay more tax to fund spending on universities	41	43	2.7	NS
Social security and prisons				
I would pay more tax to fund spending on prisons	37	45	38.0	.001
I would pay more tax to fund spending on social security benefits	37	41	7.0	.01
Defence and development aid				
I would pay more tax to fund spending on security forces	31	29	2.8	NS
I would pay more tax to fund spending on overseas aid	59	64	16.3	.001

Table 5.15   Education: men and women in the pews

	men	women		
	%	%	χ^2	p<
State provision				
Private schools should be abolished	12	10	7.0	.01
I have confidence in the state-funded education system	49	51	2.3	NS
Religious education				
Religious education should be taught in all schools	93	94	1.7	NS
Religious education in schools should teach about world religions	75	82	41.5	.001
Schools should hold a religious assembly every day	69	69	0.0	NS
Faith schools				
I am in favour of state-funded church schools	85	85	0.0	NS
The Church of England should fund more new church primary schools	75	75	0.3	NS
The Church of England should fund more new church secondary schools	76	78	3.4	NS
I am in favour of state-funded Jewish schools	41	38	5.9	.05
I am in favour of state-funded Islamic schools	37	33	9.0	.01

Table 6.1   Patterns of belief: young and old in the pews

	under 50 %	50-69 %	70 plus %	χ^2	p<
God					
I believe that God exists	98	97	96	7.5	.05
I believe that God is a personal being	83	79	76	19.2	.001
I believe that God is an impersonal power	12	14	16	10.8	.01
Jesus					
I believe that Jesus' birth was a virgin birth	65	60	64	13.2	.01
I believe that Jesus rose physically from the dead	81	77	78	7.5	.05
Jesus really turned water into wine	69	64	65	11.2	.01
Life after death					
I believe that there is life after death	89	87	87	3.3	NS
I believe that heaven really exists	82	77	75	19.6	.001
I believe that hell really exists	53	46	39	59.5	.001

Table 6.2   Paths of truth: young and old in the pews

	under 50 %	50-69 %	70 plus %	χ^2	p<
Bible					
The bible is without any errors	16	11	8	47.4	.001
Biblical truths are culturally conditioned	60	60	53	25.1	.001
Exclusivity					
I believe that Christianity is the only true religion	45	44	48	6.3	.05
I believe that all religions are of equal value	17	12	10	30.8	.001
Evolution					
God made the world in six days and rested on the seventh	20	16	18	6.5	.05
I believe that all living things evolved	67	69	65	9.1	.05

Table 6.3   Paths of spirituality: young and old in the pews

	under 50 %	50-69 %	70 plus %	χ^2	p<
Personal practices					
I am helped in my faith by praying by myself	87	85	83	10.5	.01
I am helped in my faith by reading the bible	83	83	81	4.7	NS
I am helped in my faith by reading Christian books	80	80	75	19.2	.001
I am helped in my faith by reading non-religious books	37	30	26	33.5	.001
Group activities					
I am helped in my faith by discussing my faith with others	82	81	73	59.0	.001
I am helped in my faith by bible study groups	50	57	52	18.2	.001
I am helped in my faith by prayer groups	49	50	49	8.5	.05
Wider activities					
I am helped in my faith by considering the natural world	69	69	66	4.4	NS
I am helped in my faith by going on retreat	54	51	47	13.3	.01
Often I get more spiritual help outside the church than within it	19	15	12	25.7	.001

Table 6.4   Public worship: young and old in the pews

	under 50 %	50-69 %	70 plus %	χ^2	p<
Ancient and modern					
I am helped in my faith by traditional forms of service	66	70	78	55.7	.001
I am helped in my faith by new forms of service	55	49	37	93.9	.001
I am helped in my faith by traditional hymns in services	73	75	82	39.1	.001
I am helped in my faith by new hymns in services	61	60	50	51.8	.001
Styles of worship					
I am helped in my faith by periods of silence in services	79	77	74	10.9	.01
I am helped in my faith by listening to sermons	78	77	72	22.1	.001
I am helped in my faith by ritual in services	66	69	71	6.8	.05
Children and church					
I am in favour of churches baptising only babies of regular churchgoers	17	12	11	20.5	.001
I am in favour of baptised children being admitted to communion before confirmation	56	50	38	93.5	.001

Table 6.5   Local church life: young and old in the pews

	under 50 %	50-69 %	70 plus %	χ^2	p<
Cycle of commitment					
I am coming to my church more regularly nowadays	44	44	41	4.1	NS
I am coming to my church less regularly nowadays	7	6	5	5.0	NS
Commitment and belonging					
I feel a strong sense of belonging to my church	85	91	93	51.5	.001
My church is important for my social life	64	71	75	38.5	.001
I turn to fellow members of my church when I need help	56	61	62	11.9	.01
Commitment and power					
I can influence my church's decisions	61	65	51	81.7	.001
I have too little control over the running of my church	19	15	16	12.0	.01
My church makes too many demands on my time	15	15	8	49.3	.001
My church makes too many demands on my money	7	9	8	1.9	NS

Table 6.6   Ordained ministry: young and old in the pews

	under 50 %	50-69 %	70 plus %	χ^2	p<
Women					
I am in favour of the ordination of women as priests	80	78	72	35.4	.001
I am in favour of the ordination of women as bishops	71	66	53	109.4	.001
Divorced					
I am in favour of divorced people as priests	63	54	38	182.7	.001
I am in favour of divorced people as bishops	57	45	29	226.4	.001
Divorced and remarried					
I am in favour of divorced and remarried priests	57	49	35	134.7	.001
I am in favour of divorced and remarried bishops	52	41	27	176.2	.001
Practising homosexuals					
I am in favour of the ordination of practicing homosexuals as priests	34	23	15	146.9	.001
I am in favour of the ordination of practicing homosexuals as bishops	32	19	11	184.5	.001

Table 6.7   Church leadership: young and old in the pews

	under 50 %	50-69 %	70 plus %	χ^2	$p<$
Clergy					
Clergy should be paid a better wage	64	64	63	0.8	NS
Clergy freehold should be abolished	34	43	37	28.4	.001
Clergy should be employed on short-term renewable contracts	24	33	27	34.8	.001
Clergy should live in their own houses	20	28	25	22.5	.001
Laity					
I am in favour of:					
lay people leading morning and evening prayer	88	87	80	55.8	.001
lay people preaching at morning and evening prayer	85	83	74	71.6	.001
lay people preaching at communion services	80	75	61	142.0	.001
lay people leading the first part of the communion services	71	72	59	95.0	.001
lay people taking the whole communion service	24	22	13	63.5	.001

Table 6.8   Churches and cathedrals: young and old in the pews

	under 50 %	50-69 %	70 plus %	χ^2	$p<$
My church					
My congregation can no longer afford to pay for its church building	22	21	17	15.8	.001
In order to survive my church building:					
needs more grants from the state	30	33	27	24.3	.001
needs more money from tourists and visitors	22	26	24	6.7	.05
Wider issues					
Too much money is spent on keeping old churches	33	34	23	61.5	.001
More church buildings should be taken over by the state	29	34	22	67.9	.001
Many rural churches should be closed	11	14	10	20.5	.001
Cathedrals should charge visitors for entry	16	24	31	82.9	.001

Table 6.9   Money and policy: young and old in the pews

	under 50 %	50-69 %	70 plus %	χ^2	$p<$
Church structures					
My parish pays too much for its parish share (quota)	28	33	32	7.7	.05
I am happy for some money given to my church to go to diocesan funds	69	70	67	5.4	NS
I am happy for some money given to my church to go to church central funds	53	53	48	10.2	.01
Clergy support					
I am happy for some money given to my church:					
to go to training new priests	90	90	85	33.5	.001
to go to clergy pensions	82	81	79	6.5	.05
Development and mission					
I am happy for some money given to my church:					
to go to struggling parishes	89	87	79	68.3	.001
to go to churches in developing countries	87	82	75	63.2	.001
Community regeneration					
I am happy for some money given to my church:					
to go to urban regeneration	68	61	51	83.4	.001
to go to the farming community	54	54	54	0.1	NS

Table 6.10   Anglican identity: young and old in the pews

	under 50 %	50-69 %	70 plus %	χ^2	$p<$
Ecumenism					
I would never become a member of another denomination	27	33	46	125.5	.001
I would not want my denomination to merge with another	19	20	25	18.2	.001
I would not want to be a member of an ecumenical church					
or local ecumenical project	20	23	31	52.4	.001
I would be prepared to accept the Pope as my church leader					
in some situations	26	26	27	0.9	NS
Establishment					
The Church of England should be disestablished	29	29	22	25.1	.001
Senior bishops should continue to sit in the reformed					
House of Lords	78	82	86	32.2	.001
The monarch should continue to be the Supreme Governor					
of the Church of England	39	50	62	143.4	.001
Diocesan bishops should be appointed by the state	5	5	5	0.9	NS
Parliament should retain control of Church of England					
legislation	11	13	15	9.2	.05

Table 6.11   Confidence in the future: young and old in the pews

	under 50 %	50-69 %	70 plus %	χ^2	$p<$
Leadership					
I have confidence in the:					
leadership given by my local clergy	80	77	77	4.3	NS
leadership given by my diocesan bishop	67	70	72	8.4	.05
leadership given by the General Synod	40	41	44	4.3	NS
leadership given by the Archbishops' Council	32	38	46	56.4	.001
Local church					
The membership of my church will grow in the next 12					
12 months	42	40	32	35.6	.001
I can invite other people to come to my church	32	32	27	12.9	.01
It is not easy for newcomers in my church	31	23	15	95.0	.001

Table 6.12   Sex and family life: young and old in the pews

	under 50 %	50-69 %	70 plus %	χ^2	$p<$
Sex before marriage					
It is wrong for men and women to have sex before marriage	31	41	54	147.2	.001
It is all right for a couple to live together without intending					
to get married	34	27	17	108.1	.001
It is a good idea for couples who intend to get married to					
live together first	25	19	15	42.6	.001
Separation and divorce					
Some marriages can come to a natural end . . .	73	77	69	34.4	.001
Couples should stay together for the sake of the children	26	33	52	227.1	.001
Same sex relationships					
It is wrong for people of the same gender to have sex	42	56	66	158.0	.001
Homosexual couples should have the right to marry	23	13	8	134.6	.001
Children and teenagers					
Children thrive equally cared for by father or mother	43	31	19	188.3	.001
Contraception should be available to teenagers under 16	44	36	24	134.6	.001

Table 6.13   Social concerns: young and old in the pews

	under 50 %	50-69 %	70 plus %	χ^2	$p<$
Global concerns					
I am concerned about environmental pollution	95	95	91	29.9	.001
I am concerned about the poverty of the developing world	96	95	93	15.1	.001
I am concerned about the spread of AIDS	94	95	95	2.8	NS
I am concerned about research into human genes	71	67	64	14.3	.001
Community concerns					
I am concerned about violence on television	70	84	88	155.3	.001
I am concerned about paedophiles living in the community	53	54	58	10.4	.01
I am concerned about the National Lottery	40	45	48	16.4	.001

Table 6.14   Social conscience: young and old in the pews

	under 50 %	50-69 %	70 plus %	χ^2	$p<$
Health and education					
I would pay more tax to fund spending on health	83	81	78	12.1	.01
I would pay more tax to fund spending on schools	79	75	68	45.7	.001
I would pay more tax to fund spending on universities	51	42	37	55.3	.001
Social security and prisons					
I would pay more tax to fund spending on prisons	38	43	41	8.0	.05
I would pay more tax to fund spending on social security benefits	38	40	40	1.5	NS
Defence and development aid					
I would pay more tax to fund spending on security forces	18	28	41	178.7	.001
I would pay more tax to fund spending on overseas aid	64	63	60	5.8	NS

Table 6.15   Education: young and old in the pews

	under 50 %	50-69 %	70 plus %	χ^2	$p<$
State provision					
Private schools should be abolished	14	11	7	35.4	.001
I have confidence in the state-funded education system	50	50	50	0.1	NS
Religious education					
Religious education should be taught in all schools	92	94	93	5.2	NS
Religious education in schools should teach about world religions	87	81	71	106.3	.001
Schools should hold a religious assembly every day	58	68	77	114.3	.001
Faith schools					
I am in favour of state-funded church schools	82	86	85	9.1	.05
The Church of England should fund more new church primary schools	70	75	78	18.5	.001
The Church of England should fund more new church secondary schools	75	78	78	5.6	NS
I am in favour of state-funded Jewish schools	42	41	36	15.7	.001
I am in favour of state-funded Islamic schools	38	36	30	20.4	.001

Table 7.1   Patterns of belief: Catholics and Evangelicals in the pulpit

	Cath %	Evan %	χ^2	$p<$
God				
I believe that God exists	97	99	5.2	.05
I believe that God is a personal being	89	98	26.4	.001
I believe that God is an impersonal power	10	4	12.8	.001
Jesus				
I believe that Jesus= birth was a virgin birth	54	93	179.3	.001
I believe that Jesus rose physically from the dead	73	98	98.7	.001
Jesus really turned water into wine	53	92	162.9	.001
Life after death				
I believe that there is life after death	90	98	25.5	.001
I believe that heaven really exists	82	98	55.5	.001
I believe that hell really exists	41	83	179.8	.001

Table 7.2   Paths of truth: Catholics and Evangelicals in the pulpit

	Cath %	Evan %	χ^2	$p<$
Bible				
The bible is without any errors	4	42	285.2	.001
Biblical truths are culturally conditioned	78	49	102.4	.001
Exclusivity				
I believe that Christianity is the only true religion	40	85	213.9	.001
I believe that all religions are of equal value	10	3	17.2	.001
Evolution				
God made the world in six days and rested on the seventh	4	29	155.6	.001
I believe that all living things evolved	82	47	155.9	.001

Table 7.3   Paths of spirituality: Catholics and Evangelicals in the pulpit

	Cath %	Evan %	χ^2	$p<$
Personal practices				
I am helped in my faith by praying by myself	92	93	0.6	NS
I am helped in my faith by reading the bible	91	98	18.7	.001
I am helped in my faith by reading Christian books	89	91	1.1	NS
I am helped in my faith by reading non-religious books	61	34	72.5	.001
Group activities				
I am helped in my faith by discussing my faith with others	86	96	25.4	.001
I am helped in my faith by bible study groups	45	83	147.2	.001
I am helped in my faith by prayer groups	44	80	137.3	.001
Wider activities				
I am helped in my faith by considering the natural world	71	56	24.6	.001
I am helped in my faith by going on retreat	81	60	64.9	.001
Often I get more spiritual help outside the church than within it	20	8	24.2	.001

Table 7.4   Public worship: Catholics and Evangelicals in the pulpit

	Cath %	Evan %	χ^2	p<
Ancient and modern				
I am helped in my faith by traditional forms of service	70	39	98.8	.001
I am helped in my faith by new forms of service	59	72	18.8	.001
I am helped in my faith by traditional hymns in services	77	65	19.0	.001
I am helped in my faith by new hymns in services	57	85	85.4	.001
Styles of worship				
I am helped in my faith by periods of silence in services	86	68	51.1	.001
I am helped in my faith by listening to sermons	73	86	22.6	.001
I am helped in my faith by ritual in services	94	29	566.3	.001
Children and church				
I am in favour of churches baptising only babies of regular churchgoers	6	34	162.8	.001
I am in favour of baptised children being admitted to communion before confirmation	68	63	3.8	NS

Table 7.5   Local church life: Catholics and Evangelicals in the pulpit

	Cath %	Evan %	χ^2	p<
Cycle of commitment				
I am coming to my church more regularly nowadays	33	37	2.2	NS
I am coming to my church less regularly nowadays	4	5	0.5	NS
Commitment and belonging				
I feel a strong sense of belonging to my church	92	89	2.2	NS
My church is important for my social life	64	73	9.2	.01
I turn to fellow members of my church when I need help	57	66	8.0	.01
Commitment and power				
I can influence my church=s decisions	69	78	9.6	.01
I have too little control over the running of my church	11	11	0.0	NS
My church makes too many demands on my time	23	24	0.2	NS
My church makes too many demands on my money	8	4	4.5	.05

Table 7.6   Ordained ministry: Catholics and Evangelicals in the pulpit

	Cath %	Evan %	χ^2	p<
Women				
I am in favour of the ordination of women as priests	73	81	8.4	.01
I am in favour of the ordination of women as bishops	60	59	0.1	NS
Divorced				
I am in favour of divorced people as priests	66	52	20.9	.001
I am in favour of divorced people as bishops	58	43	22.2	.001
Divorced and remarried				
I am in favour of divorced and remarried priests	60	43	27.6	.001
I am in favour of divorced and remarried bishops	51	35	26.1	.001
Practising homosexuals				
I am in favour of the ordination of practising homosexuals as priests	44	5	179.6	.001
I am in favour of the ordination of practising homosexuals as bishops	39	3	163.4	.001

Table 7.7   Church leadership: Catholics and Evangelicals in the pulpit

	Cath %	Evan %	χ^2	p<
Clergy				
Clergy should be paid a better wage	58	53	2.5	NS
Clergy freehold should be abolished	35	36	0.3	NS
Clergy should be employed on short-term renewable contracts	24	24	0.0	NS
Clergy should live in their own houses	25	23	0.5	NS
Laity				
I am in favour of:				
lay people leading morning and evening prayer	92	97	12.1	.001
lay people preaching at morning and evening prayer	78	94	44.0	.001
lay people preaching at communion services	70	91	62.0	.001
lay people leading the first part of the communion service	56	93	159.9	.001
lay people taking the whole communion service	2	37	277.0	.001

Table 7.8   Churches and cathedrals: Catholics and Evangelicals in the pulpit

	Cath %	Evan %	χ^2	p<
My church				
My congregation can no longer afford to pay for its church building	22	18	2.5	NS
In order to survive my church building:				
needs more grants from the state	38	25	18.7	.001
needs more money from tourists and visitors	27	14	24.8	.001
Wider issues				
Too much money is spent on keeping old churches	41	61	41.0	.001
More church buildings should be taken over by the state	46	53	5.6	.05
Many rural churches should be closed	19	28	10.7	.01
Cathedrals should charge visitors for entry	23	20	1.4	NS

Table 7.9   Money and policy: Catholics and Evangelicals in the pulpit

	Cath %	Evan %	χ^2	p<
Church structures				
My parish pays too much for its parish share (quota)	22	19	1.2	NS
I am happy for some money given to my church to go to diocesan funds	75	71	2.5	NS
I am happy for some money given to my church to go to church central funds	63	60	0.9	NS
Clergy support				
I am happy for some money given to my church:				
to go to training new priests	92	90	2.6	NS
to go to clergy pensions	91	85	8.0	.01
Development and mission				
I am happy for some money given to my church:				
to go to struggling parishes	93	86	13.1	.001
to go to churches in developing countries	87	89	1.0	NS
Community regeneration				
I am happy for some money given to my church:				
to go to urban regeneration	67	60	6.2	.05
to go to the farming community	57	54	1.0	NS

Table 7.10   Anglican identity: Catholics and Evangelicals in the pulpit

	Cath %	Evan %	χ^2	p<
Ecumenism				
I would never become a member of another denomination	42	26	29.8	.001
I would not want my denomination to merge with another	19	11	11.3	.001
I would not want to be a member of an ecumenical church or local ecumenical project	24	15	12.8	.001
I would be prepared to accept the Pope as my church leader in some situations	57	9	243.7	.001
Establishment				
The Church of England should be disestablished	32	37	3.5	NS
Senior bishops should continue to sit in the reformed House of Lords	74	77	1.2	NS
The monarch should continue to be the Supreme Governor of the Church of England	46	40	4.1	.05
Diocesan bishops should be appointed by the state	7	6	0.5	NS
Parliament should retain control of Church of England legislation	15	15	0.1	NS

Table 7.11   Confidence in the future: Catholics and Evangelicals in the pulpit

	Cath %	Evan %	χ^2	p<
Leadership				
I have confidence in the leadership given by my local clergy	66	69	1.2	NS
I have confidence in the leadership given by my diocesan bishop	72	78	4.7	.05
I have confidence in the leadership given by the General Synod	35	44	10.1	.01
I have confidence in the leadership given by the Archbishops' Council	28	49	49.5	.001
Local church				
The membership of my church will grow in the next 12 months	45	62	29.2	.001
I can invite other people to come to my church	55	66	13.6	.001
It is not easy for newcomers in my church	23	24	0.3	NS

Table 7.12   Sex and family life: Catholics and Evangelicals in the pulpit

	Cath %	Evan %	χ^2	p<
Sex before marriage				
It is wrong for men and women to have sex before marriage	33	82	241.8	.001
It is all right for a couple to live together without intending to get married	36	4	133.5	.001
It is a good idea for couples who intend to get married to live together first	21	3	64.8	.001
Separation and divorce				
Some marriages can come to a natural end in divorce or separation	83	68	33.7	.001
Couples should stay together for the sake of the children	37	53	26.3	.001
Same sex relationships				
It is wrong for people of the same gender to have sex together	36	85	241.9	.001
Homosexual couples should have the right to marry one another	23	3	72.2	.001
Children and teenagers				
Children thrive equally whether cared for primarily by their father or mother	33	23	12.8	.001
Contraception should be available to teenagers under 16 who want it	41	23	38.4	.001

Table 7.13   Social concerns: Catholics and Evangelicals in the pulpit

	Cath %	Evan %	χ^2	$p<$
Global concerns				
I am concerned about environmental pollution	95	93	1.3	NS
I am concerned about the poverty of the developing world	97	95	1.3	NS
I am concerned about the spread of AIDS	96	95	1.5	NS
I am concerned about research into human genes	69	74	3.4	NS
Community concerns				
I am concerned about violence on television	71	85	26.9	.001
I am concerned about paedophiles living in the community	36	53	30.0	.001
I am concerned about the National Lottery	40	71	103.6	.001

Table 7.14   Social conscience: Catholics and Evangelicals in the pulpit

	Cath %	Evan %	χ^2	$p<$
Health and education				
I would pay more tax to fund spending on health	86	84	0.6	NS
I would pay more tax to fund spending on schools	79	81	1.0	NS
I would pay more tax to fund spending on universities	49	44	2.4	NS
Social security and prisons				
I would pay more tax to fund spending on prisons	51	38	16.0	.001
I would pay more tax to fund spending on social security benefits	51	40	12.8	.001
Defence and development aid				
I would pay more tax to fund spending on security forces	25	20	4.0	.05
I would pay more tax to fund spending on overseas aid	74	79	4.3	.05

Table 7.15   Education: Catholics and Evangelicals in the pulpit

	Cath %	Evan %	χ^2	$p<$
State provision				
Private schools should be abolished	16	12	4.5	.05
I have confidence in the state-funded education system	60	61	0.0	NS
Religious education				
Religious education should be taught in all schools	89	93	3.9	.05
Religious education in schools should teach about world religions	86	80	5.5	.05
Schools should hold a religious assembly every day	61	65	1.7	NS
Faith schools				
I am in favour of state-funded church schools	87	89	1.0	NS
The Church of England should fund more new church primary schools	69	72	1.1	NS
The Church of England should fund more new church secondary schools	78	80	0.3	NS
I am in favour of state-funded Jewish schools	58	35	55.5	.001
I am in favour of state-funded Islamic schools	54	32	49.0	.001

Table 8.1 Patterns of belief: charismatics and non-charismatics in the pulpit

	charis %	non-ch %	χ^2	p<
God				
I believe that God exists	100	97	6.5	.05
I believe that God is a personal being	99	88	21.0	.001
I believe that God is an impersonal power	5	9	4.0	.05
Jesus				
I believe that Jesus' birth was a virgin birth	88	49	95.8	.001
I believe that Jesus rose physically from the dead	97	71	58.7	.001
Jesus really turned water into wine	89	51	92.4	.001
Life after death				
I believe that there is life after death	100	87	25.2	.001
I believe that heaven really exists	98	78	43.4	.001
I believe that hell really exists	80	36	121.6	.001

Table 8.2 Paths of truth: charismatics and non-charismatics in the pulpit

	charis %	non-ch %	χ^2	p<
Bible				
The bible is without any errors	35	8	97.1	.001
Biblical truths are culturally conditioned	65	80	21.2	.001
Exclusivity				
I believe that Christianity is the only true religion	81	39	109.7	.001
I believe that all religions are of equal value	1	8	13.1	.001
Evolution				
God made the world in six days and rested on the seventh	18	6	33.2	.001
I believe that all living things evolved	54	80	57.2	.001

Table 8.3 Paths of spirituality: charismatics and non-charismatics in the pulpit

	charis %	non-ch %	χ^2	p<
Personal practices				
I am helped in my faith by praying by myself	91	91	0.1	NS
I am helped in my faith by reading the bible	99	91	13.4	.001
I am helped in my faith by reading Christian books	92	91	0.3	NS
I am helped in my faith by reading non-religious books	39	61	28.4	.001
Group activities				
I am helped in my faith by discussing my faith with others	96	89	9.3	.01
I am helped in my faith by bible study groups	81	48	68.6	.001
I am helped in my faith by prayer groups	83	41	114.0	.001
Wider activities				
I am helped in my faith by considering the natural world	66	71	1.3	NS
I am helped in my faith by going on retreat	74	73	0.1	NS
Often I get more spiritual help outside the church than within it	7	22	22.5	.001

Table 8.4   Public worship: charismatics and non-charismatics in the pulpit

	charis %	non-ch %	χ^2	p<
Ancient and modern				
I am helped in my faith by traditional forms of service	32	67	81.2	.001
I am helped in my faith by new forms of service	77	58	24.3	.001
I am helped in my faith by traditional hymns in services	60	75	18.3	.001
I am helped in my faith by new hymns in services	86	59	48.6	.001
Styles of worship				
I am helped in my faith by periods of silence in services	81	81	0.0	NS
I am helped in my faith by listening to sermons	80	73	3.4	NS
I am helped in my faith by ritual in services	47	82	101.2	.001
Children and church				
I am in favour of churches baptising only babies of regular churchgoers	31	8	75.8	.001
I am in favour of baptised children being admitted to communion before confirmation	75	65	6.8	.01

Table 8.5   Local church life: charismatics and non-charismatics in the pulpit

	charis %	non-ch %	χ^2	p<
Cycle of commitment				
I am coming to my church more regularly nowadays	42	32	6.7	.01
I am coming to my church less regularly nowadays	3	6	1.9	NS
Commitment and belonging				
I feel a strong sense of belonging to my church	92	89	2.0	NS
My church is important for my social life	68	63	1.9	NS
I turn to fellow members of my church when I need help	64	55	5.9	.05
Commitment and power				
I can influence my church=s decisions	77	71	3.4	NS
I have too little control over the running of my church	12	12	0.0	NS
My church makes too many demands on my time	29	22	4.2	.05
My church makes too many demands on my money	6	7	0.3	NS

Table 8.6   Ordained ministry: charismatics and non-charismatics in the pulpit

	charis %	non-ch %	χ^2	p<
Women				
I am in favour of the ordination of women as priests	85	78	4.2	.05
I am in favour of the ordination of women as bishops	69	64	2.3	NS
Divorced				
I am in favour of divorced people as priests	67	68	0.1	NS
I am in favour of divorced people as bishops	58	59	0.1	NS
Divorced and remarried				
I am in favour of divorced and remarried priests	57	63	2.9	NS
I am in favour of divorced and remarried bishops	47	53	2.1	NS
Practising homosexuals				
I am in favour of the ordination of practising homosexuals as priests	8	40	71.5	.001
I am in favour of the ordination of practising homosexuals as bishops	7	36	62.2	.001

Table 8.7   Church leadership: charismatics and non-charismatics in the pulpit

	charis %	non-ch %	χ^2	p<
Clergy				
Clergy should be paid a better wage	57	57	0.0	NS
Clergy freehold should be abolished	43	36	2.9	NS
Clergy should be employed on short-term renewable contracts	27	24	0.6	NS
Clergy should live in their own houses	27	25	0.3	NS
Laity				
I am in favour of:				
lay people leading morning and evening prayer	99	92	11.3	.001
lay people preaching at morning and evening prayer	92	81	13.9	.001
lay people preaching at communion services	91	75	22.5	.001
lay people leading the first part of the communion service	87	65	34.5	.001
lay people taking the whole communion service	31	7	81.2	.001

Table 8.8   Churches and cathedrals: charismatics and non-charismatics in the pulpit

	charis %	non-ch %	χ^2	p<
My church				
My congregation can no longer afford to pay for its church building	23	22	0.1	NS
In order to survive my church building:				
needs more grants from the state	31	38	3.6	NS
needs more money from tourists and visitors	17	27	8.7	.01
Wider issues				
Too much money is spent on keeping old churches	68	41	44.7	.001
More church buildings should be taken over by the state	57	48	5.6	.05
Many rural churches should be closed	29	20	6.6	.05
Cathedrals should charge visitors for entry	19	23	1.7	NS

Table 8.9   Money and policy: charismatics and non-charismatics in the pulpit

	charis %	non-ch %	χ^2	p<
Church structures				
My parish pays too much for its parish share (quota)	19	21	0.3	NS
I am happy for some money given to my church to go to diocesan funds	78	74	1.1	NS
I am happy for some money given to my church to go to church central funds	67	62	1.5	NS
Clergy support				
I am happy for some money given to my church:				
to go to training new priests	93	91	0.5	NS
to go to clergy pensions	83	90	6.4	.05
Development and mission				
I am happy for some money given to my church:				
to go to struggling parishes	93	90	1.7	NS
to go to churches in developing countries	96	86	13.4	.001
Community regeneration				
I am happy for some money given to my church				
to go to urban regeneration	65	64	0.0	NS
to go to the farming community	58	55	0.6	NS

Table 8.10   Anglican identity: charismatics and non-charismatics in the pulpit

	charis %	non-ch %	χ^2	p<
Ecumenism				
I would never become a member of another denomination	30	38	4.2	.05
I would not want my denomination to merge with another	12	16	1.4	NS
I would not want to be a member of an ecumenical church or local ecumenical project	10	21	10.7	.01
I would be prepared to accept the Pope as my church leader in some situations	24	44	25.3	.001
Establishment				
The Church of England should be disestablished	46	29	21.3	.001
Senior bishops should continue to sit in the reformed House of Lords	82	75	4.7	.05
The monarch should continue to be the Supreme Governor of the Church of England	37	45	4.4	.05
Diocesan bishops should be appointed by the state	2	7	6.8	.01
Parliament should retain control of Church of England legislation	10	14	2.5	NS

Table 8.11   Confidence in the future: charismatics and non-charismatics in the pulpit

	charis %	non-ch %	χ^2	p<
Leadership				
I have confidence in the leadership given by my local clergy	73	66	2.3	NS
I have confidence in the leadership given by my diocesan bishop	81	70	8.7	.01
I have confidence in the leadership given by the General Synod	49	37	8.7	.01
I have confidence in the leadership given by the Archbishops' Council	53	29	40.9	.001
Local church				
The membership of my church will grow in the next 12 months	65	40	39.2	.001
I can invite other people to come to my church	63	52	6.6	.05
It is not easy for newcomers in my church	26	28	0.3	NS

Table 8.12   Sex and family life: charismatics and non-charismatics in the pulpit

	charis %	non-ch %	χ^2	p<
Sex before marriage				
It is wrong for men and women to have sex before marriage	73	36	84.8	.001
It is all right for a couple to live together without intending to get married	9	34	45.5	.001
It is a good idea for couples who intend to get married to live together first	5	19	22.5	.001
Separation and divorce				
Some marriages can come to a natural end in divorce or separation	73	81	6.6	.05
Couples should stay together for the sake of the children	45	39	2.5	NS
Same sex relationships				
It is wrong for people of the same gender to have sex together	76	41	79.3	.001
Homosexual couples should have the right to marry one another	5	21	25.4	.001
Children and teenagers				
Children thrive equally whether cared for primarily by their father or mother	28	30	0.2	NS
Contraception should be available to teenagers under 16 who want it	33	37	1.4	NS

Table 8.13   Social concerns: charismatics and non-charismatics in the pulpit

	charis %	*non-ch* %	χ^2	*p<*
Global concerns				
I am concerned about environmental pollution	96	95	0.6	NS
I am concerned about the poverty of the developing world	97	97	0.3	NS
I am concerned about the spread of AIDS	95	96	0.0	NS
I am concerned about research into human genes	77	67	7.1	.01
Community concerns				
I am concerned about violence on television	88	72	21.2	.001
I am concerned about paedophiles living in the community	49	41	4.4	.05
I am concerned about the National Lottery	59	47	8.4	.01

Table 8.14   Social conscience: charismatics and non-charismatics in the pulpit

	charis %	*non-ch* %	χ^2	*p<*
Health and education				
I would pay more tax to fund spending on health	86	85	0.2	NS
I would pay more tax to fund spending on schools	82	80	0.2	NS
I would pay more tax to fund spending on universities	45	48	0.7	NS
Social security and prisons				
I would pay more tax to fund spending on prisons	44	50	1.9	NS
I would pay more tax to fund spending on social security benefits	47	49	0.3	NS
Defence and development aid				
I would pay more tax to fund spending on security forces	21	25	1.2	NS
I would pay more tax to fund spending on overseas aid	82	75	4.9	.05

Table 8.15   Education: charismatics and non-charismatics in the pulpit

	charis %	*non-ch* %	χ^2	*p<*
State provision				
Private schools should be abolished	15	18	0.7	NS
I have confidence in the state-funded education system	61	63	0.5	NS
Religious education				
Religious education should be taught in all schools	90	92	0.5	NS
Religious education in schools should teach about world religions	82	86	1.3	NS
Schools should hold a religious assembly every day	64	57	2.6	NS
Faith schools				
I am in favour of state-funded church schools	89	86	1.7	NS
The Church of England should fund more new church primary schools	77	63	13.2	.01
The Church of England should fund more new church secondary schools	81	72	6.6	.05
I am in favour of state-funded Jewish schools	40	57	16.7	.001
I am in favour of state-funded Islamic schools	36	53	17.9	.001

Index